Celebrity Politics

Celebrity Politics

Image and Identity in Contemporary Political Communications

Mark Wheeler

polity

First published in 2013 by Polity Press

Polity Press
65 Bridge Street
Cambridge CB2 1UR, UK

Polity Press
350 Main Street
Malden, MA 02148, USA

ISBN-13: 978-0-7456-5248-1
ISBN-13: 978-0-7456-5249-8(pb)

A catalogue record for this book is available from the British Library.

Typeset in 10.5 on 12 pt Plantin
by Servis Filmsetting Ltd, Stockport, Cheshire
Printed and bound in Great Britain by Clays Ltd, St Ives PLC

For further information on Polity, visit our website: www.politybooks.com

Contents

Acknowledgements

I would like to thank my students, colleagues and Dean Professor Bob McKeever in the Faculty of Law, Governance and International Relations at London Metropolitan University who have enabled me to develop my interest in celebrity politics. I am particularly grateful to Wendy Stokes who read several early drafts of the chapters in manuscript form and gave me many insightful comments. I am also grateful to a number of scholars from a range of disciplines who have helped to guide my interests by giving their time, both directly and unwittingly, over the course of several years. They include Dominic Wring, John Street, Heather Savigny, Michael Higgins, Philip Drake, Nathan Farrell, Rinna Yrjölä, Ivor Gaber, Seamus Simpson, Dan Brockington, Ilan Kapoor, Jo Littler, Liza Tsaliki, Asteris Huliaras, Raymond Kuhn, Bruce Newman, Paul M. Green, Iwan Morgan and Mark White. Further, I should also like to thank the team at Polity for their interest and support. Finally, I am extremely grateful to my friends and family, and I dedicate this book to my mother and to the memory of my father.

Introduction

This book emerges from the growing interest of practitioners and academics in the notion of 'celebrity politics'. As modern public relations (PR) techniques have cross-fertilized with a commercialization of journalistic practices in the global media, there has been a personalization of politics. This has led to cultural researchers considering how celebrities are established through their media profiles and to reflect upon their political functions (Cashmore 2006). While these questions lead to a sophisticated analysis of celebrity in media studies, political science's investigation of celebrity has remained, until recently, relatively marginal (West and Orman 2003).

Those academic works that consider celebrity politicians and politicized celebrities have largely viewed celebrity as a 'manufactured product' that has been fabricated by media exposure (Louw 2005; Turner 2004). This concern about the negative effects of celebrity first emerged when the American sociologist Leo Lowenthal argued that US media coverage had replaced 'idols of production', such as politicians, with 'idols of consumption', such as film stars (Lowenthal 1944). In turn, Herminio Martins contended that celebrities were an 'elite without power' who combined maximum observability with an inability to provide life chances for the public's benefit (Martins 1964). Therefore, public interest in celebrity politics has been manipulated through 'pseudo-events' staged by cynical media to construct a perceived myth of individual aspiration (Boorstin 1971: 58). Subsequently, there has been an unfavourable emphasis on the incursion of celebrities into political communications.

There is, however, an emergent literature which has addressed (i) how celebrities are taking part in politics and (ii) whether politicians are behaving as if they were celebrities. Among these works are:

Leo Braudy, *The Frenzy of Renown: Fame and Its History* (Braudy 1997); John Corner and Dick Pels, *Media and the Restyling of Politics: Consumerism, Celebrity and Cynicism* (Corner and Pels 2003); P. David Marshall, *Celebrity and Power: Fame in Contemporary Culture* (Marshall 1997); Graeme Turner, Frances Bonner and P. David Marshall, *Fame Games: The Production of Celebrity in Australia* (Turner, Bonner and Marshall 2000); Graeme Turner, *Understanding Celebrity* (Turner 2004); Liesbet van Zoonen, *Entertaining the Citizen: When Politics and Popular Culture Converge* (van Zoonen 2005); Darrell M. West and John Orman, *Celebrity Politics* (West and Orman 2003); and Sean Redmond and Su Holmes, *Stardom and Celebrity: A Reader* (Redmond and Holmes 2008).

In dealing with celebrities in global politics, Andrew F. Cooper, in *Celebrity Diplomacy* (Cooper 2008), examines the ways in which celebrity activism is changing the nature of diplomatic practice. Moreover, the late Mark D. Alleyne considered the role of United Nations (UN) goodwill ambassadors and the organization's commitment to public relations reforms in *Global Lies? Propaganda, the UN and the World Order* (Alleyne 2003) and 'The United Nations' Celebrity Diplomacy' in *SAIS Review* (Alleyne 2005). A further series of essays in Liza Tsaliki, Christos A. Frangonikolopoulos and Asteris Huliaras (eds), *Transnational Celebrity Activism in Global Politics* (Tsaliki, Huliaras and Frangonikolopoulos 2011), has considered celebrities' impact on international affairs.

John Street's work, most especially his seminal article 'Celebrity Politicians: Popular Culture and Political Representation' (Street 2004), has led to an understanding of how celebrity politicians may give a greater expression to the representation of democratic behaviour (Street 2002, 2003, 2010).[1] Consequently, as celebrities and image candidates assume the authority to promote political agendas among target audiences/citizens, it becomes necessary to reflect upon their significance in election campaigns, political agendas and activism. Therefore, Street's concerns about the relationship between political aesthetics and democratic practice refer to a wider debate about the dynamics which are shaping in a period of late modernity (Street 2010: 259).

Here it is contended that traditional civic duties are being replaced by alternative forms of virtuous participation. Within this new political environment, different types of agency such as celebrity politics have become centrifugal forces for public engagement. Thus, as Street demonstrates that celebrity politics is consistent with a liberal democratic ethos, his work provides a basis upon which alternative forms of political behaviour may be considered in relation to their ability to enable citizens to reconnect with their societies (Street 2010: 260).

This text will outline the academic debates and methodologies which have defined the literature concerning the political and social impact of celebrity. Chapter 1 will discuss the questions associated with the worth of celebrity politics and consider how these forms of political representation segue into a wider debate about post-democratic societies wherein civic values are being replaced by new forms of participatory engagement. The chapter demonstrates the analytical frameworks which have been used to interpret celebrity politics and outlines a holistic approach to underpin this study.

The second chapter provides a historical context for the phenomenon of celebrity politics to offset the view that celebrity engagement is only a recent development. Therefore, chapter 2 considers how the principles of fame, which have been drawn upon from antiquity, were transformed into the constructs of celebrity during the tide of democratic reform in the eighteenth and nineteenth centuries. It will consider how this democratization of celebrity reached fruition in twentieth-century American political and cultural life, as politicians employed fame as part of their imagery, and as film stars and protest singers used their renown for the purposes of political endorsement and advocacy.

Chapter 3 provides a contemporaneous account of the development of celebrity politics in the United States (US) and how these matters have informed other western liberal democracies, especially the United Kingdom (UK). It employs Street's distinction of celebrity politicians who have incorporated the principles of fame for electoral achievement (CP1s) and the rise of politicized celebrities who have become activists in their own right (CP2s). On the one hand, this typology is employed to analyse how media-savvy politicians, such as Ronald Reagan, Bill Clinton, Barack Obama and Tony Blair, have utilized their celebrity as part of their political weaponry (McKernan 2011: 192–3). On the other, the chapter looks at the rise of celebrity endorsements in campaign and electoral politics in the USA and the UK.

With reference to Street's typological distinction, chapters 4 and 5 respectively provide a greater focus on the rise of celebrity politicians and politicized celebrities in modern democracies. In the fourth chapter, the analysis considers Barack Obama's 2008 presidential campaign in which image candidacy was cross-fertilized with the social media to popularize a form of 'liquid celebrity' (Redmond

2010). It compares this approach with the UK mainstream parties' employment of political imagery. In particular, the British media focused on the personalities of Gordon Brown, David Cameron and Nick Clegg as a result of the introduction of the televised leadership debates in the 2010 general election. The chapter concludes with how 'celebrity' was employed in the context of negative campaigning and the extraordinary rise and fall of the 2008 Republican vice-presidential nominee Sarah Palin.

Chapter 5 considers how far politicized celebrities have utilized their fame in terms of grass-roots political activism. It considers how modern American film and rock stars have been involved in a range of campaigns concerning political reform, health provision and social justice. The chapter discusses how such forms of CP2 behaviour have been transferred to UK politics as an instant celebrity culture has emerged in association with reality television programmes, a commercially driven news media and the viral powers of the social media. In turn, these forums have established a public 'space' wherein celebrity activism has been deemed credible and legitimate. In this respect, such behaviour was validated during the 2011 UK phone-hacking scandal when stars such as Hugh Grant led the campaign to unearth the unethical and illegal journalistic practices which had been endemic in Rupert Murdoch's News International tabloid papers. Simultaneously, CP2s have been condemned and praised in equal measure.

Such a duality has been evidenced in the increase of celebrity activism with regard to international affairs. Therefore, chapter 6 moves beyond the confines of the nation-state to consider how CP2 advocacy has been most explicit with reference to questions about international justice and fund-raising. Celebrity advocates have understood that it is their responsibility to represent oppressed peoples in global forums. These activities were given a major boost by Bob Geldof's *Live Aid, Live 8* and *Feed the World* campaigns. In tandem, the U2 singer Bono has accessed the centres of diplomatic power to place matters of global debt and aid resources on the international agenda. Andrew F. Cooper suggests that a new form of 'celebrity diplomacy' has materialized, to the mutual benefit of social reformers and the oppressed. However, many scholars and members of the international community have complained that CP2 activities have reinforced cultural stereotypes. Further, despite generating publicity, many academics remain sceptical about the ability of celebrity-directed campaigns to address the structural economic inequities which have defined relations between the global North and South.

Throughout its exploration of the theoretical, historical and thematic issues that have arisen as a consequence of celebrity politics, it is this volume's intention to consider whether political celebrity represents an imposition of ideological power over the public or if it is indicative of more deep-seated changes to new alternative mechanisms of political engagement. In effect, it will ask whether the celebritization of politics has had a positive or negative effect on the political process and what the democratic implications of these developments are.

1
Celebrity Politics in an Era of Late Modernity

In recent years, there has been an increased involvement of celebrities in the political process. Moreover, as P. David Marshall has commented, politicians have constructed 'public personalities' which have an 'affective function' in the organization of interests and issues (Marshall 1997: 203–4). Clearly, these actors perceive their usage of the mass and multi-media to be an effective means through which to influence public opinion: 'In the shift away from emphasising party ideology, the political style of individual politicians . . . [who] take on an aura of "celebrity" . . . [and the symbolism of the] stars of popular culture . . . becomes central to how audiences . . . evaluate [political] performance, authenticity and . . . capabilities' (Dahlgren 2009: 137). But how far do celebrity politicians and politicized celebrities actually affect outcomes? Traditionally, many academics view celebrity politics as a 'manufactured process' fabricated by media exposure (Louw 2005; Turner 2004). Public interest in celebrity has been manipulated through contrived pseudo-events staged by a collusion of communicators and cynical media (Boorstin 1971: 65). However, as celebrities have become politically engaged with the public sphere, this literature requires a re-evaluation. As stars have intervened in politics and political leaders have been defined by celebrity-style imagery, it may be argued critical theorists do not take into account the extensive influence of celebrity politics on decision-making processes.

An alternative literature has identified the trend towards the celebritization of politics, both theoretically (Street 2004) and empirically (Holmes and Redmond 2006), through an exploration of celebrity performance, authority and representation. As celebrities and image candidates gain credibility to assume a moral authority amongst target audiences/citizens, it becomes necessary to reflect upon their significance when mobilized for political campaigns, policy agendas and activism.

These matters of political representation segue into a wider debate wherein civic values are being replaced by new forms of participatory engagement. In a period of late modernism, there have been growing concerns that a democratic deficit has occurred with regard to a collapse in virtue and citizenship. For instance, Robert Putnam has argued that new forms of social capital are necessary to reconnect citizens with their societies (Putnam 2000). Alternatively, Henrik Bang suggests that different types of political capital are emerging as duty-bound citizens are being replaced by virtuous 'everyday makers' who utilize local narratives to reciprocate with one another (Bang 2003). Similarly, John Keane, in his analysis of 'monitory democracy', in which consumer-led forms of representation become a measurement of accountability, has considered how changes to matters of 'voice' and 'output' have reformed democratic practices (Keane 2009b).

This chapter will outline the contours of the academic debate concerning the celebritization of politics. Critical theorists have provided an analysis of the 'media spectacle' in which celebrity engagement has been defined by public relations techniques to distort political issues. Conversely, Liesbet van Zoonen, John Corner, Dick Pels and John Street have considered how the popular aesthetics employed by celebrity politicians may be linked with reconfigured democratic practices.

Therefore, this analysis will critically assess how celebrity politics operates in reference to the post-democratic changes that have been identified by Bang and Keane. It will discuss whether their analyses provide an appropriate framework to capture the worth of celebrity politicians. While these authors have focused on matters of output, this chapter will consider the extent to which celebrity politicians 'input' aggregated forms of 'agency' to affect political outcomes. From these differing perspectives, it will seek to define a normative position concerning the worth of celebrity politics.

Finally, this chapter will define a systematic taxonomy to analyse the relationship between celebrity politics and democratic behaviour. Thus, it shifts the focus of attention away from those studies which have sought to categorize the different types of celebrity political behaviour (West and Orman 2003) to the definition of a methodology through which to analyse such activism. In this context, it will review the work of Paul 't Hart and Karen Tindall ('t Hart and Tindall 2009; Marsh, 't Hart and Tindall 2010), who have sought to consider the forms of political action which are associated with celebrity politics. Elsewhere, it will be necessary to consider how van Zoonen (2005) and Street (2003, 2004) have elaborated on the analytical distinctions which can be made concerning the significance of the typologies of political personalization and celebrity performance. In turn, this analysis will draw upon Max Boykoff and Mike Goodman's model of politicized celebrity systems (PCS) to provide a framework to consider the aesthetics of celebrity political behaviour (Boykoff and Goodman 2009). The chapter will conclude by considering how these typologies may be utilized to discuss what constitutes an effective celebrity politician in a modern political culture.

The traditional paradigm: style over substance

Several commentators have contended that fame is a manufactured process. Through an industrialization of culture, an individual's 'celebrity-ness' has been facilitated by the mediatization of their public rather than their real persona (Drake and Miah 2010: 52; Louw 2005: 172). Concurrently, critics such as Neil Postman claim that the mass political communication process has led to a decline in rationality as televisual style dominates substantive debate. This critique suggests that the 'Americanization' of politics has had a negative impact on the public sphere and civil engagement (Postman 1987). In tandem, political communications have evidenced the convergence of public relations (PR) techniques with commercial pressures drawn from the global media. For instance, Thomas Meyer notes: 'Insofar as the elite actors in the political system put their faith in the basic question of media democracy – publicity equates with success – they yield to the time constraints of media production, because they suppose that it is the price they have to pay to win public support' (Meyer with Hinchman 2002: 45).

Most recently, with the escalation of media and communication outlets, together with the voluminous use of talent and reality shows such as *The X Factor* (2004 onwards) and *Celebrity Big Brother* (2001 onwards), instant celebrities can be launched in conventional and viral terms (e.g., Susan Boyle or Justin Bieber). Such ubiquity in fame has combined with a more visible and self-conscious employment of celebrity activists. Under such conditions, Daniel Boorstin has argued, illusions are mistaken for reality (Boorstin 1971).

Thus, politicians have 'packaged' themselves as commodities to be sold to voters in an era of partisan de-alignment in which the electorate no longer clearly identifies with the political parties on matters of ideology or class (Franklin 2004). This suggests the relationships between 'leaders' and the 'crowd' which have evolved in late capitalist societies are vital to 'the mass's support of the individual in mass society' (Marshall 1997: 43). Therefore, public interest in celebrity politicians and politicized celebrities has been manipulated through pseudo-events staged by a cynical media to construct a perceived myth of individual aspiration (Boorstin 1971: 58). This has created a spurious egalitarianism which 'in reality . . . [serves] only to thwart a desire for equality, and [conceals] the extent to which the practice of government [departed] from its democratic ideal' (Hatch 1960: 65). In turn, the public is presented as being culpable as it cannot understand that it has been manipulated by elite marketing tactics.

Moreover, Darrell West and John Orman contend that celebrities propagate irrelevant understandings of complex political matters, remain ignorant and do not justify their status in claiming to represent public opinion. In particular, West and Orman argue that the skills of celebrity politicians are ill-suited to statecraft as they lack knowledge or expertise of public policy so that 'serious political issues become trivialized in the attempt to elevate celebrities to philosopher celebrities' (West and Orman 2003: 118).

This anxiety over the negative effects of celebrity on the political process may be traced back to the American sociologist Leo Lowenthal, who argued that US media coverage had replaced 'idols of production', such as politicians, with 'idols of consumption' such as film stars (Lowenthal 1944). Similarly, C. Wright Mills contended that the attention placed on celebrities meant that they had become part of a new power elite (Mills 1956). Elsewhere, Herminio Martins claimed instead that celebrities were an 'elite without power' whose maximum observability combined with an inability to provide life chances for the public (Alberoni 1972; Martins 1964).

Even Graeme Turner, in his multifaceted account of celebrity, accepts the notion of celebrity as a mechanism of political inauthenticity (Turner 2004: 134). He explains celebrity politics as a means of commodification through which to neutralize consumer/citizen engagement (ibid.: 135). While Turner views the cultural consumption of celebrity as part of a new media democracy in which a heterogeneous public sphere allows for the possibilities of a do-it-yourself (DIY) citizenship, he chooses to ignore the social relations proffered by politicized celebrities. In tandem, Nick Couldry and Tim Markham remain sceptical that celebrity culture can positively contribute to the public's political engagement. They contend that the followers of celebrities will be unlikely to be politically engaged and that any claims of democratic renewal offered by celebrity politics are spurious (Couldry and Markham 2007).

Following this logic, Louw has argued that, with the exportation of the US cultural values accompanying the globalization of the mass media, branded performers have narrowed the gap between politics and entertainment (Louw 2005: 192). In his definition of 'pseudo-politics', Louw suggests there has been a PR-ization of issues 'in which celebrities are now enlisted to whip up mass public opinion' (ibid.: 191). By defining celebrity politics as the latest manifestation of the fame game, he views the media as a site of ideological control: 'Fame-game endorsements constitute the ultimate PR-ization of politics based upon pure puff and hype. The media's preference for glib sound bites, good visuals, and attractive famous faces is exploited to the full to celebrity-ize and emotionalize issues as a tool to steer mass public opinion' (ibid.: 191).

In the most sophisticated variation of this position, Douglas Kellner has developed his concept of the 'media spectacle' to suggest that the emphasis on celebrity replaces the complexities of policy with stylistic gestures (Kellner 2010b: 123). He argues that the media coverage of celebrity politics creates a form of spectacle which 'frames' politicians and celebrities as global 'superstars'. Kellner suggests that such a form of spectacle has substituted substance with a symbolism in which the norms of democratic engagement have been undermined (ibid.: 123). He concludes: 'An informed and intelligent public thus needs to learn to deconstruct the spectacle to see what are the real issues behind the election, what interests and ideology do the candidates represent, and what sort of spin, narrative, and media spectacles is being used to sell candidates' (Kellner 2009: 738).[1]

Underpinning the traditional paradigm is a normative position that suggests that celebrity politics diminishes the processes of representative democracy. In such a pessimistic extrapolation, 'politics has been subsumed within the culture industry, so that the political is now another commodity to be marketed, purchased and consumed in a cycle of false needs and unsatisfied desires' (Calcutt 2005). These critiques of celebrity activism reflect the values of the Marxist Frankfurt School whose critical theorists contended that the media had become an expression of dominant ideologies. Effectively, culture has been industrialized and distorted for the needs of political and social elites. Chris Rojek has concluded that, as celebrities express an ideology of heroic individualism and upward mobility, they standardize social conditions to perpetuate consumption and subdue the masses (Rojek 2001: 33).

These critiques share Jürgen Habermas's modernist concerns that there has been erosion of the public sphere. Instead of the mass media providing an agora in which legitimate debate may occur, the public space between the state and the electorate has evidenced an irrational political discourse. Therefore, partial or distorted information is presented as being representative when, in reality, it is controlled by powerful influences (Habermas 1992). Thus, the most common analysis of celebrity-ness has referred to the ubiquitous growth of the visual media in which fame operates as a tool with which to manipulate public opinion (Louw 2005). It is contended that such a usage of performance is pitched on artifice and sells prescriptive ideas to a disengaged public.

Celebrity politics and political aesthetics

The employment of political rhetoric has a historical continuum which offsets the modernist dismay directed at the personalization of politics (Braudy 1997; Pleios 2011: 251). As Liesbet van Zoonen comments, the classical Greek Sophists contended that virtue was a matter of great performance (van Zoonen 2005: 72). Moreover, Niccolò Machiavelli demonstrated that the proper union of personality and performance was necessary to create the appearance of a convincing 'good' political persona if it was not a requirement to actually have one. Therefore, while the conditions of the modern political communication have changed, the need to determine a persuasive political performance remains timeless.

But even without acknowledging this important historical context, the traditional paradigm may be criticized as it perceives political communication as a top-down process between political elites and a passive electorate. It disregards the polysemic range of readings that audiences take from popular culture. Such an approach ignores the effects of celebritized politicians in forging new or alternative social formations for engagement. Effectively, it does not evaluate the influence of imagery on the public's political decision-making processes. Instead, it is necessary to consider the changes in political aesthetics that have facilitated the opportunities through which celebrities have influenced politics and politicians have popularized themselves. As P. David Marshall comments, 'a leader must somehow embody the sentiments of the party, the people and the state . . . a celebrity must somehow embody the sentiments of the audience' (Marshall 1997: 203).

John Corner and Dick Pels contend that the previous forms of partisan allegiances have eroded to be replaced by a focus on post-ideological lifestyle choices which foreground matters of aesthetics and style (Corner and Pels 2003). As voters are less likely to identify with political parties, the public have favoured 'more eclectic, fluid, issue specific and personality-bound forms of political recognition and engagement' (Corner and Pels 2003: 7). Corner argues that through their 'mediated personas' – the individual's public image – film, television and music stars have created new forms of identification in which they attain public admiration, sympathy and authority to effect political expression (Corner 2003: 83). Thus, celebrities and image candidates command credibility through a conjunction of de-institutionalization, personalization and parasocial familiarity to transcend other agencies of social authority[2]: 'It is a claim that derives from a world which, says Keane [2002] . . . is marked by . . . (the) popular identities (which) derive from the role models provided by celebrities who inhabit this world' (Street 2004: 442).

Within a world in which mediated personas are taking greater shape and importance, it is necessary to investigate celebrities' integral roles in political campaigns. While symbolism and charisma have always shaped political communications, can celebrities use their reputations and charisma to invigorate politics with new ideas? Moreover, as Aeron Davis has shown, celebrity politicians have employed personalized forms of 'media capital' to define their 'performances' so that their mediated personas may connect with the electorate:

> In many modern . . . mediated democracies . . . several contemporary leaders, such as Vladimir Putin, Silvio Berlusconi and Nicolas Sarkozy, devote extensive resources to the cultivation and promotion of their public images to voters. In competitive presidential and majoritarian type systems . . . personalities often appear to be a more decisive factor in deciding election outcomes than policies and political records. Thus, the 'personal appeals' of Tony Blair and David Cameron are compared favourably to the 'technologically gifted' but 'uncharismatic' Gordon Brown. (Davis 2010a: 83)

In this respect, John Street's work provides a systematic attempt to analyse how the political aesthetics of celebrity politicians and politicized celebrities interlink with their democratic worth. As Street argues that celebrities have assumed a moral authority and provide credibility for political agendas, it is necessary to investigate their integral roles in political campaigns. He asks whether celebrities can use their reputations to reinvigorate politics with new ideas and an aggregated form of political agency (Street 2003, 2004, 2010): 'In other words, the study of politics requires study of the way in which performances are constructed and styles are articulated, because they constitute the transactions between represented and representatives in democracies. Significant political relationships are constructed through media performance' (Street 2003: 25).

This form of agency has shown how celebrities can interact with the public through their ability to be 'in touch' with popular sentiment (Street 2004: 447). Stars can achieve an 'intimacy with distant others' (Thompson 1995: 220) through fan networks, and these can be understood as the basis of political representation (Holmes 2005). Street contends that such a representational relationship is established by the 'affective capacity' of the celebrity's cultural performance and in such a manner stars 'give political voice to those who follow them, both by virtue of the political conditions and by means of their art . . . this is . . . a matter . . . of aesthetics, of creatively constituting a political community and representing it' (Street 2004: 449).

The impact of post-democratic theory on celebrity politics

David Marsh, Paul 't Hart and Karen Tindall contend that the academic debate concerning celebrity activism has been limited to a critique which has tended to focus on either a diminution or an enhancement of democratic pluralism (Marsh, 't Hart and Tindall 2010: 322). In their review article, these authors do Street's contribution a disservice as they fail to acknowledge its importance in placing the concerns about celebrity politics and political representation at the centre of the agenda (ibid.: 323). Yet, they have also undoubtedly moved the academic analysis of celebrity politics along as they have relocated the questions about such forms of representation into a discussion about the contested principles of late modernity or post-democratic behaviour (Crouch 2004). Consequently, despite such an omission, Street's ideas about the political engagement of celebrities have been placed into a broader consideration of the nature of citizenship, participation and equality (Marsh, 't Hart and Tindall 2010: 328).

Several political sociologists have defined the era of late modernism as being characterized by major transformations in democratic values (Beck 1992; Giddens 1991; Lash 1990). These ideas are comparable with but contest the notion of postmodernism, in that they suggest a self-referring modernism and fragmentation in which 'social practices are constantly examined and reformed in the light of incoming information about those very practices, thus constitutively altering their character' (Giddens 1991: 38). Moreover, as Zygmunt Bauman has argued, this has created a 'liquid modernism' in which individualist practices of social behaviour simultaneously create new opportunities for the self-realization of participation and exacerbate uncertainties in the human condition. Most notably, new patterns of social activity paradoxically facilitate an increasing fluidity in people's behaviour while producing existential fears over being imprisoned by such freedoms (Bauman 2000: 8).

In terms of post-democratic activity, late modernists contend such changes reflect: a replacement of hierarchies with networks; the hollowing out of the state; the replacement of politics policy with policy politics; a greater fluidity of identity; more reflexivity; changing forms of political participation; the rise of discursive network governance; the expansion of the media and celebrity politics; and a constantly reformed version of contemporary democracy (Marsh, 't Hart and Tindall 2010: 326). However, these characteristics have also led to concerns about the values of democratization. For instance, Wendy Stokes notes that 'the view that democracy is a device for delivering responsible, responsive, accountable and legitimate government . . . remains potent; . . . [Yet] . . . without wider and deeper social and economic equality there is radically unequal *access* to those fundamental rights, and thus unequal citizenship' (Stokes 2011: 396).

The fears of inequality have been heightened by the decline of civic virtues, the dismantlement of democratic associations and the disengagement of the public with the political classes. Robert D. Putnam has argued that communitarian agreements about what constitutes the common good have dissolved as trust has been eroded. In the post-democratic era of consumer politics, the citizenry has become disaffected with parties and social institutions. This has led to a profound 'thinning' of the political community and the formation of the atomized citizen who is 'bowling alone' (Putnam 1995). To fill the accompanying void, Putnam has argued for the extension of voluntary organizations to create 'virtuous circles' to accumulate social capital that enables citizens to agree on a set of shared aims for collective activity (Putnam 2000).

Elsewhere, Henrik Bang (2003, 2004, 2009) and John Keane (2009a, 2009b) have argued that civic forms of aggregated political behaviour have been replaced by more dispersed forms of participation which are determined by 'involvement', 'voice' and 'output'. Bang contends that new forms of citizenship occur within governance networks and partnerships between private and public organizations (Bang 2009). Similarly, Keane maintains alternative voluntary organizations create different types of ethical pluralism which are bound by an 'aversion to grandiose, pompous, power hungry actions of those who suppose, falsely, that they are God, and try to act like God' (Keane 2003: 208). As facets of these new processes, celebrity politicians and politicized celebrities will be integral to shaping the rise of alternative discourses in democratic societies.

Henrik Bang – 'everyday makers', the rise of expert–celebrity parties and reflexive celebrity politicians

Bang (2004) argues against Putnam's thesis concerning the revival of social capital through virtuous circles. Instead, he focuses on a discursive form of political activism in which solidarity exists but is not tied to any notion of the common good or of a particular ideology. Bang contends that new types of representation have emerged outside the mainstream political institutions as citizens have a minimal interest in party politics. Rather than aspire to the duties of citizenship, these virtuous 'everyday makers' want to feel 'involved' in their communities and are motivated by the beliefs that the public should:

- do it yourself;
- do it where you are;
- do it for fun, but also because you find it necessary;
- do it ad hoc or part time;
- do it concretely, instead of ideologically;
- do it with self-confidence and show trust in yourself; and
- do it with the system, if need be. (Bang 2004)

Bang contends this form of political engagement has combined individuality with commonality to re-establish different relations of self or co-governance. In his view, the public no longer have pre-constituted interests, identities or policy preferences, and participate as social constructivists in a contemporary network society. Bang argues that most people are involved in small local narratives which are founded on a mutuality of interests. Therefore, as political activity is no longer based on ideology and membership, politicians need to engage on a continuing basis with citizens to persuade them to participate. Bang 'identifies a shift away from an input–output model of politics, in which citizens via parties etc., were negotiated and aggregated into policy outputs by governments, to a recursive one, in which the demo-elite, operating through the political system acts: "in its own terms and on its own values, thereby shaping and constructing societal interests and identity"' (Marsh, 't Hart and Tindall 2010: 329).

Within this reformulated view of participatory practices, there has been a change in the relationship between citizens and the political classes. The centralized 'cartel' parties who were employed by states to realize policies have been superseded by 'expert–celebrity' parties who enact a discursive set of exchange relations aimed at achieving good governance. Although good governmental performance remains a requisite for re-election, so is the presentation of the party, the government and the policy. In an expert–celebrity party, members are not sources of policy ideas but are valued instead by their ability to communicate the 'message' of reform to convince the electorate to cast their vote. Thus, to speak to the electorate, parties have employed the media tools of celebrity, such as the appearances of leaders on popular television programmes, personalized web sites and political blogs.

This reflexivity has meant that politicians have 'celebritized' themselves to engage in a more personalized and less ideological set of political communications. Bang argues that the spectacular rise of Barack Obama as a celebrity politician from junior senator for Illinois to US president demonstrates how demo-elites must be in constant contact with their publics. For example, Obama utilized the entertainment–politics nexus to seek 'everyday maker' support when he appeared on popular talk shows such as *The Oprah Winfrey Show* (1986–2011) and mixed with celebrity artists including the singer Bruce Springsteen. In particular, this accords with Matthew Baum's (2005) arguments that 'entertainment talk shows are invested with a level of trust on the part of the viewer . . . [to sustain] . . . political fortunes . . . which (rely) more on the image of the candidate than the quality of the arguments' (Higgins 2008: 49).

Sean Redmond describes Obama as a 'liquid celebrity' who effectively communicated with those American citizens who had become disenfranchised by machine politics. He formed links with non-traditional activists by being a charismatic figure that solidified the promise of change and reform (Redmond 2010: 81). Bang is particularly impressed by how Obama's 2008 Democratic presidential campaign directly interacted with 'everyday makers' through an innovative use of new information communication technologies

(ICTs). He notes how the social network entitled 'mybarackobama.com' (MyBo) mobilized the democratic input of over two million users and, through the 100,000 profiles available, 35,000 affinity groups were organized at community level.

Such an online presence helped Obama to launch his campaign on the national scene, orchestrate campaign funds and galvanize his political support. This commonwealth of local associations was comprised of grass-roots activists drawn from youth and ethnic minority delegates who worked in an inclusive and relational manner to arrange over 200,000 events which enabled 70,000 people to raise US$35 million for Obama's campaign (Bang 2009). Obama defined a political image founded on reciprocity and shared meaning and that encouraged popular scrutiny of his political deliberations (see chapter 4):

> The Obama network was capable of establishing and reproducing relationships that were usable whether by fundraising or volunteering. This allowed the campaign to interact with people in a different way . . . Also these tools suggest . . . [a] possible long-term [development]. Following Putnam (1995) we could see 'networks of civic engagement [that] embody past success at collaboration which can serve as a cultural template for future collaboration. (Cogburn and Espinoza-Vasquez 2011: 205)

Similarly, van Zoonen has shown how the German prime minister, Angela Merkel, in her campaign against the incumbent Gerhard Schröder during the 2005 general election, employed 'an agreeable and especially visible private life and persona' (van Zoonen 2006: 296). The reserved Merkel, childless and in her second marriage, was required to open up her private life when she was presented on a fishing trip with her husband in *Der Bild am Sonntag* (1952 onwards). Moreover, as van Zoonen notes, the Christian Democratic Union (CDU) tried to popularize Merkel by employing the Rolling Stones' song 'Angie' (1973), despite the inappropriateness of the lyrics and the band's decision to sue the CDU. This demonstrated how the celebritization of politicians has become a requisite in modern democracies not only for media-savvy politicians including Schröder and Tony Blair, but also for less suitable candidates such as Merkel. Consequently:

> The celebrity politician . . . is the successful embodiment of the concurrent constituents of the political field and the stage of private life. He emerges mainly from performance on television, because television and

its many genres are the main source from which the majority of people learn about politics, with talk shows ranking high when it comes to influencing voting decisions. (van Zoonen 2005: 78)

John Keane – monitory democracy, new forms of scrutiny and celebrity voice

Bang's work concerning the reformulation of democratic relations between political elites and the public ties in with John Keane's vision of 'monitory democracy' (Keane 2009a). Effectively, Keane argues that, since 1945, governmental or parliamentary forms of democratic practice have declined. Therefore, the central grip of elections, parties and representative assemblies has weakened and behaviour in 'all fields of social and political life [has] come to be scrutinized . . . by a whole host of non-party, extra parliamentary and often unelected bodies operating within and underneath and beyond the boundaries of territorial states' (Keane 2009b).

These alternative types of accountability are linked in with monitoring mechanisms which are founded on consumer preferences, customer voting and networks of redistributed power. The new formations of monitoring have included concepts of 'empowerment', 'high energy democracy', 'stakeholders', 'participatory governance' and 'communicative democracy'. This means that monitory democracy has placed an emphasis on surveys, focus groups, deliberative polling, online petitions, audiences and customer voting. Simultaneously, the number of power scrutinizing institutions has exponentially increased to include non-governmental organizations, human rights bodies, think tanks and consumer protection agencies. For Keane, these bodies have a liberating role as 'people are coming to learn that they must keep an eye on power and its representatives, that they must make judgments and choose their own causes of action' (Keane 2009b).

Keane contends that monitory democracy is closely associated with the rise of the new communications technologies of the multimedia and the internet. These horizontal forms of information flow have led to overlapping and interlinked devices through which multiple communication and scrutiny may occur. For instance, the older mechanisms of media accountability have been replaced by a myriad of citizen-generated discussion groups. Most especially, within the content of the internet there has been a move away from journalistic 'objectivity' to the 'subjectivity' of bloggers, social networking and adversarial journalism. In this context, the malleability of 'hype' has been viewed as a profundity in which everyone's opinions are of equal worth. Thus, it may be contended that these power-scrutinizing innovations enfranchise citizens through the formation of 'bully pulpits' in which there exists '[o]ne person, many interests, many voices, multiple votes and multiple representatives' (Keane 2009a).

Through the 'communicative abundance' which exists, the private lives and romances of politicians, unelected officials and celebrities come directly into the public sphere for scrutiny by millions of people. Ordinary individuals may morph into media stars through simulated-reality television elections and as competitive news practices constantly seek to break 'scoops': 'Thanks to journalism and the new media of communicative abundance, stuff happens. Shit happens. There seems to be no end of scandal, and there are even times when "-gate" scandals, like earthquakes, rumble beneath the feet of whole governments' (Keane 2009b).

Therefore, akin to Bang's viewpoint of the relations between 'everyday makers' and expert–celebrity parties, Keane emphasizes the opportunities for citizenship to provide for accountability and exchange values between the public and political elites. He has shown how the success of maverick celebrity politicians, such as Ross Perot, Ralph Nader and Martin Bell, has been determined by their ability to champion unrepresented citizens who do not connect with the political classes (Keane 2002: 13). In this manner, celebrity politics enhances democratic processes which are no longer defined by 'interest aggregation on the input side of politics; but rather with the organization of "voice" and accountability on the output side' (Marsh, 't Hart and Tindall 2010: 331).

Another variation of monitory democracy in relation to celebrity politics occurred in the UK 2010 party leader debates which brought a heightened level of consumer-led scrutiny to the election. They placed a focus on the celebritization of political leadership by being a media spectacle. Consequently, the performances of former Labour prime minister Gordon Brown, Conservative Party leader David Cameron and the Liberal Democrat Nick Clegg were constantly monitored through the speculation of political commentators, pollsters, bloggers and tweeters to declare who had won and who had lost the debates.

A normative position for the democratic worth of celebrity politics

Bang and Keane have focused on the relative worth of the values of voice and output as against the requirements of aggregated input and agency to define a normative position of post-democratic behaviour. Yet, while accepting the theoretical sophistication of Bang's analysis concerning 'everyday makers', Marsh, 't Hart and Tindall (2010: 330) bring into question the validity of several of his key assertions. First, to what extent has the politics of late modernity actually witnessed a rise of network governance and the decline of hierarchical relations? Second, does such a reliance on 'voice' to garner support from lay people ignore the traditional sources of information? Third and most importantly, to what degree does this thesis choose to ignore the structured inequalities as political elites market themselves through the media and celebrity to the public?

Similarly, Keane's emphasis on the desirability of consumer-led forms of scrutiny may be seen to underestimate the divisions which exist in modern democracies. In failing to address the nature of power in post-democratic societies, Bang's and Keane's focus on output does not deal with matters of inequality (educational, material and access to information) and may be seen to reinforce Putnam's fears concerning the democratic deficit. Most especially, it may be suggested that 'everyday makers' and monitory-democratic practices favour the voices of the ill-informed over the enlightened. This means that populist attitudes define a distorted version of the common good, and these reconfigured forms of behaviour may operate akin to what Alexis de Tocqueville termed soft tyranny (de Tocqueville 1830). In effect, normative democratic ideals have been undermined by the vagaries of public opinion, conformity to material security, the absence of intellectual freedom and the prejudices of the ignorant.

Subsequently, Bang's and Keane's approaches provide a partial analysis of the true worth of celebrity politics. Their arguments show how celebrity politicians such as Obama may create 'spaces' to define links between the political classes and the public. Yet, if the normative expectations of celebrity politics are limited to a measurement of voice and output alone, it can be posited that such activity has no greater merit than relaying the values of the demo-elite to the public or allowing disaffected, oppositional groups the means by which they can articulate their interests to the public.

Further, such an emphasis upon the 'form' of Obama's campaign (liquid celebrity, MyBo) rather than the ideological 'content' (founded on a variation of Keynesism and smart power in foreign policy) of his campaign may be seen to demonstrate the limitations of his political profile (Redmond 2010). For instance, Redmond relates how he took immense pleasure in the emotional commitment he felt towards Obama's cause at the time of the campaign. However, in retrospect, he grew to view Obama's utilization of personal communication and public celebrity as being 'watery'. Redmond contends that Obama replaced a fixed set of meanings with an emphasis on a passionate sense of 'feeling', resulting in profound discomfort:

> I *felt* a sharing in the injustices of capitalism, the history of slavery and racism, and the opportunity we had . . . to make the world anew again. One feels stronger, almost superhuman, when one is taken over by a belief or a conviction such as that. Surely, this sensorial transformation *is* something? . . . But such imagined strengthening of the self, and of the consumerist world, is the exact way in which liquid celebrity . . . ensure(s) that it holds the imaginary or mythical centre together. . . . As I reflect upon my love for Obama now . . . the transient nature of the connection and the emotional seduction he once offered but no longer does is what I most *feel* (ibid.: 93–4).

Within this context, Obama's transience as a celebrity politician may be seen to be reflected in the rapid rise of the reactionary Tea Party, which included its own set of liquid celebrity politicians such as Christine O'Donnell, Michelle Bachmann, Rand Paul and the 2008 Republican vice-presidential candidate Sarah Palin. Like Obama, the Tea Party utilized internet-based social networks to facilitate grass-roots participatory practice, political organization and the mobilization of the electorate. In turn, through their communicative abundance, the Tea Party candidates articulated a personalized sense of disaffection to define a collective sense of belonging. Their inchoate populism demonstrated a volatile expression of popular disempowerment, emotional commitment, nativism and racism (Bretherton 2011). Consequently, these celebrity politicians benefited from the same forms of 'everyday maker' involvement and monitory democracy that had enabled Obama to achieve his electoral victory, yet their success indicated a markedly different set of ideological values:

> All the talk of long-term realignment that accompanied President Obama's win now appears misguided. The message from this electoral cycle [2010] is that Americans are no longer loyal to any brand in politics and the country is entering a phase where movements, founded

> by frustrated voters who use social networking tools to organize and spread their message, can take the lead every two years (Bai 2010: 1).

Therefore, for celebrity politics to have an appropriate value, it must enhance civic virtues through the mechanisms of input and agency as much as illustrating the openings for voice and output. For celebrity politicians and politicized celebrities to have a democratic worth, they need to demonstrate ideological substance and provide a political clarity to a fixed range of meanings so people achieve a real sense of connection with causes. Celebrity politics may be employed not only as a means to involve disaffected members of the electorate. More vitally, it should provide the representational basis upon which those citizens can participate in terms of their own political efficacy to define a wider sense of the common good.

Developing an effective taxonomy for celebrity politics: (1) Categorizations

This normative position means that it is necessary to establish an effective taxonomy through which to analyse, assess and explain the aggregation of the worth of input and output of celebrity politics. In particular, a systematic methodology is required to consider:

- Under what conditions can celebrity politics thrive?
- How do celebrity politicians and politicized celebrities reconvene a sense of democratic worth?
- What are the opportunities and the pitfalls?
- How far does celebrity politics operate as a form of social or political capital?
- In whose interests does it occur? and
- What are the outputs of celebrity politics in effecting real and meaningful reform?

Darrell M. West and John Orman have categorized the emergence of a celebrity class of politicians (West and Orman 2003: 1–16). They have formulated a typology which defines five categories of political celebrity including: political newsworthies who use their performance skills when engaging in public communication; 'legacies' who have invariably descended from political families; famed non-politicos (elected officials) who are responsible for their own prominence when moving into office; famed non-politicos (lobbyists and spokespersons) who utilize their celebrity for causes without seeking office; and event celebrities who become famous due to a specific predicament or tragedy (ibid.: 2). While useful in defining the 'charismatic' personalization of politics, West and Orman's typology may be criticized as it categorizes celebrity activity rather than provides a consideration of how it operates as a form of political agency. Moreover, this analysis does not effectively consider the interlinkage between the realm of politics and popular culture (Street 2010: 245).

Subsequently, Paul 't Hart and Karen Tindall have considered the types of political action associated with celebrities' and politicians' use of fame to define their personas. They have listed the following typologies: long-term celebrity advocates (Angelina Jolie, Bob Geldof, Bono) who pay more than lip-service to a cause; celebrity endorsers (Oprah Winfrey) who use their A-list celebrity to endorse political candidacy; celebrity politicians (Ronald Reagan, Arnold Schwarzenegger) who seek office but use their 'outsider' status so they are not tainted by compromises but ultimately become part of the system; and the politician-turned-celebrity who is an established politician who uses entertainment values and celebritizes their image.

Through these categories, 't Hart and Tindall have speculated on the worth of celebrity politics. On one hand, they contend that the low level of public trust directed towards the political establishment has enabled celebrities to benefit from populist support and that celebrity politicians have achieved a relative degree of success within office. Yet, 't Hart and Tindall demonstrate a modernist distaste for what they describe as the 'anti-politics' of celebrity engagement. They remain concerned that politicians have 'branded' their leaderships to become political 'stars'. Further, 't Hart believes that there has been a decline in political efficacy as politicians have tried to appeal to disaffected members of the electorate through their employment of celebrity endorsers because '[if] you can bring stars, people may notice you more than if you bring in a trade unionist or real estate developer' (Edwards 2008).

Consequently, 't Hart and Tindall contend that the outcomes drawn from celebrity politics are often negligible. They focus on the transience of celebrity politicians by contending that the average tenure of such an actor is far shorter than that of most professional politicians. In part, this occurs due to the party systems which stop celebrity politicians from entering a political race. Moreover, 't Hart and Tindall maintain that the very characteristics that attract voters tend to alienate legislators (Marsh, 't Hart and Tindall 2010: 4). Their approach, however, is qualified by their notion of a 'successful' celebrity politician or politicized celebrity which is limited to a measurement of the impact of a candidate's personality within the general marketization of political communications. This is seen as a virtue as 'the majority of the literature [has focused] . . . on the way in which . . . pre-existing celebrities [have engaged] . . . with citizens who are normally apolitical or . . . [act] as a check on executive power or to which they constrain democracy because they have undue power or influence' (ibid.: 325).

Yet such an approach is myopic. It is not only necessary to consider celebrity personas in terms of parliamentary politics but it remains requisite to discuss how celebrity politicians and politicized celebrities have mobilized public support for issue-based campaigns or social movements (see chapter 5). Most especially, it ignores the conscious understanding within the celebrity classes themselves that their fame may draw public attention to a range of causes (Dreyfuss 2000). Effectively, 't Hart and Tindall do not go beyond party systems or political institutions to seek the meaning of the democratic worth of celebrity activity. This ignores celebrity engagement in entertainment-driven or populist forms of politics. Further, with the fragmentation of information and communication services, the purposes of such celebrity advocacy have evolved in relation to technological reform:

> The new model is more narrowcasting than broadcasting, more about mobilizing small groups of motivated people than about changing the opinions of millions all at once, and more about building the long-term infrastructure of change than producing short-term influences on the news media agenda. . . . Thus . . . the rise of celebrity advocacy should not be seen . . . as a sign of the declining substance of . . . politics, but rather as an indicator of sea change in how politics works (Thrall et al. 2008: 364–5).

Therefore, it is necessary to establish how and why the usage of celebrity represents a broader re-configuration of economic, political and social change. For example, in the USA and Great Britain, there has been a long-standing linkage between celebrity and campaign politics and the rise of the phenomenon of celebrities as politicians (most notably in the cases of Ronald Reagan and Arnold Schwarzenegger). Celebrities engaging in partisan or causal affairs can bring a guile and persuasiveness in using the media, which may reinvigorate politics with new ideas. This does not mean scholars should uncritically embrace celebrity activism. Instead, analytical tools are required to consider the relative impact of celebrity politics in order to assess the worth of this activity in an ever-widening political culture.

Developing an effective taxonomy for celebrity politics: (2) Typologies for political persona and performance

A more sophisticated typology has been defined by van Zoonen who argues that celebrity politics is founded upon a paradoxical combination of an individual's ability to be mediated as being both ordinary and extraordinary (van Zoonen 2005: 82–3).[3] For example, van Zoonen notes that Princess Diana's global appeal was defined by her membership of the royal family which meant that she was quite clearly 'one of them', while as a self-proclaimed 'Queen of Hearts', she could equally be perceived as 'one of us'. In turn, the former UK prime minister Tony Blair frequently reiterated that he was just 'a regular guy' and therefore an ordinary representative of the public, while seeking to demonstrate his capability to be a special political leader.

Moreover, van Zoonen notes that the political stage adds a further dimension in defining a celebrity persona: that of being an outsider as well as an insider. She notes that the political field contains many routines to create a barrier between the elites and the public. Consequently, celebrity politicians and politicized celebrities may promote populist promises to bring the establishment back in line with the needs of the people. This has been a persistent theme in the fictional representations of politics. For instance, the Hollywood film-maker Frank Capra produced motion pictures such as *Mr Smith Goes to Washington* (1939), which demonstrated how a naive but righteous junior senator Jefferson Smith (James Stewart) uncovered the corruption in Washington between machine politicians and business interests. In spite of being overwhelmed by his opponents, Smith fights a lost cause to bring virtue back to the political capital. In turn, van Zoonen contends that celebrity politicians have used such iconic narratives as templates to renew politics projects for subsequent generations.

To substantiate her thesis, van Zoonen establishes a typology of four political personas that have emerged through the convergence of politics and entertainment. First, she describes the run-of-the-mill politician who is an insider and has few private qualities to define his or her popular appeal. Second, there is the political insider who has earned celebrity appeal by attracting extensive media attention.

Third, there is the outsider politician who operates as an 'ordinary citizen'. And in her fourth category, there is the political outsider and celebrity performer who has definite appeal but whose fame maintains a 'special' relationship with the public. Thus, van Zoonen comments that each category has it deficiencies: the political insider could be considered too boring for mass appeal while an exceptional celebrity outsider may raise expectations that cannot possibly be realized:

> The ultimate celebrity politician, then, the one who is able to balance the contradictory requirements of politics and celebrity, is located right in the middle of the plot. He or she projects a persona that has inside experience with politics but is still an outsider; his (or, in some cases, her) performance builds on a unique mixture of ordinariness and exceptionality. (van Zoonen 2005: 84)

Like van Zoonen, John Street considers how the aesthetics of celebrity politicians' performance provides a representation of their democratic worth. First, Street makes a distinction between those celebrity politicians (CP) who have used populist techniques when seeking elected office (CP1s) and those celebrities who have employed their fame to promote political issues (CP2s). In establishing these typologies, Street provides an analytical framework through which to consider the extent to which celebrity 'performances' may effect new forms of political engagement (Street 2004: 447; 2010: 256).

Street turns the focus of attention on politicized celebrities, commenting that they utilize their status and the medium they work in to speak out on specific causes to influence political outcomes. He notes that film and music stars, including Tim Robbins, Susan Sarandon, Robert Redford, Cher, Madonna and Ms Dynamite, have employed petitions and platforms to express outrage against the war in Iraq and a host of social issues. Moreover, Bono (Paul David Hewson) has been able to enter into key forums by having audiences with former US President George W. Bush and the late Pope John Paul II. Similarly, *Live Aid* founder and spokesman Bob Geldof provided a report card commentary on the 2005 G8 meetings and became a policy advisor to the Conservative Party's political leader David Cameron in forging his Global Poverty Group. This has meant that their views are treated with respect by the political classes because of their fame and affinity with audiences.

Second, Street is concerned to demonstrate how celebrity politics is consistent with a liberal democratic ethos. Therefore, Street is interested in the impact of celebrity performance on political outcomes as he sees fame as neither an exceptional or exaggerated form of representation, but a vital characteristic of modern political culture (Street 2003, 2004, 2010). He refers to Joseph Schumpeter's analogy between the worlds of commerce and politics to demonstrate how modern political communication has been dominated by marketing as the parties 'compete' for electoral support. Street suggests politics should be seen as a type of show business in which the currency is fame and the products are the stars' performances:

> In focusing on the style in which politics is presented, we need to go beyond mere description of the gestures and images. We need to assess them, to think about them as performances and to apply critical language appropriate to this. . . . To see politics as coterminous with popular culture is not to assume that it is diminished. . . . The point is to use this approach to discover the appropriate critical language with which to analyze it. (Street 2003: 97)

As celebrities legitimize political agendas, it becomes appropriate to consider how and why they define political campaigns. Thus, Street asks whether celebrities can use their reputations to reinvigorate politics with new ideas. These matters have been taken up by Philip Drake and Michael Higgins who note that 'the relationship between celebrity and politics needs to take into account the particular celebrity, the mode of performance they adopt, their earlier image, and the political claims they make' (Drake and Higgins 2006: 99–100).

Developing an effective taxonomy for celebrity politics: (3) Politicized celebrity systems as a model of celebrity political behaviour

Van Zoonen and Street have been concerned with how effective the political persona of CP1s and CP2s have been in shaping the democratic worth of their performance. Elsewhere, Max Boykoff and Mike Goodman's politicized celebrity systems (PCS) model has sought to situate such political behaviour within a contested and dynamic global space. They consider how a celebrity's political identity is captured through a range of media representations in which there has been a framing or typecasting of such activity.[4] Consequently, they expand on P. David Marshall's pioneering work which employs political theory to frame a co-dependency of complex relations between celebrities and their public. On the one hand, celebrity 'rationalizes' the social domain as it 'celebrates the potential of the individual and the mass's support of the individual in mass society' (Marshall 1997: 43). On the other, celebrities achieve their power due to the audience and the media's investment in propagating their 'exceptional' role within society. In turn, Boykoff and Goodman focus on the iconic and material: the technologies of the media; the orchestration of representations through ownership and entertainment 'markets' and how audiences sustain the power of the celebrity sign.

They maintain that five interlocking factors may define the political behaviour of a celebrity: celebrity performance; celebrity branding; celebrity artefacts; the political economy of celebrity; and audience responses. Celebrity performance encapsulates how the media representations of celebrities in their public and private lives have filled up the airtime due to the insatiable growth of 24/7 rolling news and entertainment channels. Celebrity branding demonstrates how certain celebrity brands enable the media to typecast stars in terms of their style and backgrounds. For instance, if U2's Bono or Coldplay's Chris Martin played a particular genre of music such as 'death metal', the public perception of their stumping up for global poverty reduction and fair trade would be indubitably different! In terms of celebrity artefacts, attention may be paid to the range of media through which celebrity performances may be channelled, such as newspapers, television, magazines and the internet. The political economy of the media demonstrates how a celebrity's desire to 'sell' his or her message in a competitive media landscape will demarcate the 'market' for this information. Finally, audiences sustain the power of the 'celebrity sign':

> Celebrities represent subject positions that audiences can adopt or adapt in their formations of social identities. Each celebrity represents a complex form of audience-subjectivity that, when placed within a system of celebrities, provides the ground on which distinctions, differences and oppositions are played out . . . The celebrity's strength or power as a discourse on the individual is operationalized only in terms of power and position of the audience that has allowed it to circulate. (Marshall 1997: 65)

Consequently, Boykoff and Goodman consider how the interconnected forces of celebrity performance *circulate* among one another, the media landscape and the audience. The reception that celebrity politicians are accorded by the public is vital in defining their image, persona and ability to define their sense of agency. The measurement of the worth of a celebrity politician is not only characterized by the ability to maintain a powerful voice or actualize a space for engagement, but must be understood in terms of the interface of 'mediated deliberations' which occurs within the medium of transaction between the celebrity and the audience. This more holistic approach shows how the context of celebrity engagement is as important a determinant as the political outcome of these activities in the wider community (Boykoff and Goodman 2009: 396). Finally, the PCS model has a further advantage in providing an understanding of the extent to which a celebrity activist may enjoy any real autonomy or whether the 'success' or not of their activism will be shaped by the forces of publicity, propaganda and opinion formation.

Conclusion

This chapter has sought to theorize a normative position for celebrity politics in an era of late modernism and post-democracy. It has outlined the academic debates which have emerged between critical theorists and writers who argue for a more holistic approach to political aesthetics. The traditional paradigm needs to be critically evaluated as it oversimplifies passivity in terms of celebrity activism and public engagement. In particular, it has been noted that politically conscious celebrities have brought about new forms of engagement which indicate a dialectical transformation of high-politics with a more populist approach to cultural citizenship.

These concerns have segued into a broader debate about a democratic deficit and the construction of a post-democratic order. Bang's notion of 'everyday makers' and Keane's monitory democracy allow for alternative ways of theorizing about political participation and accountability by placing an emphasis on space, voice and output. In turn, Street and van Zoonen have shown that celebrity politicians and politicized celebrities may fill the void that has been left by the contemporary political classes by re-establishing points of identification with the public. Bang has cited Barack Obama's 2008 US presidential election campaign as exemplifying how associative democratic practices were legitimized through the candidate's celebritization of his political message. In particular, Obama used Web 2.0 to construct a social network which was founded on the principles of inclusion to engage in a reciprocal relationship with the US electorate (see chapter 4). However, the success of the Tea Party in the 2010 Congressional elections in utilizing 'liquid' forms of political celebrity suggests that different types of political 'form' have overtaken ideological 'content'.

Therefore, while Bang and Keane capture the dynamics which accompany celebrity politics, it is necessary to consider the role that celebrities play in enhancing civic virtues and utilizing their agency to input into participatory practices. Celebrity politics must not only be seen to have social value but needs to provide the conditions through which a transformation in democratic behaviour may occur. From this normative position, this analysis has demonstrated that appropriate analytical tools are required to measure the worth of the democratic input of celebrity politics in an era of late modernity.

Thus, in the final section of this chapter, several analytical approaches have been outlined to develop a systematic taxonomy wherein the celebrity political engagement can be considered in terms of the personalization of politics, the rise of celebrity performance and the impact on audiences. Through such a synthesis of personal and political communication, van Zoonen, Street, Boykoff and Goodman have provided the analytical frameworks to consider the range of celebrity politics engagements that have occurred. These have placed an emphasis on the ordinary and extraordinary, the insider and outsider status of celebrity politicians and the relationship between celebrity politics and democratic form. Moreover, there is a corollary to these analyses in which such types of celebrity engagement must be contextualized through a process of political 'mediatization'. In particular, Davis has employed the French philosopher Pierre Bourdieu's concept of 'symbolic capital' to show how celebrity politics may be founded on mutual acquaintance and recognition:

> In one key Bourdieu tract (1991: 192): 'Political capital is a form of symbolic capital, credit founded on *credence* or belief or *recognition* or, more precisely, on the innumerable operations of credit by which agents confer on a person.' In other words, political capital is made up of capital forms, which include the symbolic, but this political capital is also conveyed symbolically, and bestowed by others. To succeed, therefore, politicians must be able to acquire symbolic capital amongst several audiences, including other politicians, intermediaries and ordinary citizens. (Davis 2010a: 85)

As celebrity politicians and politicized celebrities have utilized their fame to reinvigorate politics in terms of symbolic capital, a typology of celebrity politics should consider how these forms of imagery have been orchestrated across a range of campaigns. Therefore, celebrity engagements must not be restricted to mainstream politics but need to be referenced to a wider vision of political participation. Consequently, this book will provide a holistic approach to consider the different 'types' of celebrity activism. It will focus its attention on celebritization of political elites, the politicization of celebrity, the role of celebrity endorsements, expert advocacy, populist forms of activity and celebrity diplomacy. And it will situate its analysis within the contested nature of celebrity politics in the contemporary mass and social media to consider how symbolic forms of capital may shape audience expectations and the electorate's political efficacy.

Yet, paradoxically, while the majority of attention has been placed on the role of celebrity activism during the period of late modernity, it remains necessary to show that celebrity politics has had a distinct and long-running history. As George Pleios has commented, the history of fame parallels the formation of western civilization. Moreover, the transformation from the renown to be drawn from fame into the phenomenon of celebrity politics has been dictated by the reconfiguration of cultural practices from the 'training of man . . . (to the perception) of achievements . . . as the total sum of . . . [such] forms . . . (to the centrifugal position of) culture . . . as a way of life' (Pleios 2011: 252).

This book will consider how the historical continuum of fame and renown has interfaced with contemporary developments to shape the formation and reception of celebrity politics. As these matters are ongoing, they will continue to define the nature of celebrity politics into the twenty-first century across a variety of national, international and global forums. Thus, this analysis will remain mindful of the continuous reconfigurations of political aesthetics on modern democratic behaviour to demonstrate an intellectually curious approach to the topic of celebrity politics (Stanyer 2007: viii).

Questions

- Why have academics traditionally remained critical of celebrity activists?
- To what extent have celebrities demonstrated an 'affective capacity' to successfully intervene in political campaigns?
- How far is celebrity politics representative of new or alternative forms of political efficacy and democratic behaviour?

Further reading

Alberoni, F. 1972: The powerless elite. In D. McQuail (ed.), *Sociology of Mass Communications*. Harmondsworth: Penguin.

Bang, H. P. 2009: 'Yes we can': identity politics and project politics for a late-modern world. *Urban Research & Practice* 2(2): 117–37.

Keane, J. 2009: *The Life and Death of Democracy*. New York: Simon and Schuster.

Kellner, D. 2005: *Media Spectacle and the Crisis of Democracy*. Boulder, CO: Paradigm Press.

Marsh, D., 't Hart, P. and Tindall, K. 2010: Celebrity politics: the politics of the late modernity? *Political Studies Review* 8(3): 322–40.

Street, J. 2004: Celebrity politicians: popular culture and political representation. *The British Journal of Politics and International Relations* 6(4): 435–52.

2

A Historical Analysis of Celebrity Politics: The American Experience

This chapter provides a historical review of celebrity politics to offset the common perception that this phenomenon only emerged in an era of late modernity. The introduction of fame in politics can be traced back to antiquity and came to maturity with the advent of mass communications in the early twentieth century (Street 2010: 250; Pleios 2011: 251–2). Consequently, this survey will consider how kings, emperors, political leaders, writers, thinkers and poets achieved renown through the publicization of their heroic virtues or achievements.

Moreover, as Leo Braudy has noted, fame became democratized with the collapse of feudalism in the eighteenth century (Braudy 1997). Simon Morgan has suggested that the rise of celebrity was a key development in the process of modernity as it played 'a crucial role in the growth of the public sphere, the emergence of consumer society and the global expansion of western culture' (Morgan 2010: 367). In turn, this chapter will consider how the forms of social mobility associated with fame were reconfigured by the utilization of the mass media to manufacture a celebrity's persona. Further, with the rise of mass communication technologies, including newspapers, radio, film and television, celebrity became important for a leadership class which was increasingly defined by political imagery.

Subsequently, these developments had positive and negative outcomes for the celebritization of politics. In the 1920s and 1930s, continental Europe saw the rise of fascism and Nazism in Italy and Germany, which coupled together with the totalitarianism of the Soviet Union, produced charismatic leaders such as Benito Mussolini, Adolf Hitler and Joseph Stalin (Inglis 2010: 158–69). These dictators utilized the available media to perpetuate the cult of personality and public obedience to their unquestioning rule. Elsewhere, the dynamics of celebrity politics meant that democratic politicians started to use favourable imagery to connect with the electorate. Therefore, American presidents, including Franklin Delano Roosevelt and John Fitzgerald Kennedy, realized that radio and television could be employed to gain access to the United States public.

Alongside this employment of the media by the political classes, the twentieth century saw the rise of the modern celebrity. This can be traced back to the construction of the Hollywood star system in which the studios created iconographic personas for comedians or actors such as Charlie Chaplin, Mary Pickford and Douglas Fairbanks to market their films to a mass audience (Huddart 2005: 14). Subsequently, as the stars' fame grew, politicians realized the benefits of getting celebrities to endorse their candidacies to appeal to a wider constituency of support. The most extensive use of celebrities coincided with the ascendancies of the two most media-savvy chief executives, Franklin D. Roosevelt and John F. Kennedy, thereby establishing a template for modern endorsements.

However, this incorporation of celebrity into campaign politics went hand in hand with a growing tendency amongst film and music stars to attach themselves to causes. They became associated with the protest movements of the 1960s and 1970s concerning civil rights, the war in Vietnam and the plutocratic nature of politics. These forms of activism had their antecedents in the writings of Mark Twain, the political radicalism of singers including Woody Guthrie, Pete Seeger and Paul Robeson, and in the Hollywood liberal-left's links with the anti-fascist Popular Front. The Centre-Left in the US entertainment community became the focus of the right-wing 'McCarthyite' anti-communist paranoia which affected all areas of American public life during the Cold War of the 1940s and 1950s. These controversies meant that many singers, writers and actors were blacklisted while others shied away from political activity.

Celebrity activism, however, would enjoy a rebirth in the social, political and cultural ferment of the 1960s and 1970s. As the Hollywood studio system declined, stars were freed from the tight publicity controls that had existed to engage with causes on the Left (Jane Fonda, Donald Sutherland, Robert Vaughn and the anti-Vietnam movement), in civil rights (Harry Belafonte, Sidney Poitier, Sammy Davis Jr), for Native Americans (Marlon Brando) and within mainstream campaigns (Robert Redford and Warren Beatty) (McDonald 2008: 167). Moreover, these trends gave expression to the 'baby-boomer' generation's engagement with alternative values and radical ideals. With varying degrees of involvement, rock stars such as Bob Dylan, John Lennon and Mick Jagger became associated with social movements that challenged authority and propagated rebellion.

Heroic virtues: the history of fame, celebrity and renown from antiquity to modernity

While the celebritization of politics has become a focus of attention in recent years, the utilization of fame, renown and performance in political affairs is a historical phenomenon. Daniel Boorstin contended that during antiquity a 'golden age' existed in which honour and heroism were recognized without any form of public expression (Boorstin 1971: 57). Instead of fame becoming an end in itself, recognition of an accomplishment was secondary to the achievement itself: 'In more theoretical understandings of fame and celebrity, the two are defined regularly as distinct from each other. "Celebrity" is a product of the publicity produced by the twentieth- and twenty-first century mass media, whereas "fame" has a longer history as the typification resulting from outstanding . . . achievements' (van Zoonen 2006: 290).[1]

Conversely, Braudy has contended that such a distinction is arbitrary as the accomplishment of fame has always been subject to a form of image management (Braudy 1997: 8). Rather than there being a golden age, he has shown that famed individuals had their actions mediated by long-standing forms of publicity as 'whatever the field, in public life fame is a contract between the audience and the aspirant' (ibid.: 9).

In Ancient Greece, the principles of fame were constructed through the worship of heroic deeds as popularized in the *Iliad* (800 BC) and the *Odyssey* (800 BC), and by the Greek Sophists who concluded that virtue was a matter of great performance. Liesbet van Zoonen has contended that the Sophists were the 'spin doctors' of their age as they refined the art of rhetoric so leaders could persuasively communicate to the public (van Zoonen 2005: 71). Further, Braudy has shown how Alexander the Great grappled with the vicissitudes of fame while understanding the need to publicize his accomplishments (Braudy 1997: 32). Popular discourses on fame, talent and state triumphalism came to fruition within the Roman empire, which celebrated its generals' victories with parades to construct a vision for its imperial manifest destiny. Most especially, Greek and Roman warriors achieved a mythical status in the heroic nature of their deaths, thereby fostering the glories of their empires.

These values of leadership, rhetoric and renown were apparent in the *ancien régime* as feudal autocrats employed the principles of fame to differentiate themselves from the rest of society. Niccolò Machiavelli's treatise on statecraft, *The Prince* (1532), contended that an apparently virtuous persona was a requirement of political leadership even while exercising coercive force to maintain power (Corner 2003: 68). This understanding was reinforced by the activities of kings and emperors to maintain the appearance of popularity. Jessica Evans has commented that Louis XIV staged pseudo-events, including 'spontaneous' public rejoicings at political or military victories, to advance his public appeal (Evans 2005: 21–2). Further, the image of the 'Roi-Soleil' ('Sun King') was perpetuated across France: '[Louis XIV's] advisors aimed to project a triumphal image modelled on Alexander the Great. . . . His image was everywhere, inscribed on clocks, ceilings and furnishings, paintings, tapestries, monuments, sculptures, shop signs and cheap pottery plates . . .' (ibid.: 20).

Such representations of politicians would become commonplace in the seventeenth and eighteenth centuries. However, instead of reinforcing the absolutism of monarchs, this imagery reflected the democratic reforms of the age as fame equated with social mobility (Braudy 1997). The American and French revolutions toppled monarchical power to create societies 'in which aspiration was not determined by birth or money but by talent and ability' (ibid.: 613). Consequently, the 'democratization' of fame meant that it was '[n]o longer . . . restricted to . . . individuals holding privileged positions, such as kings and popes . . . [as] it was possible for ordinary people to be elevated to social and political prominence' (West and Orman 2003: 8).

This flowering of fame became available to men of letters, social reformers, scientists, artists and actors. For instance, famed non-politicos such as John Milton, John Dryden and Andrew Marvell contributed to the debates about the English Civil War (Street 2010: 250). Moreover, the politics of fame resonated through the age of the Romantic, the European *fin de siècle* and the Gilded Age in New York and Washington (Inglis 2010). One figure of note was the poet George Gordon, Lord Byron, who became characterized by his paradoxical tendencies towards seductive passion and the defence of reason. Byron understood that as a libertine he could receive the adoration of the public and this allowed him to live his life 'on the split between sense and sensibility' (ibid.: 67). Yet he also employed his fame to push forward the causes of equality, fraternity and liberty, a fight for which he ultimately died when supporting Greek democratic rights against the Ottoman empire. His death was explicitly politicized when it made international headlines, while his romanticism became a key determinant in creating his celebrity persona.

The popular expression of fame and renown coincided with the industrialization of the printing press in the second half of the nineteenth century. Subsequently, writers such as Oscar Wilde and Charles Dickens became public intellectuals. Dickens, along with other authors such as Ralph Waldo Emerson and Henry David Thoreau, used his fame to support the abolitionist crusades against slavery. These developments would be taken further with the advent of photography as indicated by Matthew Brady's images of US President Abraham Lincoln which popularized the chief executive during his struggles in the American Civil War.

Moreover, the inventions of the telegraph and cinematic film meant that heroic deeds could be recorded and disseminated to mass audiences. Therefore, wartime heroes such as T. E. Lawrence, whose fame in the First World War's British Middle East campaigns against Turkey was orchestrated by the American documentary film-maker Lowell Thomas, became international celebrities. These developments proved to be key determinants in defining political imagery within the USA as the 'New World' was born within the context of the American democratic experiment. Consequently, with the USA's position as the world's most advanced economy, there would be an accompanying industrialization of leisure practices throughout the twentieth century.

The rise of US celebrity politicians in the nineteenth and twentieth centuries

There has been a special coalescence of celebrity and politics in the USA. This reflected the framers of the Declaration of Independence's desire to affect an American Republic which was defined by liberty, fraternity and equality. These constructions placed an emphasis on the formation of a meritocracy in which there could be opportunities for all. This dynamic intensified the demands to learn new ways of being as:

> New Worlds required new selves, and actors, who could play a variety of roles, had a professional expertise in the new etiquettes. Being on

> stage did not limit or debase who you were. It expanded it. Fame could wear the guise of freedom. No wonder then that in this new democratic world, the performer should become the model of how to be and how to be seen. (Braudy 1997: 613–14)

These values would become mythologized in the principles of the 'American Dream' and would take shape across a range of media. Therefore, Lincoln's rise from his birth in a log cabin to the presidency became part of the national mythology; Horatio Alger's courageous heroes would be mentored by upper-class benefactors to set them on their way to success, and Hollywood films would perpetuate a vision of a meritocratic and just society.

Moreover, such ideals combined with the American exceptionalism that was noted by Alexis de Tocqueville in his book *Democracy in America* (1830). This model of US democracy contended that individual liberties and communitarian responsibilities should define what it meant to be an American citizen. As de Tocqueville commented, Americans formed political associations and 'in towns it is impossible to prevent men from assembling, getting excited together and forming sudden passionate resolves' (de Tocqueville 1830). According to Inglis, this call for passion operated in parallel with the rise of reason in defining democratic behaviour (Inglis 2010: 19).

Thus, in the light of these forms of mobility, association and feeling, American political candidates constructed a form of heroism to relate to the electorate. Former generals employed their profiles to attain electoral support and many leading presidents were famed for their exploits on the battlefield. For instance, George Washington, Andrew Jackson, William Henry Harrison and Ulysses S. Grant used their military fame to gain high office. It has been speculated that General George Armstrong Custer, who achieved a lasting place in the national mythology due to his 'Last Stand' at Little Big Horn when defeated by the Sioux Indians in 1876, had intended to use his exploits to enter the White House (Braudy 1997: 507–8).

Other leaders were legacy politicians drawn from celebrated families, including the Roosevelts, the Adams and the Harrisons, who produced six presidents (Theodore 'Teddy' Roosevelt and Franklin D. Roosevelt, John and John Quincy Adams, and William Henry and Benjamin Harrison). Later, Joseph P. Kennedy, a Wall Street financier who was appointed by Franklin D. Roosevelt to become the US Ambassador to the Court of St James in the United Kingdom, started a dynasty which included John F. Kennedy and his brother Senator Robert F. Kennedy. As Stephen Hess has commented, 700 families have accounted for '1,700 of the 10,000 men and women who have been elected to the federal legislature since 1774' (Hess 2000).

In turn, with the mass circulation of newspapers, the barriers between the public and private face of politicians were breached as the personalization of politics became of greater concern in the early decades of the twentieth century. This was apparent in a 1907 article by Willis J. Abbot entitled 'At Home with William Jennings Bryan' which emphasized that, for all of the so-called 'Great Commoner's' achievements, his heart lay in his home (Evans and Hesmondhalgh 2005: 26).

US presidents became icons whose images were readily identifiable with the aspirations of 1900s' society. Teddy Roosevelt's politics owed much to the theatrics of vaudeville, which emphasized his 'larger-than-life' characteristics. Thus, Roosevelt transformed himself from a sickly, asthmatic child into a rugged outdoors man. Despite his background as an Ivy Leaguer, Roosevelt, along with his friend and fellow Easterner, the painter Frederic Remington, became indelibly associated with the Wild West. He became an advocate for the national parks movement, a hunter of great bears and celebrated cowboys in his bestselling book, *Ranch Life and The Hunting-Trail* (1888).[2] These values underpinned Roosevelt's belief that it was the USA's manifest destiny to become an international power once the western frontier had been tamed in the 1890s.

As a committed expansionist, Teddy Roosevelt resigned from his post as assistant secretary of the navy when the *USS Maine* was attacked by Spain and joined the Rough Riders in their spectacular cavalry charges during the 1898 Spanish–American War. In defining his all-American action image, Roosevelt benefited from the publicity he engendered from writing about his adventures and from commissioning Remington to paint the charge in heroic form. Further, several short film 'actualities' were produced and exhibited to US audiences in 1898–9. These one-minute documentaries were faked re-enactments and included *US Troops Landing at Daiquiri, Cuba* (1898) and *Roosevelt's Rough Riders* (1898), which showed the cavalry charging at the camera (Neve 2011: 69). Therefore, when Teddy Roosevelt became president in 1901, he had established a strong bond with the US public to reinvigorate '[t]he *idea* of America similar to that of Lafayette . . . [that demonstrated that] . . . personal success, fame and honour were not self-interested [individuals who were] opposed to national glory but [were] intimately connected with it' (Braudy 1997: 552).

In the Great Depression, Roosevelt's fifth cousin, Franklin

D. Roosevelt, expanded the executive prerogative to restore confidence in US leadership. To define his image as a benign authority who preached populist common sense, Franklin D. Roosevelt developed his rhetorical abilities. Most notably, he stated in his 1933 inaugural speech that 'the only thing we have to fear is fear itself.' He established a rapport with the American public through his 'fireside chats' delivered on the National Broadcasting Company (NBC) radio coast-to-coast network.[3] These were designed to reiterate his skills as a leader and to provide hope during a period of outstanding crisis. In Roosevelt's first broadcast on 12 March 1933, he explained how he would deal with the collapse of the banks and asked for the public's support by concluding 'Together we cannot fail.' As he informed Orson Welles, this was a matter of performance: 'There are two great actors in America today. You are one of them' (Keyishian 2011: 127). This image of Franklin D. Roosevelt was further perpetuated in the Hollywood films of the era in which 'the movie Roosevelt . . . [was] one with big ideas for the country's future and expressing special concern for the poor and disadvantaged' (ibid.: 110).

Further, despite his paralysis resulting from the life-threatening polio he had contracted in the 1920s, Roosevelt maintained the pretence of being an apparently healthy president. This was vital for national confidence, and the US media made no mention of his disability. While he was privately confined to a wheelchair, the newsreels of the day demonstrated Roosevelt walking to engagements from his car with the aid of hidden steel leg braces and always linked arm in arm with an aide or one of his sons.

A similar confluence of image, celebrity and oratory skills would mark the candidacy and presidency of John F. Kennedy. Kennedy, due to his seductive image, personal charm and understanding of the dynamics of television, affected an even greater degree of political style than his predecessors. In this respect, he built on the personalization of politics which had been apparent in Dwight D. Eisenhower's presidential administration. Eisenhower had appealed to voters after his role in the Second World War as Allied Chief Commander in the European theatre; his likeability was epitomized in the 'I like Ike' mantra of his landslide victory in 1952 (West and Orman 2003: 44).[4]

Similarly, part of Kennedy's mythology referred to his heroic war record as the commander of PT Boat 109. Elsewhere, he achieved national recognition as a precocious political talent from the publication of his bestselling, Pulitzer prizewinning book *Profiles in Courage* (1955) which chronicled the acts of integrity in the careers of eight

US senators. This would be enhanced by his decision to stand for the Democratic Party's vice-presidential nomination in 1956.

Most famously, in his 1960 presidential election debates with Vice-President Richard M. Nixon, Kennedy affected an appropriate dress sense by wearing a dark suit against a grey background, appeared suitably healthy and tanned as opposed to his opponent's drained expression and five o'clock shadow, provided discernible sound bites, remained reactive as well as active in cut-away shots and performed in a relaxed manner in accordance with the editorial grammar of television.[5] Theodore H. White's *The Making of the President, 1960* (1961) concluded that Nixon had provided the more substantive answers and won over the radio audience. However, for the 70 million viewers who had watched the debates, Kennedy had developed a 'star quality' which coincided with the positive message of the 'New Frontier'.

Moreover, the celebritization of the Kennedy administration was reinforced by the glamour of his wife Jackie who transformed the White House into 'Camelot'. On Valentine's Day 1962, she invited national television cameras into the presidential home to show the restorations she had made to the building. Inglis notes that both Kennedys melded their images of private individuals and public figures to be simultaneously ordinary and extraordinary (Inglis 2010: 177). Consequently, Kennedy interlinked his public figuration with his actual character to perform like a movie star so that he effortlessly 'filled the frame'. As Mark White comments, the Kennedy image became a brand in which Kennedy, his family and supporters constructed 'a multifaceted and potentially alluring image of his personality' (White 2011: 132). This was bolstered by Kennedy's stylish conduct, his status as a family man and his sexual allure. Moreover, both Kennedy's and Franklin D. Roosevelt's presidencies would be noted for their cross-fertilization of the politics of fame with the marked increase of celebrity endorsements.

Early forms of US celebrity endorsement

Throughout the nineteenth and early twentieth centuries, several presidents mixed with show-business personalities. It is said that during the civil war, Lincoln left a cabinet meeting to greet two superstars of the day – Tom Thumb and his wife Lavinia. Moreover, the comic film star Marie Dressler paid a social call on Teddy Roosevelt whom she considered to be 'the most vigorous and magnetic personality' she had ever encountered. In 1918, Woodrow Wilson invited Mary Pickford, Douglas Fairbanks, Charlie Chaplin and Marie Dressler to sell war bonds during the First World War (Schroeder 2004: 18). Dressler embarrassed Pickford when she told an off-colour story to the austere Wilson who neither passed comment nor smiled at her wisecracks!

During the 1920 presidential campaign, the Republican candidate Senator Warren Harding garnered support from vaudeville and film stars such as Al Jolson, Pickford, Fairbanks and Blanche Ring. Notably, Jolson led a delegation of fifty Broadway entertainers to Harding's home town of Marion in Ohio to endorse the candidate. On arrival, Jolson serenaded the candidate and his wife Florence with a song written for the occasion (Schroeder 2004: 115):[6]

> We think the country's ready,
> For a man like Teddy,
> One who is a fighter through and through.
> We need another Lincoln,
> To do the nation's thinkin',
> And Mr Harding, we've selected you. (*Time Magazine* 1924)

Metro-Goldwyn-Mayer's (MGM) Louis B. Mayer became the vice-chairman of the Southern Californian Republican Party and formed alliances with President Herbert Hoover. Yet, throughout the 1920s, Presidents Harding, Calvin Coolidge and Hoover largely kept at a formal distance from show business.

Celebrity endorsements became more significant in the 1930s when a close relationship emerged between the US film industry and the political classes. As films became the key entertainment form for US audiences in the first half of the twentieth century, their worth became apparent as 'movies [were] . . . part of the social glue of American life' (Ross 2002: 2–4). Therefore, leading American politicians realized the political capital that could be drawn from the endorsement of film stars. Moreover, the relations between Hollywood and politicians were a two-way street. For the Jewish film moguls, mixing with the powerful indicated an acceptance by America's elites. Thus, there were strong links between Franklin D. Roosevelt and Warner Brothers' studio, which prided itself on making 'good films for good citizens' and whose movies supported New Deal values. Through his flamboyant presentation of his New Deal policies, the 'tribune of the people' was favourably received by many of the stars in Tinseltown.

Hollywood Democrats and their support for Franklin Roosevelt

Throughout his 1932 presidential campaign, Roosevelt received the backing of film celebrities including Will Rogers, Stan Laurel, Oliver Hardy and Katherine Hepburn. And he was the recipient of endorsements from glamorous stars at an enormous Motion Picture Electrical Parade and Sport Pageant at the Los Angeles Olympic Stadium organized by Jack and Harry Warner. Sitting in a flag-draped box, the future president was courted by the Hollywood royalty who were as much in thrall to him as he was to them. Roosevelt's liberalism appealed to those members of the Hollywood community who were concerned about injustice at home and the encroachment of fascism abroad. In particular, the comedian Rogers was deemed, from 1933 until his untimely death in 1935, to be the 'number one new dealer' through his advancement of Roosevelt's Keynesian policies on his radio show: 'On the radio he mixed the humorous advice . . . with words of support for "Franklin's" effort to pass social security, to levy high income taxes on the rich, and to provide jobs through public works. In the world of foreign affairs, Rogers was also one of the first to recognize the rise of fascist threats' (May 2002: 45).

Roosevelt was the first president to understand the public worth of mixing with Hollywood's popular celebrities (Schroeder 2004: 17). Thus, stars were invited to galas where Roosevelt charmed favoured actors and actresses into lending themselves to election campaigns and public works schemes. Even the conservative comic Bob Hope described himself as a 'Republocrat' on being received in 1944 (ibid.: 65). Most especially, Roosevelt formed close relations with liberal supporters, including Melvyn Douglas, his wife Helen Gahagan Douglas, Orson Welles and Frank Sinatra:

> FDR was prescient enough to recognize that in a democratic society, elected officials had much to gain by embracing the people's choice. Millions of moviegoers – the same people who put Roosevelt in the White House – had ratified the popularity of actors and actresses invited to the birthday balls. Combining forces with the big names of screen could only enhance a politician's standing. (ibid.: 18)

Consequently, the Hollywood Democratic Committee (HDC) was formed to support Roosevelt throughout his election campaigns in 1936, 1940 and 1944. And film and music stars such as Humphrey Bogart, John Garfield and Judy Garland appeared at the presidential rallies and whistle-stop tours. As *Life Magazine* (1883 onwards) commented: 'Since the New Deal's salad days, Tin Pan Alley has almost been as staunchly Democratic as Tammany Hall. Broadway and Hollywood have consistently expended most of their political enthusiasm on Franklin D. Roosevelt' (*Life Magazine* 1944: 32).

The 1944 campaign marked a high point for the relationship between Franklin D. Roosevelt and the entertainment community. During this campaign, entertainers engaged in a four-week musical revue in Boston entitled the 'FDR Victory Bandwagon' and film stars hosted a 'Hollywood is FDR' Democratic Club dinner. Politics attracted leading actresses such as Rita Hayworth and Evelyn Keyes, who provided their support because of the thrill of the campaign.

Frank Sinatra entered the political fray when Roosevelt invited him to the White House for tea and the singer noted that Roosevelt was 'the greatest guy alive today and here's this little guy from Hoboken shaking his hand' (Sinatra 1944). Further, at a Democratic Political Action Committee luncheon in New York, Sinatra declared that he spoke for the youth of America 'who are thinking in the right way and the right way is the Roosevelt way' (*Life Magazine* 1944: 32). Roosevelt's Republican opponents criticized his relationship with a mere 'crooner' who had been exempt from the draft. In riposte, Sinatra dropped a new lyric concerning his meeting with 'Franklin D' into his popular song, *Everything Happens to Me* (1940) (Brownstein 1990: 94). Moreover, to prove their adoration, his bobbysoxer fans wore buttons which read 'Frankie's for FDR and so are we.'

Orson Welles was another energetic supporter of Roosevelt's cause when he endorsed him on his radio shows, in his weekly political column and by tirelessly appearing at election rallies and banquets. Indeed, he collapsed with exhaustion in the final days of the campaign. For Welles, the experience had been so intoxicating that he considered standing for the junior senatorial seat in Wisconsin in 1946. Later, he berated himself not only for his naivety for dropping out because of his belief that as an actor he could not achieve office, but also because his Republican opponent would have been Joseph R. McCarthy, who came to personify the Red Scares of the Cold War.

Celebrity endorsement for Franklin D. Roosevelt reached a pinnacle when the HDC ran a national radio broadcast for the Democrats' final appeal on the eve of the election. The writer and producer Norman Corwin enlisted Bogart as the show's narrator, Garland to sing an opening song, *You Gotta Get Out and Vote* (1944), James Cagney and Groucho Marx to provide satirical sketches and lyricist

Figure 2.1 'Everything happens to me': Frank Sinatra, 'Franklin D' and Eleanor Roosevelt

E. Y. Harburg, writer of *Somewhere over the Rainbow* (1939), to orchestrate the songs. Wisely, Corwin interspersed his famous contributors with ordinary voices drawn from a range of workers, farmers and housewives. The show proved to be a triumph and an effective tone was set when Bogart stated: 'This is Humphrey Bogart . . . Personally, I am voting for Franklin D. Roosevelt because I believe he is one of the world's greatest humanitarians: because he's leading our fight against the enemies of a free world' (ibid.: 101).

Consequently, for Hollywood, the 1944 campaign was a milestone in demonstrating that the film industry's support had been integral to Franklin D. Roosevelt's victory (ibid.: 102).

Celebrity politicians and political celebrities

As the first televisual commander-in-chief, John F. Kennedy inherited Roosevelt's mantle as the entertainment community's favoured political son. For the New Frontier generation, Kennedy personified the hopes of liberalism against the previous conformity of the 1950s. His enormous cultural and symbolic impact upon American politics proved to be a rallying call for celebrity endorsers: 'More than any president before or since, Kennedy testified to the irresistible attraction between power and glamour. Inadvertently perhaps, he thus restored the frayed idea that stars had a legitimate place in the political world' (ibid.: 145). He realized how his association with Frank

Sinatra and his 'Rat Pack' created a popular vision of the union of politics with the aristocracy of fame. This relationship had been mediated by Kennedy's brother-in-law and second-string to Sinatra, the film and television actor Peter Lawford. In particular, Sinatra was in thrall to Kennedy as both men shared a mutual admiration for each other's talents, politics and womanizing.

During the 1960 Democratic National Convention, Sinatra inveigled his friends Janet Leigh, Tony Curtis, Sammy Davis Jr, Nat King Cole and Judy Garland to participate in a range of events to glamorize Kennedy's candidacy. Moreover, Sinatra and Leigh worked the convention floor by lobbying delegates and promoting Kennedy to the press. Throughout the campaign, Kennedy feared that too much chumminess with show-business people might damage his image. Yet he appeared at star-studded rallies in New York and Los Angeles organized by Sinatra, and in an unusual campaign advert with the singer-actor/activist Harry Belafonte. This spot ad had Kennedy mostly listening while Belafonte, as 'a Negro and as an American', pleaded the candidate's case for him.

Sinatra was responsible for producing Kennedy's inaugural ball which notably integrated white and black artists. And its roster of stars included Belafonte, Jimmy Durante, Laurence Olivier, Sidney Poitier, Gene Kelly, Leonard Bernstein, Ethel Merman and Bette Davis, who declared 'the entertainment world to be the new sixth state' (Purdum 2011). When Sinatra closed this 'show of shows' with a 'Kennedyized' version of *High Hopes* (1959), his relationship with John F. Kennedy reached its apotheosis. However, his association with organized crime meant that Kennedy ultimately dropped the entertainer.[7] Yet, the die had been cast and Kennedy would (in) famously consort with Marilyn Monroe and be serenaded by rising stars such as Barbra Streisand at his birthday galas (White 2011: 133).

Subsequently, other celebrities campaigned for politicians. A small number of stars attached themselves to the Republican Party. John Wayne, who had been the president of the right-wing Motion Picture Alliance, demonstrated his fervent anti-communism by joining the John Birch Society and publicly endorsing Nixon in his 1960 and 1968 presidential election campaigns. When promoting his patriotic film *The Alamo* (1960), in a dig at Kennedy's use of Theodore Sorenson to write *Profiles in Courage*, Wayne claimed 'There were no ghost-writers at the Alamo' (Wills 1997: 202). In turn, he became an icon for right-wingers, a good friend of Arizona Senator Barry Goldwater and was asked by Republicans to stand for office.

The most visible right-wing film star was Charlton Heston, who shed his former liberalism to become an arch-conservative in the 1970s. Previously, Heston had been an activist within the civil rights movement and an advocate of fellow actors when serving terms as the Screen Actors Guild (SAG) president and the chairman of the American Film Institute (AFI). However, he had an epiphany in 1964 and decided to give his soul, if not his vote, to the hard-line conservative Republican presidential candidate Goldwater:

> [w]hile driving by a billboard with . . . Goldwater's face and the slogan, 'In your heart you know he's right.' The slogan . . . with its double meaning of being correct and to the right of the political spectrum . . . was not lost on Heston. By his own recollection, he said out loud as he passed by the billboard, 'Son of a bitch . . . he [Goldwater] is right!' (Rabidoux 2009: 142)

But his ultimate conversion to Republicanism only occurred in his support for Nixon in 1972, and his rightwards drift from a moderate conservative to hard-line activist would be later confirmed when he became president of the National Rifle Association (NRA) in 1998. In the meantime, he was even approached by the Democratic Party to stand as a senator, although his transformation to conservative values had been hastened by a trip to Vietnam in which he became an advocate for US intervention in South-East Asia (Ross 2011: 208–304).

Yet the rest of the US entertainment community was a bastion of centre-left politics in the 1960s. In 1968, Paul Newman appeared at campaign rallies for the anti-Vietnam war candidate Eugene McCarthy in the Democratic primaries, commenting 'It's not enough to sit around at parties and be concerned about the war . . . If you don't participate, you're not entitled to anything' (*Life Magazine* 1968). In addition, Newman appeared in campaign commercials and acted as the master of ceremonies at a telethon to raise money for McCarthy. However, it was his early support for McCarthy in the New Hampshire primary that proved vital in raising the candidate's visibility to national political figure. This was reflected in McCarthy's strong showing of 42 per cent of the vote in the primary as compared to Lyndon B. Johnson's 49 per cent of the poll. This political earthquake affected the respective decisions of Lyndon Johnson to withdraw from seeking the nomination and of Robert Kennedy to enter into the Democratic race. Throughout the rest of the election, Newman would continue to campaign for McCarthy and was accompanied by Alan Arkin, Woody Allen, Barbra Streisand, Burt Lancaster, Tony Randall, Dick Van Dyke and Leonard Nimoy.

In 1972, Warren Beatty and his sister Shirley MacLaine put their careers on hold to work for the Democratic presidential nominee George McGovern, whose anti-Vietnam war stance had attracted a liberal constituency of support. Further, McGovern represented a direct challenge to what Beatty and MacLaine saw as the moral and ethical hypocrisy of the Nixon administration (Rabidoux 2009: 42). MacLaine's front-of-house activism led to her interests in the Women's Movement. Indeed, she claimed that she was one of the 'new politicians' who would use her celebrity to influence voters (Schroeder 2004: 84). Beatty preferred to operate behind the scenes as a campaign manager. In this capacity, he established a formidable relationship with the chief Democratic organizer, Gary Hart, to become one of McGovern's inner circle of key advisors (Biskind 2010: 167–71).

Most especially, Beatty pioneered fund-raising concerts with Streisand, James Taylor and Quincy Jones to net US$1 million for the Democratic nominee (Schroeder 2004: 130–1). To canvass votes, he coordinated friends such as Jack Nicholson, Gene Hackman, Dustin Hoffman, Julie Christie and Goldie Hawn to knock on doors and usher at rallies. These celebrity events reached a crescendo when Beatty persuaded acts such as Simon and Garfunkel and Peter, Paul and Mary to reform at a 'Together for McGovern Reunion Concert' held at Madison Square Gardens in June 1972:

> Good ole George, honest and bland, is being transformed into . . . George the Hip . . . because of a powerful new magic weapon in his campaign. The weapon not only attracts Now Hollywood and rock royalty to the McGovern fold, but . . . raises enough dough in a single night to give the contributors at ITT a run for their money. The magic weapon is . . . Warren Beatty. (Orth 1972)

Beatty provided a celebrity formula that could be utilized by lesser-known candidates to announce their arrival on the national scene. For instance, Jimmy Carter, in the early period of his presidential campaign, relied on monies drawn from southern country rock groups such as the Allman Brothers, the Marshall Tucker Band and Charlie Daniels before receiving funds from traditional donors.

Throughout the 1970s, Beatty remained the entertainment community's most regular fixture in liberal Democratic politics. In 1976, he helped a reluctant Carter court the entertainment community, and it was suggested that Beatty might seek electoral office. However, by the second half of the decade, Robert Redford's approach to act as a citizen activist who engaged in environmental causes rather than acting as an endorser of Democratic candidates became prevalent. Redford's position reflected his belief that showbiz and electoral politics functioned more effectively when each side honoured their differences. Moreover, his activism was illustrative of a growing perception among celebrities that they could use their clout for causal rather than partisan effect: 'By the late 1960s, the stars feel involved enough and the politicians have been diminished enough, that they look across the stage and say, "Hey, maybe I belong up there. If people will listen to me, the act of giving me the microphone validates me"' (Brownstein 2000).

The history of US celebrity activism: authors, famed non-politicos, singers and songwriters, the Hollywood Popular Front and the blacklist

There has been a tradition in US public life in which celebrities have spoken out on the matters of the day. The author Mark Twain (Samuel Langhorne Clemens) criticized TR's advocacy of Big Stick diplomacy in the 1898–1902 Spanish–American war in Cuba and the Philippines (Schama 2008). Twain denounced the atrocities which were committed against Spanish and Filipino independence fighters. And his savage satirical essay, 'To the Person Sitting in Darkness' (1901), argued that there were 'two Americas: one that sets the captive free, and one that takes a once-captive's new freedom away from him . . . then kills him to get his land' (Twain 1901: 162). Such a critique of US imperialism led to Twain being censored as his writings were pulled from the newspapers of the time.

When the aviator Charles Lindbergh gained global fame for becoming the first pilot to fly solo non-stop across the Atlantic, he became a spokesman for America's isolationist movement, was an honoured guest of Adolf Hitler's Nazis and received an Iron Cross from Herman Goering. He addressed several thousand members of the anti-interventionist America First Committee rallies in Chicago and New York in the summer of 1941 and his speeches were broadcast to millions more. Lindbergh was accused by the Roosevelt government of being an anti-Semite and an apologist for Nazi Germany (Roth 2005: 371). Despite Lindbergh contributing to test flights and flying combat missions in the Pacific campaign against Japan as a civilian pilot, Roosevelt refused to renew Lindbergh's commission as a flying officer.

One of Lindbergh's most vocal critics on the American left was the folk singer Woody Guthrie, who wrote the song 'Mister Charlie Lindbergh' (1943) which commented on the aviator's collaboration with Hitler. Guthrie, with Pete Seeger, popularized the values of working-class life, solidarity and trade union organization. As an economic migrant from the 'dust bowl' state of Oklahoma, he suffered from the simultaneous calamities of natural disaster and the Great Depression. Like thousands of fellow 'Oakies', when arriving in California he was subjected to hatred and injustice. Consequently, Guthrie produced songs detailing the plight of the dispossessed. He pilloried corrupt politicians, lawyers and bankers, and championed Jesus Christ, outlaws Pretty Boy Floyd and Jesse James, and the union leader Joe Hill.

When Guthrie moved to New York he was welcomed by the leftist actor Will Geer, who introduced him to Seeger. In the 1940s, he wrote songs such as 'This Land is Your Land' (1944) and performed with Seeger in The Almanacs, the predecessor to The Weavers, and together they established a small but commercial form of urban folk music. Yet, in 1951, Guthrie's output ended when he was diagnosed with Huntington's disease. Despite his rapid demise, Guthrie had been prodigious, writing over two thousand songs and producing two autobiographical novels. Indeed, he would achieve greater fame in the legacy of his work than he ever achieved in his lifetime as his compositions had a profound effect on his successors, most notably Bob Dylan, Phil Ochs and his son Arlo.

The popular African-American singer Paul Robeson was another outspoken spokesman for progressive causes. For instance, Robeson co-founded the Council on African Affairs to support anti-colonialism in Africa and visited Spain during the civil war to rally Republican troops. Further, he denounced the Nazi's anti-Semitic treatment of Jews and donated the proceeds of his performance in *The Emperor Jones* (1934) to Jewish refugees. Later, he became a vocal supporter of Jawaharlal Nehru and the Indian independence movement; publicly repudiated the anti-communism of the 'McCarthyite' witch-hunts; criticized the Central Intelligence Agency's (CIA) coup in Guatemala in 1954; and endorsed the Reverend Martin Luther King, Jr for his protest against racial segregation.

In tandem in Hollywood, the Popular Front was formed from a coalition of centre-leftist organizations to act against fascism. One group was the Anti-Nazi League for Defence of American

Democracy, which included writers and directors such as Philip Dunne and John Cromwell and film stars and actors like Edward G. Robinson, Gloria Stuart, Frederic March, his wife Florence Eldridge, and the Douglases. The League was accompanied by the Motion Picture Democratic Committee and the Motion Picture Artists Committee to Aid a Republican Spain (MPAC), whose membership peaked at 15,000 (Ceplair and Englund 2003: 97).

For the Front's leaders, the recruitment of celebrities allowed them to publicize an anti-fascist agenda throughout the US media. The Anti-Nazi League mounted petitions, held public meetings, broadcasted a weekly radio programme, published a bi-weekly paper and picketed the German Embassy. In 1939, it sponsored several labour and Quarantine Hitler rallies while coordinating with the MPAC for a 'Save Spain' rally at the Hollywood Legion stadium. Simultaneously, the MPAC raised funds for the Republican cause when it staged a successful political cabaret called 'Sticks and Stones' whose skits were written by some of Hollywood's top writers to criticize fascists, reactionaries and appeasers: 'The entertainment world closed ranks solidly . . . with anti-Nazi forces to form an international bloc of artists and intellectuals against fascism . . . Most big Hollywood parties [would include a] guest of honour who might be Andre Malraux or Ernest Hemingway, here to raise money to send ambulances to Loyalist Spain' (Dunne 1980: 115).

While the Hollywood Popular Front had been affiliated to liberal and anti-fascist causes, it was bolstered by a sizeable minority who had become members of the Hollywood Communist Party (CP). And despite enmities between liberals and communists, right-wing politicians would later cite such infiltration as evidence of the Front being a cover for communism. These concerns would come under specific scrutiny in the aftermath of the Second World War with the collapse of New Deal liberalism and the right-wing political complexion of Washington that had emerged in the Cold War. The Truman Doctrine's concept of containment against the Soviet Union unleashed a fearful paranoia of communist subversion on the home front.

The intensity of this political climate meant that the US film, television and music communities became subject to the investigations of the House Committee on Un-American Activities (HUAC). In the 1930s, the Hollywood CP became a small but potent force whose membership was committed, with the exception of some radicals who were in thrall to Stalinism, to its stands on rights, justice and equality and anti-fascism, rather than to its ideology, structure or hierarchy. Consequently, in 1946, the CP's foothold in Hollywood meant that the newly permanent HUAC could make significant political capital when investigating the film community for potential subversion.[8]

Led by reactionary congressmen, such as J. Parnell Thomas, John S. Wood, and John S. Rankin, the committee focused its attention on 'unfriendly witnesses' and subpoenaed ten Hollywood CP writers, producers and directors: Lester Cole, Dalton Trumbo, John Howard Lawson, Albert Maltz, Alvah Bessie, Ring Lardner Jr, Samuel Ornitz, Adrian Scott, Edward Dmytryk and Herbert Biberman – the so-called 'Hollywood Ten' – who refused to recognize the legitimacy of HUAC or name other communists. Their refusal to answer HUAC's questions led the Hollywood Ten to be considered in contempt of Congress. They were blacklisted and served custodial sentences when found guilty of obstructing HUAC's investigations.

Such concerns about smears and damages to careers were played out across the rest of the US entertainment community. For instance, Robeson had his passport revoked in 1950 as Congress declared his presence abroad 'would be contrary to the best interests of the United States' (Lynskey 2010: 49). Other left-wing actors and musicians, such as Geer and Seeger, would be blacklisted for many years. As a consequence of Seeger's refusal to testify in front of HUAC, the Weavers were dropped by their label Decca and he was found guilty of obstructing HUAC's investigations. However, his obstinacy persisted and he continued to play 'We Shall Overcome' (1947) to a variety of different audiences, linking up with the British Marxist folk singer Ewan MacColl. Seeger's seven-year nightmare only ended when his conviction was overturned on a technicality in the US Court of Appeal in 1962. Therefore, celebrity activists were either blacklisted or, in the case of many liberals, withdrew themselves from political controversies. Such an engagement of celebrities with causes was renewed during the tumultuous events within the American and European societies of the 1960s and 1970s.

Transformative celebrity activism in the 1960s and 1970s: the social and political revolution of fame

> Being a celebrity is a powerful weapon . . . people listen to you and tell other people about you. You are myth. You are media.
>
> Jerry Rubin, quoted in Doggett (2007: 18)

Rock and film stars used their celebrity to draw public attention to causes such as anti-Vietnam war protest movements, the May 1968 student riots, environmental activism, civil rights and personal liberties. Consequently, musicians and actors came to influence the times they lived in and in some cases it became difficult to separate them from the social movements they represented. In part, this occurred as young people rejected the privations of the Second World War and the conformity of the 1950s. Instead, they identified themselves with the social rebellion that was reflected in the popularity of rock bands like the Beatles, the Rolling Stones, the Byrds, the Who and the White Panthers' house band the MC5, along with singer-songwriters such as Bob Dylan, Kris Kristofferson, Country Joe MacDonald, Gil Scott-Heron and Johnny Cash. When David Crosby, Stephen Stills and Graham Nash formed a supergroup, in which they were sporadically joined by Neil Young (CSNY), either individually or collectively they wrote and performed the anti-war songs such as 'For What It's Worth' (1967) (as Buffalo Springfield) and 'Ohio' (1970) about the shooting by the National Guard of protesting students at Kent State University.

In their advocacy of 'sex, drugs and rock 'n' roll', John Lennon, Mick Jagger, Jim Morrison, Jimi Hendrix and Janis Joplin became symbols of the youth movement's refutation of traditional values and revolutionary ambitions. In the case of Lennon, he associated himself with leaders of the UK left-wing students, such as Tariq Ali, and American radicals, including Abbie Hoffman, Jerry Rubin and Bobby Seale of the Black Panthers. Moreover, he became famous for his 'bed-ins' for peace with his second wife, Yoko Ono, wrote the songs 'Give Peace a Chance' (1969) and 'Imagine' (1971), and returned his Member of the Most Excellent Order of the British Empire (MBE) award to the Queen due to British support for the war in Vietnam. On taking up residence in the USA, Lennon was persistently harassed by the Federal Bureau of Investigation (FBI) who held a dossier on him that ran to several hundred pages, and in 1971 President Nixon attempted to have him deported.

Similarly, Jagger made a legendary appearance at the Grosvenor Square anti-Vietnam war protests in 1968 when taking photographs of the revolt. Yet, he was even more famous for being arrested and charged on a police raid for drugs at Redlands House in 1967, along with his bandmate Keith Richards, gallery owner Robert Fraser and girlfriend Marianne Faithful. Despite the fact that those arrested had been on a country walk at the time, it was rumoured the police had interrupted a drug-fuelled orgy in which Faithful had strategically placed a Mars Bar in a compromising position. The infamous event demonstrated the generation gap between the authorities and the hippies. Consequently, the then aspiring Granada Television producer John Birt invited the newly released Jagger to act as a spokesman for his peers on *World in Action* (1963–1998). After being 'helicoptered' from jail to a country house lawn, Jagger spoke about youth culture with establishment figures including the editor of *The Times* William Rees Mogg and the Bishop of Woolwich John Robinson.

Lennon and Jagger quickly tired of their roles as spokesmen for youthful rebellion. Further, their caustic positions concerning the revolutionary ferment of the 1960s had been apparent in their writing and recording of 'Revolution' (1968), 'Sympathy for the Devil' (1968) and 'Street Fighting Man' (1968). Therefore, to some degree, the cross-fertilization of leaders of radical movements with rock stars had been defined by the fashions of the times:

> Rock and soul music fuelled the revolutionary movement with anthems and iconic imagery. Soon the musicians themselves, from John Lennon to Bob Dylan to James Brown and Fela Kuti, were being dragged into the fray. Some joined the protestors on the barricades, some were persecuted for their political activism and some abandoned the cause and were dismissed as counter-revolutionaries (Doggett 2007: i).

However, other celebrities consciously attached themselves to the mass protests of the era. By causing millions to listen to their music, folk revivalists such as Dylan, Seeger, Ochs, Tom Paxton, Joan Baez, Donovan and Peter, Paul and Mary brought attention to the plutocratic nature of American politics. As Dylan put it, 'I always thought that one man, the lone balladeer with the guitar, could blow an entire army off the stage if he knew what he was doing' (Huddart 2005: 8).

Civil rights and the war in Vietnam

In the early 1960s, Martin Luther King's civil rights movement drew support from many singers, actors and artists. Baez, Dylan, Belafonte and Marlon Brando proved to be key members of the campaign to end racial segregation in the American South. Baez had first heard King speak at her Quaker high school in 1956 and, after touring in the Southern states in 1962, she insisted that she would only play to integrated audiences. Similarly, Dylan sang about racial segregation in 'Oxford Town' (1962) and criticized the right-wing in 'Talkin' John Birch Paranoid Blues' (1962). Most especially, he courageously

Figure 2.2 'The times they are a-changin': Joan Baez and Bob Dylan as protest performers

performed his song about the white supremacist murder of the civil rights activist Medgar Evans in 'Only a Pawn in Their Game' (1963) at Greenville, Mississippi. The movement reached its peak with the March on Washington in August 1963 in which Baez led 350,000 in 'We Shall Overcome' and Dylan sang several of his songs along with Seeger and Peter, Paul and Mary.

Therefore, for a period in the early 1960s, Dylan appeared to become the spiritual heir to Guthrie. Seeger and the US folk Left claimed Dylan as a prophet and he wrote the majority of his political songs, including 'The Times They are a-Changin'', 'Blowin' in the Wind' and 'Masters of War', from 1962 to 1963. For Dylan, 1963 was a pivotal year, not only because of his engagement with civil rights but also because his appearance at the Newport Folk Festival fixed him in the popular imagination as the quintessential protest performer. However, Dylan became disillusioned with being characterized as the voice of political activism, disengaged with the folk movement and controversially electrified his set to become a rock star at the Newport Festival of 1965.

Yet civil rights remained the clarion call for many of the USA's politicized celebrities. In 1956, Belafonte met King and participated in civil rights marches. In the early 1960s, he worked with black artists, including Sidney Poitier and Sammy Davis Jr, to support the movement by raising monies, performing at concerts, crafting strategy and liaising with the Kennedy White House. He bailed King when he was imprisoned by Birmingham's racist police chief Bull

Connor. As the cause spread, Belafonte enlisted white stars such as Newman, Heston, Burt Lancaster, Marlon Brando and James Garner. This celebrity delegation attended the Civil Rights March on Washington; this was no small feat as J. Edgar Hoover had ordered FBI agents to dissuade them from attending.

Throughout the 1960s, Marlon Brando marched on numerous demonstrations, pledged 12 per cent of his earnings to King's Southern Christian Leadership conference and worked strenuously with the United Nations Children's Fund (UNICEF) to stem famines in India (see chapter 6). In 1968, he was distraught when King was assassinated and focused his fight against racism by forming the American Indian Movement (AIM). This led to Brando supporting the AIM's occupation against injustices concerning housing and employment at Wounded Knee, South Dakota. When he won the Best Actor Oscar for *The Godfather* (1972), he sent 'Sacheen Littlefeather' (actually activist Maria Cruz of Yaqui descent) to the 1973 Academy Awards to explain his refusal to accept the award due to the treatment of Native Americans in film and history. He was castigated by old-line Hollywood for violating the ceremony, but he had shown his disgust in front of a television audience of millions. Yet Brando's activism was nothing compared to those who opposed the war in Vietnam (Brownstein 1990: 229).

In the late 1960s, Lyndon B. Johnson's escalation of the Vietnam war divided the nation. Further, Nixon's violation of his electoral pledge of 'Peace with Honour' with expansion into Cambodia angered many Americans. The first star to criticize the USA's commitment in South-East Asia was Robert Vaughn, best known as Napoleon Solo in *The Man from U.N.C.L.E* (1964–8). In January 1966, he made an anti-war speech at a Democratic rally in Indianapolis. In 1967, Vaughn debated with the arch-conservative William F. Buckley on the national television show *Firing Line* (Vaughn 2008: 170–9).[9] He became a close ally of Robert Kennedy and chaired the Dissenting Democrats against Lyndon B. Johnson. His scepticism led to other Hollywood stars openly questioning the government.

In this respect, Jane Fonda changed her image from that of a star in *Barbarella* (1968) to that of a revolutionary spokesperson for radical causes and an opponent of militarism. In 1969, she supported the occupation of Alcatraz Island by Native Americans and protested against Nixon's intention to reclaim Indian land at Fort Lawson in Washington State. Shortly afterwards, she allied herself to Huey Newton and the Black Panthers, peppering her speeches with references to the police as 'pigs' and closing with 'Power to the People'.

However, it was as the darling of the anti-war movement that she achieved everlasting notoriety. Throughout the early 1970s, she attended marches and raised monies for the Vietnam Veterans Against the War. Additionally, in 1971, in response to Bob Hope's United Service Organization (USO) shows, she performed 'Free the Army' (FTA) shows with Donald Sutherland, Dick Gregory and Len Chandler to 64,000 disaffected General Infantry (GI) across a range of US air bases in Japan and the Philippines (Parker 1972; Shiel 2007: 216–24). In 1972, she visited North Vietnam to exchange 'revolutionary greetings' in defiance of US imperialism. On the trip, she broadcasted to GIs on Radio Hanoi, attacking those American prisoners of war (POWs) who had been captured in the act of bombing Hanoi, and accused Nixon of 'war crimes': 'We deplore that you are being used as cannon fodder for US imperialism. . . . And so we know what lies in store for any third world country that could have the misfortune of falling into the hands of a country such as the United States and becoming a colony' (Critchlow and Raymond 2009: 182–4).

Most controversially, she was photographed laughing while seated on an anti-aircraft tank and was given the sobriquet of 'Hanoi Jane'. Fonda's unapologetic support of the Vietcong led to her being publicly censored as a traitor, placed under domestic surveillance by Nixon, who opened a dossier entitled 'Citizen Jane Fonda: Activist', and to the studios' refusal to hire her, even though she had won the 1971 Best Actress Oscar for *Klute*. Indeed, the chairman, Richard H. Ichord, of the House Internal Security Committee (HISC) which had replaced HUAC, sought guidance from the Attorney General Richard G. Kleindienst to see if Fonda could be charged with treason (HISC 1972). Unsurprisingly, she appeared on Nixon's infamous 'enemies' list with a handful of other stars including Streisand, Newman, MacLaine and Tony Randall when it was released in the summer of 1973.

Although Fonda apologized for her appearance in the anti-aircraft tank photo, she remained a pariah for many Vietnam veterans. In April 2005, while she was on a book-signing tour, Michael Smith spat tobacco juice into Fonda's face, claiming she was a 'traitor who has been spitting in the faces of war veterans for years' (Vendel 2005). Alternatively, liberals and radicals such as Martin Sheen and Haskell Wexler maintained that Fonda showed considerable courage and fortitude in taking such a stance: 'To many Americans, the simple utterance of [Fonda's] name is a political Rorschach test: how people respond, what they see, tends to say a lot more about them than . . .

a once very famous or infamous Hollywood star-turned-politico-turned-fitness-guru' (Rabidoux 2009: 129).

Conclusion

The relationship between show business and politics has had an important history in US public life. In several respects, the long-standing dynamics of fame, celebrity and renown crystallized within the New World as social mobility and democratic rights went hand in hand with American politics. Therefore, US politicians quickly understood the need to popularize themselves and to achieve an appropriate image wherein they balanced their political abilities with their personal attributes. Consequently, the presidencies of Teddy Roosevelt, Franklin D. Roosevelt and John F. Kennedy indicated a conscious deployment of celebrity with political substance to affect a vital form of leadership. In turn, politicians realized the worth of seeking celebrity endorsements to connect with a wider constituency.

In this history of star power, John Street's typology of celebrity performance provides an effective framework through which to define the stages of activism within the American entertainment community (Street 2003, 2004). In the early stages of celebrity activity, stars endorsed candidates and lent their voices to promote national campaigns. However, with the greater blurring of the lines between celebrities and political classes, music and film stars engaged in an era of transformative celebrity activism in the 1960s and 1970s. This form of activism had its antecedents in the activities of authors, famed adventurers and radical performers who had used their status to speak out on the issues of the day. Therefore, protest singers such as Dylan and Baez lent themselves to causes, and other politicized celebrities, including Newman, Beatty and Redford, became critical of the US government. In the case of Fonda, she offered radical solutions to matters of domestic governance and foreign policy.

This more politicized approach to celebrity engagement exemplified both the strengths and difficulties of utilizing stars for active causes. In particular, celebrity activists and politicians indicated a more conscious employment of fame. Thus, performers took public stands on social issues, endorsed charities, participated in benefit performances and became involved in a range of forms of celebrity activism. This demonstrated how they could mobilize public opinion across a range of issues and utilize their stardom as a form of political agency. Consequently, stars popularized campaigns and drew public attention to their causes through an authentification of the worth of their actions.

Alternatively, radicals like Fonda and Brando were accused of being naive at best or traitors at worst. These criticisms may be seen to demonstrate that, while star power may bring public attention to politics, it is limited in effecting real change. Therefore, as this history has shown, the recalibration of fame within an expanding range of media sources has had positive and negative connotations for matters of celebrity political performance. And as this survey will show, such concerns have been thrown into greater relief as contemporary star power has become associated with the rise of celebrity politicians and an even more ubiquitous phase of celebrity behaviour.

Questions

- How can we compare the principles of fame to the practices of celebrity?
- Why did celebrity politics become so associated with American exceptionalism?
- To what degree has the 'politics of showbiz' been a defining historical factor in US election campaigns?

Further reading

Braudy, L. 1997: *The Frenzy of Renown: Fame and Its History*. New York: Vintage Books.

Brownstein, R. 1990: *The Power and the Glitter: The Hollywood–Washington Connection*. New York: Vintage Press.

Doggett, P. 2007: *There's a Riot Going On: Revolutionaries, Rock Stars and the Rise and Fall of the '60s*. Edinburgh, New York, Melbourne: Canongate.

Lynskey, D. 2010: *33 Revolutions per Minute: A History of Protest Songs*. London: Faber and Faber.

May, L. 2002 (2000): *The Big Tomorrow: Hollywood and the Politics of the American Way*. Chicago and London: University of Chicago Press.

Rabidoux, G. R. 2009: *Hollywood Politicos, Then and Now: Who They Are, What They Want, Why It Matters*. Lanham, Boulder, New York, Toronto, Plymouth, UK: University Press of America.

3

The Mediatization of Celebrity Politics in Modern Partisan Affairs within the United States and the United Kingdom

This chapter provides an analysis of modern celebrity politics in America and its exportation to other mass democracies, particularly the United Kingdom (UK). With the commodification of media services, the lines between politics and entertainment have blurred. Moreover, with the advent of the new media, there has been an exponential rise within competitive international news channels. Further, '[t]he political communication systems of mature representative democracies . . . have undergone a fundamental change – a "paradigmatic shift" . . . In simple terms [this means] the global process of modernization . . . has impacted on each of the components of national political communications systems, unleashing in its wake a series of reactions and counter-reactions' (Stanyer 2007: 1).

Therefore, the trends that have characterized celebrity politics have been thrown into sharp relief. These include: the introduction of mass media techniques designed to manufacture a celebrity's persona; the rise of a leadership class which has been defined by political imagery; and the growth of celebrity endorsers. With the rise of talent shows, 'infotainment' rolling news channels, Web 2.0 social media networks and user-generated content, celebrity has become instantaneous. Moreover, celebrity culture may be orchestrated in conventional and viral terms. These concerns have placed a greater emphasis on the personalization of political leaders and the increased engagement of prominent celebrities associating themselves with partisan endorsements.

This chapter will consider celebrity politicians (CPs) who have employed marketing techniques to achieve electoral office (CP1s).

The construction of an appropriate political persona has become a central aspect in modern electioneering (Stanyer and Wring 2004: 2; Street 2011: 53). Thus, in US politics, CP1s have built upon the personalized forms of communications that were apparent in the presidential administrations of Franklin D. Roosevelt and John F. Kennedy. When the former film star Ronald Reagan entered the White House, the 'Great Communicator' had refined his folksy political image to propagate his right-wing ideologies. Further, Bill Clinton became associated with the sobriquet 'Slick Willy', while Barack Obama has been established as a 'celebrity president', due to his close ties with film, television and music stars.

Subsequently, this analysis will consider how celebrity politics has been exported from the USA to other western democracies. Therefore, political leaders in Britain, France, Germany and Italy have placed a greater reliance upon the employment of style, personality and performance. Consequently, UK prime ministers such as Tony Blair and David Cameron, along with the previous French president Nicolas Sarkozy, German chancellors Gerhard Schröder and Angela Merkel, and the Italian media mogul and former prime minister Silvio Berlusconi, have exhibited CP1 characteristics. John Street has commented that CP1s may be identified through their growing reliance on popular cultural values and adherence to celebrity endorsements (Street 2004, 2010). For instance, Blair developed an iconic image of himself as a 'good bloke' who was interested in football and rock music. Further, he inveigled himself with 'Britpop' stars including Damon Albarn and Noel Gallagher to promote 'Cool Britannia' in the mid-1990s (Harris 2003).

Finally, this chapter will consider how politicized celebrities (CP2s) have utilized their fame as a form of political capital to endorse candidates or propagate partisan ideologies. It will refer to Street's concept of CP2s as 'performers as representatives' who may 'represent' a viewer or constituency in a broad political sense (Street 2004). However, the focus here will be on the celebrity endorsement of political candidates because a 'two-way' street has occurred in which a politicized star's persona may add credence to a campaign while demonstrating their adherence to a party, policy or political cause. Consequently, within the relationship between politicians and celebrities, close affiliations in terms of personal and financial support have emerged, alongside some significant questions about the efficacy of this form of political behaviour. This analysis will consider the positive and negative implications of such forms of behaviour in modern partisan politics.

Modern celebrity politicians (CP1s)

Celebrity politicians have utilized their imagery, style and rhetoric to operate effectively within a public space (Corner 2000: 396; Street 2004: 446). Thus, for John Corner, CP1s are required to 'perform' in an 'attempt to convince us that [they operate] congruently with the political demands placed upon [themselves]' (Drake and Higgins 2006: 89). This enables politicians to 'condense' their values to the section of the electorate they represent. For instance, American talk shows such as *The Oprah Winfrey Show* (1986–2011), *The Late Show with David Letterman* (1993 onwards) or *The Tonight Show* (1954 onwards) allow politicians to show the 'personal' side of their characters to connect with the public (Baum 2005).

In this respect, television has been (until the rise of social networking) the most effective medium whereby CP1s can establish a definitive performance to remove the barriers between their known and the unknown selves:

> [Schickel] argues [television] . . . 'brings famous folk into our living rooms in a psychically manageable size. We see them not from the alienating distance of the stage, which is where we were forced to view them from the pre-electronic age.' Through television citizens could witness a political event . . . [and] it could be argued that leading politicians gained the status of celebrities. (Stanyer 2007: 73)

Consequently, as Street comments, there has been the construction of a political aesthetic that refers to 'the realm of show business and the world of the celebrity' (Street 2004: 446) wherein a politician's performance becomes a vital form of democratic representation. He argues that, by rendering themselves as celebrities, politicians legitimize the breach between their public and private personas. This enables them to make their motives more transparent, thereby providing the public with greater insight into their conduct (Street 2003).

In part, this development refers to the concept of 'packaging politics', as defined by Bob Franklin and Kathleen Hall Jamieson, wherein modern leaders use campaign commercials, sound bites and photo opportunities to stay 'on message'. Further, politicians construct their images through spin, marketization and advertising (Franklin 2004). And throughout the celebrity branding of politicians, there has been an increased usage of public relations techniques which has been associated with the promotion of film, television and music stars (Street 2010: 246). Therefore, spin doctors are the political equivalent of entertainment PRs in managing their clients' images and audience expectations: 'Explaining the political success of Governor Jesse Ventura, his media advisor said, "Jesse's worked in movies, he's been a pro-wrestler, and he understands pop culture. He gets it. He know what's going to play in public and he's not afraid to take chances"' (West and Orman 2003: 11).

Such an orchestration of a CP1's performance has meant that, to achieve popularity, they have to appeal to a diverse range of audiences across a vast array of stages and genres. Therefore, CP1s have sought the appropriate iconography through which to connect to the electorate by employing popular cultural attributes. For instance, in the USA there has been the phenomenon of the celebrity as politician. Ronald Reagan's ascendancy to the presidency marked the apotheosis of a tradition in which American celebrities became politicians (George Murphy, Clint Eastwood, Sonny Bono, Arnold Schwarzenegger and Al Franken) (see chapter 5). Elsewhere, Peter Garrett in Australia, Imran Khan in Pakistan and Indian 'Bollywood' film stars, such as Amitabh Bachchan and Govinda, have stood for office (Bennett 2011: 86).

Further, CP1s have engaged in 'celebrity formats', including appearances in situation comedies, reality television programmes (e.g., Respect Party Member of Parliament [MP] George Galloway on *Celebrity Big Brother* [2001 onwards]), talk shows or topical satire programmes such as the American *The Daily Show* (1996 onwards) or British comedy quiz shows like *Have I Got News for You?* (1990 onwards).[1] For example, the former Liberal Democrat leader Charles Kennedy appeared on so many radio and television programmes that he became known as 'Chat-show Charlie' (Drake and Higgins 2006: 88).

CP1s have associated themselves with celebrity endorsers to enhance their status and to effect their messages. Invariably, this has been in the form of the photo opportunity: UK prime ministers have posed with the English national football team; German chancellors have appeared with the heavy metal band the Scorpions; and Nelson Mandela has had his picture taken with Naomi Campbell and the Spice Girls. This linkage has created an ideological shorthand for politicians to broaden their appeal to the electorate. For instance, in 1984 the Labour Party leader Neil Kinnock appeared in the comedy star Tracey Ullman's promotional music video for 'My Guy's Mad at Me' to show the humorous side of his character in order to bolster his personal ratings. Since the 1980s, these concerted attempts to mix renown with commonality have been played out in the US presidencies of Reagan, Bill Clinton and Barack Obama. All of these CP1s enhanced their uniqueness while seeking to attain a popular proximity with the American public. They have personalized their appeal to US voters, made populist appearances in the media and courted stars to endorse their campaigns.

The Great Communicator: Ronald Reagan – the celebrity as president

When Ronald Reagan defeated the incumbent president Jimmy Carter in the 1980 presidential election, he had established his political persona as the 'Great Communicator', benefiting as he did from his previous career as a film star and from being 'some forty years . . . in the public eye' (West and Orman 2003: 46) (see chapter 5). During his presidential campaign, he could repeat his lines many times over and make them sound fresh. Further, he was the master of the sound bite, putting down Carter in the televised debates with 'There you go again!', and hitting his marks with practised ease. Although Democrats criticized him for his background as an actor, Reagan used this to his advantage when he invoked the spirit of the late John Wayne as the symbolic representation of 'the American dream'. He promised an optimistic future, thereby challenging Carter's arguments that a malaise had sapped the nation of its will (Brownstein 1990: 276–7).

Reagan's success as the Great Communicator tied in with his New Right ideologies to install the marketization of political communications at the heart of government. During his presidency, his hawkish agenda was mediated by his folksy image. Reagan demonstrated a masterful use of television, photo opportunities and phrases drawn from films such as Clint Eastwood's 'Go ahead and make my day' or his own line as George Gip in *Knute Rockne* (1940), 'Win one for the Gipper'. His administration was praised for bringing glamour back to the White House, for the celebrity status of the First Lady Nancy Reagan, who led the 'Just Say No' anti-drug campaign, and for the coverage which Reagan generated when he appeared in the National Broadcasting Corporation's (NBC) celebration of the comedian Bob Hope's eightieth birthday.

Through his ability to manipulate the public space around him, Reagan maintained a popularity that meant that the media could not hold him to account. Thus, he became the 'Teflon president' to whom mud did not stick, despite his repeated personal gaffes, inaccurate claims and scandals which marred his administration during its second term. Even after Reagan's failures on housing and urban development programmes and the Iran–Contra affair in which he claimed to have lost his memory, the president managed to avoid political scrutiny with a well-timed quip: '[Reagan] became the quintessential media president who elevated style and image over substance with the help of an uncritical, protective American establishment media' (West and Orman 2003: 48).

His administration marked the point wherein there was an institutionalization of the long-standing CP1 trends towards imagery, style, performance and personalization. He effected a Republican Party communications machinery that would enable George H. W. Bush and his son George W. Bush to determine the agenda during their presidencies. These developments combined with permanent campaigning and the construction of a public relations state so that spin would become a defining force in US public life: 'It couldn't have made for a better presidency in the age of entertainment ... [Reagan's] programmes [represented] a return to bedrock American values and his optimism [shielded] the country from bitter realities such as burdensome debt, social inequity and international challenge' (Gabler 1998: 112).

The modern celebrity presidency: Bill Clinton and Barack Obama

Throughout the 1992 election campaign, Bill Clinton's charismatic abilities as a celebrity politician became evident in a series of well-staged speeches, photo opportunities and appearances on talk shows, most notably when he played 'Heartbreak Hotel' on the saxophone on the *Arsenio Hall Show* (1989–94). Subsequently, he was interviewed about racism, the Los Angeles riots and his plan for the nation. In shaping his image, he was aided by his long-term friendship with the Arkansas-born television producer Harry Thomason and his wife, Linda Bloodworth-Thomason, who employed marketing and advertising techniques to help define Clinton's political persona.

Thomason came up with Clinton's 'rock star' walk to the 1992 Democratic National Convention (DNC) in New York City, in which he was trailed by handheld cameras from Macy's across Manhattan to Madison Square Garden. Once in the hall, and accompanied by a rising crescendo of enthusiasm, Clinton delivered a last-minute line to his speech contributed by Bloodworth-Thomason: 'Tomorrow night, I will be the Comeback Kid.' Further, Bloodworth-Thomason wrote and produced the campaign biopic *The Man from Hope* (1992) which made capital of the grainy footage that existed of a brief handshake which had taken place between John F. Kennedy and the teenage Clinton when the latter had visited the White House on 26 June 1963 as part of an Arkansas representation to Boys Nation, an annual visit to Washington made by outstanding students sponsored by the American Legion (Herman 2003: 314–15). As a celebrity politician, Clinton understood the worth of making a direct link between Kennedy and himself as successor to the 'Camelot' legacy to determine his political imagery and 'in Clinton, public service finally found an artisan who understood exactly how to shape the mythology Hollywood services for his own indefatigable ends' (Scott 2000: 154).

In addition, Hollywood celebrities flocked to be at Clinton's side during political rallies and the rock band Fleetwood Mac contributed their song 'Don't Stop' (1977) as the soundtrack to his campaign. Clinton persuaded the disbanded group to perform and stand in line with many other stars to shake his hand at his four inaugural events in 1993. In the first term of his presidency, Clinton invited actors such as Christopher Reeve, Michael Douglas and Harrison Ford to the Oval Office, while Barbra Streisand spent the night at the White House after performing at his inaugural ball. In the 1996 election, celebrities such as Robin Williams, Paul Newman, Whoopi Goldberg, Sharon Stone and Sarah Jessica Parker endorsed the president. And, despite his illustrious predecessors, no other president moved with such ease within Hollywood's leading circles as Clinton. 'Presidential scholars [complained] there [had] been a diminution of the executive office, a downsizing – a general feeling of less presidential dignity . . . Bill Clinton as a man [had] gained something. As a tabloid star – rather than just a president – he [was] . . . allowed addictions, debts, weight fluctuations, degenerate family members, [and] an unusual marriage' (Sherrill 1998: 74).[2]

Similarly, Barack Obama has continued as a CP1 by employing 'telegenic' imagery in relation to the 'hyper-reality' of the Hollywood/entertainment/Washington nexus (Scott 2011a: 27). At the 2004 Democratic National Convention (DNC), then State Senator Obama made a well-received keynote speech in which 'he [became] more than a candidate seeking votes; people were seeking him' (Freedland 2008). Moreover, he employed the social networks of Facebook, YouTube and Twitter, along with his own inclusive web site, mybarackobama.com (MyBo), to galvanize a grass-roots

Figure 3.1 From satirist to politician: Al Franken and Bill Clinton call for change

political support (Heilemann and Halperin 2010: 107) (see chapter 4). For Paul M. Green:

> Obama's rise has been rapid from being State Senator, then in 2004 becoming the Junior Senator for Illinois and 2008 the President. It is a remarkable rise in eight years and almost unprecedented in US politics. I can only think of Woodrow Wilson emerging as President of Princeton and becoming President in three years in 1912. Obama became the black JFK. And remember JFK had been a Congressman in 1946 and it took him fourteen years to become the President. (Green 2011)

Throughout his presidential campaigns, Obama used 'media spectacles' to cultivate his persona. He has presented himself as an educated and articulate African American with an international background who simultaneously exemplified the American Dream (Kellner 2009: 715). In 2008, his image became available on a host of magazine covers, including the iconic 'Africa' edition of *Vanity Fair* (1983 onwards); he became the first presidential candidate to receive the endorsement of *Rolling Stone* (1967 onwards) and he was named as the 'Person of the Year' in *Time* (1923 onwards) magazine. Before he had declared his candidacy, Obama had appeared on popular talk shows such as *The Oprah Winfrey Show* (1986–2011) and he effortlessly mixed with celebrity endorsers, including Winfrey herself.

Further, Obama's celebrity image became intertwined with fictional representations of the American presidency in US films and television (Kellner 2010b: 35; Scott 2011b). America had been made ready for the rise of a black president through a range of anticipatory representations of African-American chief executives. For example, Dennis Haysbert played the charismatic black leader, President David Palmer, in the popular television thriller *24* (2000 onwards) for five seasons. However, the most revelatory anticipation of Obama's election occurred in Aaron Sorkin's *The West Wing* (1999–2006), which in its final two seasons conducted a fictionalized presidential campaign between a Democratic Mexican-American candidate, Matthew Santos (Jimmy Smits), and a maverick liberal Republican Californian senator, Arnold Vinick (Alan Alda) (Scott 2011a: 27–8).

Obama's fictional counterpart was a coalition-building newcomer who had only served a short period in Congress, was an attractive liberal, had a photogenic family and was a candidate of colour. These coincidences were not a matter of chance as a *New York Times* (1851 onwards) article demonstrated that one of *The West Wing*'s writers, Eli Attie (a former speechwriter for Vice-President Al Gore in 2000), had contacted David Axelrod, Obama's chief strategist and media advisor, to find out more about him after the 2004 DNC address (Selter 2008): '"We're living your scripts," joked Axelrod in an e-mail to Attie as the gathering momentum of Obama's campaign encouraged hope that it would emulate Santos's success' (Scott 2011a: 28).

During his time in office, Obama has employed CP1 attributes to enhance his popularity, despite considerable domestic and foreign policy difficulties. To boost his ratings shortly before the Congressional mid-term elections, he became the first sitting president to appear on Jon Stewart's satirical *The Daily Show* on 27 October 2010. In this interview, Obama hoped to appeal to the younger, liberal members of the electorate and to acknowledge that his reforms would take a longer time to be effective.

Similarly, after his success as an 'activist president' when ordering the US forces' assassination of Osama bin Laden, Obama reinvigorated his position as a global icon on a trip to Europe in May 2011. Along with his wife Michelle, he provided political glamour when attending the G8 conference at Deauville in France, pulling pints of Guinness in Ireland and meeting Queen Elizabeth II and Prime Minister David Cameron in a state visit to Great Britain:

> It was hard, watching Barack Obama and David Cameron play table tennis together for the benefit of cameras recently, not to be struck by their synthetic similarities. Wearing crisp white shirts, nearly identical in height and both left-handed except in their high-fiving, these two

young leaders with picture-perfect families embodied the telegenic imperatives of democracy in the internet age. (Rajan 2011: 12)

Obama mingled with Cameron at a stage-managed barbecue for injured war veterans at 10 Downing Street. At the subsequent Group of Eight (G8) conference, he made pleasantries with the former French president, Nicolas Sarkozy, and his singer wife, Carla Bruni. In seeking to attain reflective glory during Obama's visit, both Cameron and Sarkozy demonstrated how celebrity politics had become an international phenomenon in an era of late modernity.

The exportation of celebrity politicians to western democracies: France, Italy and Germany

Throughout modern European democracies, there has been a rise in CP1s, including Tony Blair and David Cameron in the UK, Nicolas Sarkozy in France, Silvio Berlusconi in Italy and Gerhard Schröder and Angela Merkel in Germany. In relation to their national cultures, these European CP1s imported celebrity values that existed in American politics. As Raymond Kuhn notes: 'Image projection focuses on the mediated transmission of values, capabilities and competences in a coherent fusion of the personal and the political. A positive media image remains an integral part of executive leadership in all Western democracies' (Kuhn 2010).

Throughout his presidency (2007–12), Sarkozy used public relations techniques in an attempt to dominate the media's coverage of French politics. He became a prominent CP1 via a mixture of controlled briefings, interviews, press conferences, formal speeches and numerous personal appearances. Sarkozy shaped his image as 'Mr Bling-Bling' through his usage of the official Elysée web site with its web channel PR TV1, his own Facebook page and consorting with celebrities such as Johnny Hallyday. Controversially, he broke down the distinction between a French politician's public and private life to present himself as a man of strength. Yet Sarkozy's personalization of his image proved to be a double-edged sword, not least when his extramarital affairs were played out in the public domain and his populism backfired. This meant his failure to stimulate the French economy was matched by his unpopularity, resulting in him losing the 2012 presidential election to the socialist François Hollande.

Within Italy, Berlusconi constructed a CP1 image of himself as a self-made man. He transformed his persona from that of a cruise ship crooner to one of a property magnate, and then to a media tycoon who would ultimately become the Italian prime minister. Berlusconi was aided by his ownership of the Mediaset Corporation which controls the three commercial Italian terrestrial television channels – Canale 5, Italia 1 and Rete 4. With the aid of compliant journalists, he promoted himself as a major personality in Italian public life. Indeed, he orchestrated his party 'Forza Italia', named after a national football chant, and employed the local fan associations of the club he owns – AC Milan – to develop his political movement.

In 2001, during one of his many comebacks, Berlusconi published a glossy brochure which portrayed him as a family man and national icon. However, his personal peccadilloes, numerous divorces, sexual infidelities and constant battles with the judiciary were played out in the full glare of publicity. Therefore, Berlusconi's leadership proved to be untenable and it ended on 12 November 2011 with his resignation when the Italian economy collapsed due to the Eurozone crisis.

Similarly, in Germany, Schröder's ascendancy to the federal chancellorship indicated a greater personalization of the political processes. In the 1998 and 2002 elections, he used his fame to humanize his image and define his celebrity status so he could relate to the electorate (Holtz-Bacha 2003). This was part of a long-standing process in which Schröder and his former wife had been known as the 'Clintons of Lower Saxony' when he was prime minister for the state. In 2002, he utilized his wife and family as a means to appeal to the public. Again, in Schröder's case, this proved to be double-edged as it came to light in 2003 that he had engaged in an extramarital affair.

His successor, Merkel, followed Schröder's example as a CP1 by engaging in photo opportunities, popularizing her image, utilizing web sites and appearing in glossy magazines such as *Bild am Sonntag* (1952 onwards). Moreover:

> While Merkel herself does not care much about her appearance and style . . . her position as CDU leader forced her into a complete makeover. Her pudding-basin hair was transformed into a Hillary Clinton-like soft wave, and while her usual black trouser suits matched the CDU colours well, she also began to wear softer orange-shaded jackets (also a CDU colour), complete with matching make-up and jewellery (van Zoonen 2006: 295–6).

This reformulation of Germany's 'Iron Frau' (Paterson 2010) had a precedent in the transformation of Britain's own 'Iron Lady' (as dubbed by the Soviet Union) and Conservative Party prime minister of the 1980s, Margaret Thatcher.[3]

Celebrity politicians in the United Kingdom

In the UK, the introduction of celebrity politics can be traced back to the premierships of Harold Wilson and Margaret Thatcher. The populist Wilson supported his home football team of Huddersfield Town, smoked a pipe and insisted on having brown sauce on his food. He understood the political capital that could be achieved by honouring the Beatles as Members of the Most Excellent Order of the British Empire (MBEs) and by associating with the 1966 World Cup-winning England football team. As Colin Seymour-Ure comments, Wilson professionalized the post of prime minister as a former economist, meritocrat and civil servant (Seymour-Ure 2003: 42).

However, the office of prime minister was presidentialized when Thatcher came to power in 1979. Within the Conservative Party's electoral campaign, the public relations specialists Gordon Reece and Tim Bell, along with the advertising agency Saatchi and Saatchi, radically altered Thatcher's appearance, hair, make-up and the tone of her voice. As a CP1, she became a guest on the BBC Radio 2's *Jimmy Young Show* (1973–2002), the chat show *Wogan* (1982–1992) and the children's programme *Saturday Superstore* (1982–1987) (where her endorsement of the band the Thrashing Doves on the show's Pop Panel ended their career!). As leader of the opposition, she had appeared on the perennial favourite of British politicians, *Desert Island Discs* (1942 onwards).

Over her eleven-year period in office, Thatcher's electoral success, strident political views, wartime victory in the Falklands crisis, privatization policies, anti-communism and anti-trade unionism saw her define herself as the Iron Lady. This apparent invincibility would be shattered in 1990 when she lost the confidence of the Conservative Party by pursuing the electorally disastrous poll-tax legislation and an anti-European Union stance. As befitting her status as a celebrity politician, Thatcher's removal contained elements from the Shakespearean tragedy *Julius Caesar* (1599), with Michael Heseltine cast as Cassius and Sir Geoffrey Howe as an unlikely Brutus! Howe's use of cricket as a political metaphor in his resignation statement describing Thatcher's dealings with the cabinet sealed her demise: 'It is rather like sending your opening batsmen to the crease only for them to find, the moment the first balls are bowled, that their bats have been broken before the game by the team captain' (Howe 1990).

However, for the Labour Party, the lessons learned from the Thatcher era would be put to use in the 1990s.[4] It rebranded itself as 'New Labour', advocated the ideology of the Third Way and elected a charismatic politician – Tony Blair – as its leader in 1994. As a CP1, Blair emulated 'relationship marketing' strategies (Kuhn 2007: 212) that have been associated with US political leaders, most notably Clinton. In opposition, he developed his 'telegenic' skills by making speeches which were littered with sound bites, provided numerous photo opportunities and he engaged in many stage-managed appearances. Blair was booked onto chat shows such as *Good Morning Television* (GMTV) (1993 onwards), *Des O'Connor Tonight* (1977–2002) and *The Frank Skinner Show* (1995–1999). He formed his celebrity persona with public accounts of his time as an aspiring singer in a band called Ugly Rumours. Consequently, as a rock'n'roll candidate, he presented awards at the *Q Magazine Awards* and *The Brits* in 1996. Like Thatcher, as leader of the opposition he appeared on *Desert Island Discs*. Here he talked about his career, his courtship of his wife, Cherie, and his decision to send his sons to the London Oratory School which had opted out of taking local authority status.

Further, Blair associated himself with the burgeoning 'New Lad' culture of the mid-1990s in which magazines such as *Loaded* (1994 onwards) took an 'ironic', postmodernist approach to the previously unreconstructed masculine pursuits of girls, drinking, music and football. The 1996 England football team's European Championship matches had been accompanied by the release of a single entitled 'Three Lions', written and performed by the laddish comedians Frank Skinner and David Baddiel, along with the Lightning Seeds' singer Ian Broudie. The song had become a favourite on the terraces with its chant of 'Football's coming home'. Therefore, at the 1996 Labour Party Conference, Blair finished his speech with a craftily populist rallying call lifted from the song: 'Eighteen years of hurt never stopped us dreaming . . . Labour's coming home' (Harris 2003: 303).

For New Labour, football became a matter of obsession, and Blair associated himself with Premier League managers such as Alex Ferguson and Kevin Keegan, with whom he was photographed playing a game of 'keepie-uppie'. Blair proclaimed that he was a lifelong Newcastle United fan, although doubts were expressed about his claims that as a boy he had watched the club's most famous player, Jackie Milburn, when seated in the Gallowgate End, not least because he would have been only four years old, living in Australia at the time and in the 1950s there was no seating, only terracing!

In carefully cultivating his CP1 image, Blair employed spin doctors such as Alastair Campbell and Peter Mandelson to orchestrate the 1997 general election campaign. This was noted for its utilization of public relations techniques and its emphasis on Blair's electoral persona. He was defined by his youth, his commitment to the Third Way and his determination to reform the sleazy political landscape. The Labour Party produced an innovative 'fly-on-the-wall' ten-minute party election broadcast (PEB), made by Molly Dineen, to focus on Blair's dynamic character, his concerns as a parent and his likeability as a 'decent bloke' (Wring 2005: 146). In addition, the campaign included PEBs featuring the late stage, television and film star Pete Postlethwaite and employed pop act D:Ream's *Things Can Only Get Better* (1994) as its signature track. It successfully climaxed with a celebrity-laden gala event held at the Royal Festival Hall: 'These formats underscored Blair's desire to communicate with a wider range of voters and demonstrated his awareness of popular culture and sentiment . . . Blair's presentational style both responded to and encouraged an increasingly emotionalized public discourse' (ibid.: 150).

As the 'people's prime minister' (ibid.: 150), Blair's administration marked the high-point of the absorption of CP1 characteristics in UK politics. From 1997 to 2007, his premiership was noted for its presidential style and its use of spin in presenting policy. In office, Blair continued to appear on 'sofa programmes' (Neveu 2005) wherein he fused the 'ordinariness' of personality with the 'extraordinariness' of his position as the 'first among equals'. Most especially, he emphasized his role as a figure of national unity in the aftermath of the death of Princess Diana and as a conviction leader in the 'war on terror'. In accordance with US politicians, he brought his wife and children into the public limelight. Indeed, Cherie Blair had four assistants working for her, including Fiona Millar (Campbell's partner) as her chief spin doctor. Notably, Cherie Blair became pregnant during her husband's period of office and the birth of their son Leo became a national news event. Further, her involvement in the dubious mortgage arrangements for a flat she bought for her son Euan marked the advent of 'Cherie-gate'.

Blair's successors, Gordon Brown and David Cameron, along with Liberal Democrat leader Nick Clegg, would utilize similar CP1 attributes in their attempts to appeal to the electorate in the 2010 general election (see chapter 4). However, Blair's premiership would reflect another facet of the CP1s involvement in modern politics – the conscious employment of celebrity endorsements. Most especially, New Labour would be celebrated, and then vilified, in its attempt to incorporate 'Cool Britannia' into its political brand.

The characteristics of politicized celebrity endorsers (CP2): Cool Britannia, legitimacy, endorsement and activity

In the summer of 1995 Blur and Oasis (the two bands which had headed the 'Britpop' movement) competed with one another for the Number One spot in the UK Singles chart. The competition between the bands reflected a return in confidence within Britain's creative communities. Therefore, the political gains that could be achieved by association with Cool Britannia, which included artists like Damian Hirst and Tracey Emin, were not lost on the New Labour spin doctors. In 1996, Blair made a speech in which he celebrated the return of UK popular music to its rightful place 'at the top of the world' (Harris 2003).

First, Damon Albarn of Blur was courted by Blair, Campbell and Deputy Leader John Prescott. However, Albarn wavered in terms of his support of the New Labour agenda. Consequently, Margaret McDonagh, a key strategist in Blair's abolition of Clause IV and the Labour Party's general election coordinator, met with Creation Records' mogul Alan McGee to see if Oasis would lend itself to the cause. Thus, McGee and Oasis lead guitarist Noel Gallagher were co-opted by New Labour to provide endorsements at awards shows, to make donations and to appear at a range of party events (ibid.: 306–7). In the short term, New Labour's courting of celebrities enhanced its electoral chances and the maverick McGee proclaimed that Blair could 'do for British politics what Creation Records has done for British Music' (ibid.: 309). This collaboration marked an American-style confluence of celebrity endorsers with the political classes. An ecstasy-fuelled Gallagher enthused at the 1996 *Brit Awards*:

> There are seven people in this room who are giving a little bit of hope to young people in this country . . . That is [sic] me, our kid, Bonehead, Guigs, Alan White, Alan McGee and Tony Blair. And if you've all got anything about you, you'll go up there and you'll shake Tony Blair's hand, man. He's the man! Power to the people! (Gallagher 1996)

However, the partnership was short-lived as both sides realized each other's shortcomings. For the politicians, the unpredictable nature of rock stars meant that they might go vehemently off-message. This occurred at the 1998 *Brit Awards* when the Deputy Prime Minister Prescott had a bucket of water thrown over him by Danbert Nobacon from the anarchist group Chumbawumba (Street 2010: 247).[5] For the stars, whose 'coolness' had been defined by their apparent rebellion, they could lose their popularity if they were seen to be cosying up to the establishment. The gulf between politicians and pop stars became conspicuous at a reception to celebrate Blair's electoral success at 10 Downing Street on 30 July 1997:

> Looking at the picture of Noel and Blair, in which Alan McGee hovered in the background; one was assailed by all kinds of questions. Who was more compromised: the politician, whose aspirations to upright statesmanship suddenly seemed swamped by star-struck superficiality, or the musician, whose presence spoke volumes about just how tamed his art form, once built on scattershot dissent, had become? (Harris 2003: 345)[6]

The Cool Britannia initiative had had its origins in previous attempts to integrate pop stars with Labour Party politicians, such as 'Red Wedge' led by Paul Weller and Billy Bragg. Bragg had enjoyed a close relationship with the Labour Party leader Kinnock, who had a detailed knowledge of popular culture, stretching back to his youthful membership of the Gene Vincent fan club. Further, left-wing collectives such as 'Rock Against Racism' (RAR) incorporated Punk acts like the Clash to perform at anti-Nazi League concerts organized by the Trotskyite Socialist Workers Party (SWP) (Street, Hague and Savigny 2008: 277). Although the respective success of these forms of celebrity activism had been mixed, they indicated a growing consciousness within British rock acts that they bring public attention to a variety of causes.

These activities were accompanied by an increasing amount of celebrity involvement in promoting human rights bodies, such as Amnesty International, for whom the *Secret Policeman's Ball* shows were initially organized by the *Monty Python* (1969 onwards) and *Fawlty Towers* (1975–1979) comedian John Cleese. Furthermore, the UK and US comedic establishments constructed the telethon *Comic Relief* along with a range of national offshoots to raise funds for charities dealing with African poverty (see chapter 5). Ultimately, there would be the global televised spectacle of *Live Aid* in 1985 which made Bob Geldof *the* celebrity activist of the modern era. In this respect, Geldof would be influenced by the United Nations Children Fund's (UNICEF) concert for Bangladesh organized by George Harrison in 1971 and by UNICEF's *Music for UNICEF* run by David Frost, Robert Stigwood and the Bee Gees in 1979 (Wheeler 2011) (see chapter 6).

All of these events, endorsements and activities have contributed to Street's analytical distinction of the politicized celebrity who engages in causal or partisan politics (CP2). He defines CP2s as those celebrities who are not seeking electoral office but have utilized their fame to speak out on political and international affairs. Their effect may be measured in terms of the media attention and the public reception their engagement attracts. However, the modern CP2 has been transformed from acting as an endorser of a political leader or party into an engaged activist who not only participates in but leads campaigns (Richey and Ponte 2011: 32). Consequently, CP2s have associated themselves with environmental causes, protested against wars or fronted human rights campaigns (see chapters 5 and 6). Therefore, this more ideologically driven type of celebrity engagement has meant that CP2 has created greater opportunities for new forms of partisan expression, along with more problematic examples of these endeavours.

Modern partisan celebrity endorsements in the United States: public and financial contributions

In modern American politics, Hollywood film stars, musicians and sportsmen and sportswomen have continued to endorse political candidates. Indeed, such a form of celebrity engagement reached a crescendo during Bill Clinton's and Barack Obama's presidencies. CP2s have moved beyond appearing on platforms or in television commercials to support candidates as they have understood that it is their responsibility to propagate the values of the campaign itself. The ubiquity of celebrity has meant that there has been a shift in public attitudes in which stars have assumed a moral authority for political agendas among target audiences (Cashmore 2006: 218).

This was important to Clinton: he understood that his Hollywood supporters enabled him to propagate his New Democratic values concerning fiscal responsibility and social liberalism. Moreover, Obama's close affiliation with Oprah Winfrey enabled him to establish a creditable image with black supporters which could be crucially translated into votes during the Democratic Primaries against Hillary Clinton. In addition, within the USA, due to electoral rules, celebrity financial endorsements have become an important means through which to raise campaign funds. Therefore, Hollywood has become a lucrative fund-raising stop for Democratic politicians (West and Orman 2003: 38–9).

For many years, the Hollywood–Washington linkage was presided over by the head of the Music Corporation of America (MCA), Lew R. Wasserman, who channelled monies into the campaign coffers of presidential candidates from Kennedy to Clinton. Clinton was shrewd enough to charm Wasserman who, in his last major act of campaign funding, organized a US$10,000-a-couple dinner that raised US$1.7 million. Indeed, Wasserman remarked, 'If you are going to get me going on the subject of Bill Clinton, I'll sound like a love-struck teenager' (Bruck 2004: 464). Clinton further benefited from the ascendancy of a new generation of key players within Hollywood's permanent governance in the 1980s. He received support from a group of film executives, such as Mike Medavoy and Dawn Steel, and stars, including Barbra Streisand, Warren Beatty and Richard Dreyfuss, who became known as the 'Friends of Bill' (FOB).

Subsequently, other industry players, such as Sid Sheinberg, David Geffen, Steven Spielberg and Jeffrey Katzenberg, contributed funds to Clinton's presidential campaigns in 1992 and 1996. They favoured him as they saw that his centrist New Democratic values accorded with their own positions concerning fiscal responsibility and social liberalism. In Clinton, they also saw a figure who would advocate their interests in government with regard to their Jewish heritage, environmental matters, multiculturalism, health care, abortion and gay rights.

Moreover, they were attracted to Clinton because of his star presence, charisma, rigorous intellect and avowed desire to be a participant in the entertainment elite (Medavoy with Young 2002: 269). From the late 1980s, Clinton's Arkansas allies in Hollywood, the Thomasons, hosted a set of informal receptions to introduce him to the Hollywood community. Despite some resistance, the persistent FOBs helped to launch Clinton from being a relatively unknown governor of Arkansas to becoming a recognized player on the national scene:

> Long before Clinton was even on the national radar as a presidential candidate, I [Medavoy] set up a dinner for him to meet some of the

> entertainment community . . . Clinton and I kept in touch, and in September 1991 . . . he called me . . . (as) . . . he wanted to meet with me and some supporters to discuss his run for the White House. It was clear to him that we would be able to bring money and glamour to the campaign, both of which are crucial to political success in our media-centric age (ibid.: 270).

Beginning in late 1991, when Clinton announced his candidacy, the Thomasons ran a series of modest fund-raisers to increase his standing in the film community. These events enabled him to win the support of their television colleagues, including the actors from Thomason-produced shows, including *Designing Women* and *Night Court*. By the time Clinton had clinched the Democratic nomination, he enjoyed support from Hollywood unrivalled since John F. Kennedy.

In September 1992, the entertainment community bestowed its 'formal blessing' on his candidacy by hosting a US$1 million fund-raiser at the Los Angeles estate of producer Ted Fields. The Hollywood elite, including Jack Nicholson, Dustin Hoffman, Annette Bening, Michelle Pfeiffer, Rhea Perlman and Danny DeVito, basked in Clinton's attention. He benefited from the endorsement of two heavyweight Hollywood political hitters, Barbra Streisand and Warren Beatty, by informing them that, as 'some of the most gifted, creative and caring Americans in the country . . . I want you to be part of the administration – not just part of the campaign' (Schroeder 2004: 136).

During the main campaign against the incumbent president, George H. W. Bush, the music impresario David Geffen bankrolled Clinton's war chest which was plagued by a deficit of US$1 million. Clinton promised the homosexual Geffen that he would represent gay rights and he became one of his closest friends. In tandem, Streisand hosted a US$1.5 million Beverly Hills fund-raiser which was broadcast by satellite in New York, Washington, Atlantic City and San Francisco. And this extended to other executives and film-makers, including Mike Ovitz, Peter Guber and Steven Spielberg, as he was as much in thrall to the entertainment establishment as they were to him.

In his second presidential campaign, Clinton received donations from Wasserman of US$507,833 and from his protégé Sheinberg US$321,362, along with further monies from Geffen (US$575,697), Spielberg (US$503,123), Katzenberg (US$408,320), Edgar Bronfman Jr (US$318,000), Streisand (US$142,825) and Newman (US$72,500) (McDougal 1998: 520).

Additionally, the Democratic National Committee received US$7 million in 1996 with three fund-raisers organized by Spielberg, Katzenberg and Geffen (who had formed Hollywood's newest studio DreamWorks SKG in 1994) which were emceed by Tom Hanks and featured Streisand, Don Henley and Maya Angelou. Moreover, the Clinton campaign attained soft money contributions from Seagrams, Disney and DreamWorks SKG which meant that the Democratic Party could raise US$8 million per election cycle throughout the 1990s (Dickenson 2006: 47). Elsewhere, Kevin Spacey declared Clinton to be 'one of the shining lights' of the political process and appeared in a humorous satire entitled *President Clinton: The Final Years* (2000): 'The affair between Hollywood and Clinton . . . was love. Clinton made the neurotic folk of Hollywood feel special. He went to their parties; he tucked them up in the Lincoln Bedroom and gave them a storyline to die for . . . Even at its lowest points, his presidency was performance art' (Macintyre 2000: 18).

Similarly, in 2008, the Hollywood establishment provided Obama with substantial campaign contributions totalling US$4.8 million. In this respect, he profited from his organization being well connected:

> For instance, Obama's former Chief of Staff Rahm Emanuel is Ari Emanuel's older brother who is the top talent agent in Hollywood. Ari Emanuel hosted a $2,300 a plate fund-raiser for Obama in 2008 and he received monies from such luminaries as Steven Spielberg due to this linkage in Hollywood. Celebrities like to support celebrity politicians. The Hollywood contingent is full-tilt for Obama! (Green 2011)

In addition, Obama utilized the US entertainment–politics nexus to enhance his status as neophyte presidential candidate in 2008. Consequently, he received CP2 endorsements from Leonardo Di Caprio, George Clooney, Bruce Springsteen, Robert De Niro, Chris Rock, Kerry Washington, Tim Robbins, Susan Sarandon, Ben Affleck, Jennifer Aniston, Halle Berry, Will Smith, Matt Damon and Stevie Wonder. Other film and music stars, including Scarlett Johansson, Kelly Hu, John Legend, Herbie Hancock, Kareem Abdul Jabbar, Adam Rodriquez, Amber Valetta and Nick Cannon, produced a pro-Obama video with the Black Eyed Peas, entitled *Yes We Can*, which became one of the most downloaded items on YouTube in 2008.[7] In tandem, the comedienne Sarah Silverman appeared in an online advertisement, *The Great Schlep* (2008), to implore Jewish grandchildren to fly to Florida to 'force' their grandparents to vote for Obama! Further, the Asian-American actor Kal Penn became such an active supporter that he quit his role in the popular medical drama *House* (2004–2012) to work directly for Obama as his associate director of public engagement from 2008–9.

Crucially, the talk show hostess Oprah Winfrey endorsed Obama on Cable News Network's (CNN) *Larry King Live* (1985–2010) in May 2007. She hosted a star-studded fund-raiser in Santa Barbara for 1,600 guests, including Stevie Wonder, Sidney Poitier and George Lucas at US$2,300 a head (Coburn 2008). This event raised US$4 million for the Obama campaign coffers. More importantly, Winfrey launched Obama on the national scene by appearing at rallies and, as her show was syndicated to nearly 150 countries worldwide, this made him an internationally recognized figure. In 2008, she held the top spot in *Forbes Magazine*'s (1917 onwards) hundred most powerful American celebrities and she endorsed Obama via her popular monthly magazine and book clubs. As key strategist David Plouffe noted, Winfrey enabled the Democratic nominee to reach those unorthodox sections of the electorate that were key to him winning the election (Plouffe 2009: 118). Most significantly, Winfrey helped Obama to mobilize political support within the African-American community: 'Oprah Winfrey's endorsement of Barack Obama prior to the 2008 Democratic Presidential Primary generated a statistically and qualitatively significant increase in the number of votes received as well as in the total number of votes cast. . . . In total, we estimate the endorsement was responsible for 1,015,559 votes for Obama' (Garthwaite and Moore 2008: 3).

Such a distribution of votes proved crucial in the 2008 Democratic Primaries as 'Hillary Clinton would have garnered more votes than Obama if not for Winfrey . . . her power was great enough to help throw the nomination to her preferred candidate' (Ross 2011: 412).

Moreover, Obama was a beneficiary of Geffen's fallout with the Clintons as the music impresario moved his support from them to the then senator for Illinois's campaign. This change in attitude occurred because Bill Clinton refused the studio boss's request to pardon Leonard Peltier, an American-Indian activist, for murder. On the other hand, in the last days of his administration he agreed to pardon the fugitive fraudulent financier Marc Rich. When Geffen found out that Rich's ex-wife Denise had been a major contributor to the presidential library and Hillary Clinton's 2000 senatorial campaign, he accused the Clintons of gross hypocrisy (Rabidoux 2009: 302–3).

In accordance with previous Democratic candidates, Obama understood that the support of film and rock stars allowed him to

Figure 3.2 Barack Obama lends a helping hand to his most crucial celebrity endorser, Oprah Winfrey

appeal to a wider range of constituencies within the American electorate. He shrewdly demonstrated a critical awareness of popular culture when he proclaimed that the highly praised yet cult Home Box Office (HBO) 'policier' *The Wire* (2002–8), which dealt with the impact of the drugs war on an African-American underclass in West Baltimore, was one of his favourite shows (Fletcher 2010: 39). In turn, when calling for voter registration in North Carolina and New Orleans, he received support from several cast members.

However, as his popularity has waxed and waned in the Hollywood film community, Obama's relationship with film stars proved to be more tentative in the run-up to the 2012 presidential election:

> Team Obama has known of the curdling of Hollywood's affection for months. In May [2011], at the annual White House correspondent's dinner, the President felt obliged to crack a joke at the expense of Matt Damon, who was already sniping about the President's performance . . . 'Well, Matt I just saw *The Adjustment Bureau* (2011), so right back atcha, buddy,' he quipped, referring to a new Damon film (Usborne 2012: 30).

Yet Obama remained in the ascendancy as a celebrity president when compared to his Republican opponent Mitt Romney, who was described as the 'celebrity apprentice' due to his courting of the outspoken billionaire and US *Apprentice* (2004 onwards) reality television show host Donald Trump. Moreover, although

Republicans continued to damn Obama because of his links with the Hollywood liberal elite, the Democrats made greater political capital from Romney's association with traditional right-wingers, such as a rambling Clint Eastwood, who addressed an imaginary Obama in an empty chair on the stage of the 2012 Republican National Convention, and loose-cannon rock stars, such as Ted Nugent and Kid Rock. Therefore, in the caustic 2012 US presidential campaign cycle, celebrities became weapons of attack as much as popularizers of their causes (Johnson 2012).[8]

Celebrity endorsements in British electoral politics

With the exception of Cool Britannia and Red Wedge, there has been a general reluctance among UK politicians and entertainers to become reliant upon each other. Furthermore, the British public has distrusted such affiliations and the mobilization of UK celebrity supporters has tended to spectacularly backfire. In 1983, the Conservative Party utilized celebrity supporters in an American-style youth rally held at Wembley Conference Centre. This was hosted by old-stager comedians like Bob Monkhouse and Jimmy Tarbuck. It included such 'luminaries' as the World Snooker champion Steve 'Interesting' Davis and *Death Wish* (1974) film director Michael Winner. To appeal to the Young Conservatives who attended, the organizers booked the popular disc jockey (DJ) and comic performer Kenny Everett. However, the Tories got rather more than they bargained for when Everett, replete with giant foam hands, outrageously yelled 'Let's bomb Russia!' and 'Let's kick Michael Foot's [the Labour Party leader] stick away!' The footage of his performance was endlessly replayed on television, caused offence and proved a source of embarrassment. Everett regretted his involvement, claiming that he only went along to the rally as the Conservatives had asked him before the Labour Party.

Elsewhere, partisan celebrity endorsements were largely restricted to the smaller parties. For instance, the astronomer Sir Patrick Moore put forward his anti-European Union views for the right-wing United Kingdom Independence Party (UKIP). UKIP also fielded the permanently tanned former Labour MP and chat show host Robert Kilroy-Silk as a member of the European Parliament (MEP), although this marriage of interests ended in bitter acrimony. Moreover, the Green Party inadvertently became a source of public mirth when it signed up the ex-BBC sport presenter David Icke, only to discover that he had decided that he was the Son of God! The Liberal Democrats at least employed a real comic 'messiah', John Cleese, to appear in a number of their PEBs in the 1987, 1992 and 1997 general election campaigns. Within these appearances, Cleese utilized his comedic persona of 'Basil Fawlty' to demonstrate the unrepresentative nature of the British electoral system.

Yet the blurring of the lines between politics and entertainment has meant that CP2 endorsements have become increasingly commonplace in UK politics. In the 1997 general election, the MP Barbara Follett, along with her novelist husband Ken, film producer Lord David Putnam, television presenter Lord Melvyn Bragg and theatrical impresario Sir Cameron Mackintosh became known as 'Labour luvvies'. In addition, throughout the 2001 and 2005 general elections, Blair could rely on a number of UK celebrities to endorse his leadership, although the relationship diminished after the high point of 'Cool Britannia' and the campaigns remained moribund, due to the inevitability of further Labour Party victories.

In 2010, a revitalized Conservative campaign machine unveiled the film star Sir Michael Caine to promote its plans for sixteen-year-olds to volunteer as 'national citizens' as part of 'the Big Society'. Caine was joined by other CP2s, such as Carol Vorderman, Kirstie Allsop, Gary Barlow and Chris Rea. Within this campaign, the Labour Party used the comedian Eddie Izzard in a Labour Party PEB, stating that a Conservative victory would be a disaster and that 'Britain is brilliant'. Elsewhere, David Tennant and Richard Wilson provided voice-overs for Labour Party PEBs and its audio manifesto. Finally, there were a growing number of Liberal Democrat supporters, including the film stars Colin Firth and Daniel Radcliffe.

Yet the British political and entertainment classes have remained generally wary of one another. This use of celebrity endorsement in mainstream politics leads to questions about whether the public has been unduly influenced by the merging of imagery, glamour and ideology. A key allegation has emerged that celebrity style has impoverished the rights of citizens because the democratic polity has been undermined. Consequently, Neil Postman claims that there has been a decline in rationality as televisual style dominates substantive debate (Postman 1987). P. Eric Louw complains that these activities have created a 'pseudo-politics' based on 'pure puffery and hype' (Louw 2005: 191). Alternatively, with the new configurations of political communications in an era of social networking, celebrities have filled the void in public trust left by unscrupulous politicians, as exemplified by the UK parliamentary expenses scandal in 2009. This enables CP2s to make creditable interventions within the polity and to empower the public to take up political candidates and their causes (Street 2004: 447–8; Thompson 1995).

Conclusion

This chapter has shown that there is a distinction between celebrity politicians (CP1s) and politicized celebrities (CP2s). CP1s have emerged from a combination of image candidacy, spin and political marketing so that a leader's political persona has been defined by both his or her common reach and renown. In the USA, this has been evident in the presidencies of Reagan, Clinton and Obama, who engaged in populist communications and benefited from celebrity endorsements. Thus, the modern CP1 can be characterized as follows:

- they should be well-known;
- they should construct a clear political narrative;
- they should be able to communicate effectively within the popular culture;
- they can draw a crowd;
- they should be able to voice an opinion so that their ideas have an impact upon events; and
- they can employ their celebrity to mobilize a political movement that refers to their personal values.

Such a celebritization of political leadership has been transferred to the major offices of state in France, Italy, Germany and the UK. In Britain, Tony Blair utilized CP1 attributes to make New Labour electable. In part, this development has been led by the growth of non-ideological parties in which skilful public relations techniques were employed to market political leaders. However, Blair distinguished himself from other UK politicians by propagating his image as a cultural icon who enjoyed close proximity to the entertainment classes.

In this respect, he sought endorsements from actors, writers and rock stars. Therefore, the New Labour leader was characterized as a rock'n'rolla who retained the requisite cool to be associated with the Britpop acts of Blur and Oasis. For Blair, such an association would enable New Labour 'to reach the people who listened to Duran Duran and Madonna' (Blair 2010: 91). However, the failure of 'Cool Britannia' demonstrated the extent to which British politics and popular cultures were more comfortable with one another when they maintained an arm's-length relationship. Moreover, by the 2010 general election, the political fashions had dramatically changed and such celebrity politics proved to be 'a far cry from the heady days of 1997, when "Things Could Only Get Better." Whither the glitz of soap stars, the razzamatazz of rock gods?' (Woods 2010).

Conversely, in the USA, the long-standing relationship between CP1s and CP2s has been enhanced by the use of television to mediate political messages. Furthermore, politicians and celebrities have transmitted messages through social networks such as Twitter and Facebook. In turn, the Clinton and Obama administrations were characterized by their close affiliations with Hollywood film stars and popular musicians. And Obama owed a considerable debt to celebrity endorsers, such as Oprah Winfrey, for helping him to launch his campaign and to achieve electoral success.

It is the contention of this chapter that such a celebritization of politics should be viewed within the framework of a change in political aesthetics in which there will be both positive and negative outcomes. While some aspects of their performances have been more successful than others, partisan celebrity endorsers have made credible interventions to bring about effective political outcomes (Tsaliki, Huliaras and Frangonikolopoulos 2011: 16). Therefore, these interventions demonstrate a greater political efficacy among CP2s and a willing consumption of their activities from national electorates. Thus, celebrity politicians and politicized celebrities have utilized their 'star' power to communicate political messages effectively.

Questions

- How have modern American and British politicians become 'celebrities'?
- What has been the value of celebrity endorsements for political leaders?
- Why have celebrities been more valued in American election campaigns than in British ones?

Further reading

Baum, M. A. 2005: Talking the vote: why presidential candidates hit the talk show circuit. *American Journal of Political Science* 49: 213–34.

Bennett, J. 2011: Celebrity and Politics. *Celebrity Studies: Special Edition on Celebrity and the Global* 2(1): 86–7.

Corner, J. and Pels, D. (eds) 2003: *Media and the Restyling of Politics: Consumerism, Celebrity and Cynicism*. London, Thousand Oaks, New Delhi: Sage Publications.

Dickenson, B. 2006: *Hollywood's New Radicalism: War, Globalisation and the Movies from Reagan to George W. Bush*. London: I. B. Tauris.

Harris, J. 2003: *The Last Party: Britpop, Blair and the Demise of English Rock*. London: Harper Perennial.

Street, J. 2010: *Mass Media, Politics and Democracy*, 2nd edn. Basingstoke: Palgrave Macmillan.

4

Celebrity Politicians as Campaign Stars

Contemporary political elites have continued to draw on the forms of celebrity and renown which previous leaders used to signify their power and status. These methods of popular representation have segued into a range of political advertising techniques as elections have been fought on television and are being contested within the social media. Whereas image candidates had previously incorporated elements of fame into their personas, celebrity politicians (CP1s) have incorporated matters of performance, personalization, branding and public relations into the heart of their political representation.

Moreover, there has been a cross-fertilization of show business and political values where the 'narrative' of an election has defined the success or failure of a campaign (Renshon 2008: 391). This accords with the commercial news media's demand for a 'story' in which 'there are heroes and villains, conflict . . . and . . . a major dose of drama' (Wolfsfeld 2011: 73). Therefore, it becomes vital to discern the type of story a campaign is presenting: '[Barack Obama] the Illinois Senator understood the importance of storyline and steered clear of unsuccessful narratives of hope and guilt. Instead he shifted his party's mantra to hope and "change we can believe in". . . Obama's storyline appealed to the emotions and inspired millions of voters' (Ross 2011: 412–13). Further, CP1s must 'perform' across a range of media to define their personas, demonstrate their fortitude and enhance their appeal to the electorate.

This chapter will provide case studies concerning the deployment of celebrity politics in the United States' and the United Kingdom's electoral processes. It will consider how the 'media spectacle' (Kellner 2010a: 121) has shaped the coverage of the US primaries and the general election. Most especially, the 2008 Democratic Party presidential nominee Senator Barack Obama, as an articulate African-American politician, became the personification of a progressive movement (Sanders 2009: 96). As the first black man to win either of the US parties' nominations, Obama offered a sharp break from his predecessor, President George W. Bush. Moreover, his cosmopolitanism contrasted with the Democratic Party primary front runner, Hillary Clinton, and his youth compared well with the septuagenarian Republican nominee, John McCain. Further, Obama would establish inclusive relations with grass-roots organizations, online sites and social media networks (Redmond 2010).

Subsequently, this chapter considers how celebrity politics was exported to Britain in the 2010 UK general election. This campaign was conducted with a focus on the positive and negative connotations of political leadership. The Labour Party tried to shoehorn the prime minister, Gordon Brown, into becoming an effective CP1. Yet his discomfort was evident when he appeared on talk shows and user-generated web sites to widen his appeal. At the same time, David Cameron and Nick Clegg engaged as CP1s to gain credence with the electorate. However, there were perceived shortcomings in terms of their popular appeal. Therefore, while the election was fought on the UK's economy, all three leaders believed they could make significant gains from engaging in the televised prime ministerial debates. Although commonplace in the USA, these were the first televised debates of their kind within British politics and they placed an unprecedented focus on the leaders' celebrity.

Finally, the chapter will consider whether CP1 techniques have enhanced or diminished the democratic process. Within the 2008 American presidential campaign, McCain used negative advertisements such as 'the One' and 'Celeb' to accuse Obama of being a shallow celebrity. Therefore, the use of 'celebrity metaphor' (Alexander 2010a: 163–91) indicates how fame may prove to be a double-edged sword. On one hand, politicians utilize imagery to make themselves electable. On the other, this can lead to the public's disengagement with the political classes as candidates may be seen to be lightweight and to mislead the electorate. Further, McCain's decision to choose the unknown Republican Governor of Alaska Sarah Palin as his vice-presidential running mate was seen to be the apotheosis of a celebrity-driven campaign. In turn, this led to criticisms that the celebritization of politicians will perpetuate a long-standing disjuncture between a candidate's image and his or her appropriateness for office.

Barack Obama – From 'Yes we can' to 'Change we can believe in': leadership, story, narrative appeal and a political movement

'What modern American political leader, at any level of office, cannot afford to be a celebrity? To be a successful celebrity politician, you need to connect your personal status as a leader with a strong political movement. Barack Obama was able to bring these two elements together extremely successfully in 2008' (Newman 2011).

As Bruce Newman notes, there has been a linkage of celebrity politics with social movements to mobilize the public's emotional response to issues. In America, the US political system's emphasis on a candidate's endeavour, rather than on a more fixed set of partisan attachments, has facilitated the rise of CP1s. In 2008, Obama reached out to conventional voters and to a largely ignored young, black and disaffected section of the electorate. In this respect, he built up his position 'in the air' as a legitimate political leader whose celebrity status was defined by his cosmopolitan background (Sanders 2009: 97). Moreover, Obama was accompanied by a photogenic wife and family who appealed to young voters (Green 2011). Additionally, he employed a team of strategists to engage in a 'ground war' to establish an upsurge of support:

> We started our campaign with the firm but risky belief that we could radically expand the electorate and that we could count on our grassroots supporters to execute the plan . . . We – most importantly the candidate himself – refused to accept the electorate as it was. We thought we could make it younger and more diverse, and that's exactly what we did. (Plouffe 2009: 381)[1]

To develop this multicultural appeal, Obama provided an intriguing narrative that suggested the elements of a fable – wherein he rose from humble origins to triumph over adversity. He made evident his personal history as the son of an African father, Barack Obama Sr, from Kenya and a white American mother, Stanley Ann Dunham, from Kansas. As his parents separated when he was very young, Obama was brought up by his mother in Indonesia and Hawaii before she died from ovarian cancer at the age of fifty-two. Furthermore, Obama only saw his alcoholic father on one further occasion before his death in Africa. This exotic and tragic upbringing was popularized by Obama when he wrote two bestselling books, *Dreams of My Father* (2004) and *The Audacity of Hope* (2006).

Subsequently, he won two Grammys for the audio versions of these memoirs.

From then on, the rest of Obama's story completed the legend. This included: his attendance as a scholarship student at the Occidental College in California, then Columbia University and the Harvard Law School; community organizing on Chicago's South Side; legal work in a firm specializing in civil rights law and teaching constitutional law at the University of Chicago; and finally his budding political career. 'Obama has a great story. . . . It's very deep and archetypal. It's got all the elements of the mythological hero. The long road of trials he went through – that's important in mythology' (Vogler 2009).

While Obama embraced his international background, he made it apparent that his values were drawn 'as much from Kansas as they were from Kenya' (Green 2011). Therefore, he took the advice of former congressman and mentor Abner Mitka, who recounted an anecdote in which Cardinal Richard Cushing had advised John F. Kennedy to be 'less Harvard and more Irish' in the 1960 presidential campaign. In turn, Obama 'learned to speak more Chicago and less Harvard' (Scott 2007). Consequently, he demonstrated the CP1 characteristic of being simultaneously different and familiar in terms of public appreciation.

The other part of Obama's popular appeal was as a 'new force' in US politics whose ethnicity, international status and cool intellect could be sold to the US electorate. His well-received speech at the 2004 Democratic National Convention (DNC) launched him as an overnight sensation on the national stage. Before then, Obama had been barely known outside Chicago as an 'articulate speaker with a strange sounding name' (Green 2011). Subsequently, he was 'described as the most eloquent African-American public speaker since the late Martin Luther King Jr . . . [who could transform] . . . a well-written speech into an awe-inspiring testimony for change' (Wilbekin 2008). Thus, he became an instant celebrity whose autograph was sought after and who appeared on magazine covers and on numerous television shows. Obama's campaign for the senatorial seat of Illinois became a national news event.

However, despite this rapid rise, it should be remembered that Obama had refined his political image for well over a decade. His experience in his adopted home town of Chicago proved to be vital in defining his attraction to voters. The 13th District seat that Obama occupied as a state senator covered the affluent area of Hyde Park, composed of University of Chicago academics, through to the South

Side, and then up to the Near North of the city. This meant that while Obama represented black voters in the poor South Side, at either end of his constituency he had to construct an image through which he could connect with white members of the electorate (Green 2011). In 2008, he would transfer this local appeal to the national stage.

Moreover, his background allowed him to set up a campaign organization formed from a close circle of political consultants who had worked for the election of the Chicago mayor, Richard M. Daley, in 1989. Notable members of this group included David Axelrod, Rahm Emanuel, Valerie Jarrett, William M. Daley and Michelle Obama (née Robinson) (Green and Holli 1991). The speech was '[t]he work of Axelrod as the DNC needed a black politician who was articulate as hell and available. Obama was able to sell the story of being a mixed race African American who could get out the black vote but did not frighten the white voters. As it was said by Richard Daley, "Obama was f***ing golden!"' (Green 2011).

It brought him to the attention of an American public that remained open to the prospect of change. Everything about Obama promised a sharp break from the discredited President George W. Bush and this enabled him to differentiate himself from the apparently invulnerable Democratic Party front runner, Hillary Clinton.

Obama gained early momentum by winning the Iowa caucus in January 2008, which opened up a political route that would ultimately take him to the White House (Heilemann and Halperin 2010: 6). Throughout the hard-fought primaries, Obama's campaign strategists Axelrod and David Plouffe realized that his intense social energy could be employed to renew the political project. With his catchphrase of 'Yes we can', Obama promised the US electorate a palpable, yet undefined, sense of 'togetherness' to deal with the nation's economic, political and foreign policy ills. Within the general election, this phrase was refined to become 'Change we can believe in'. Obama's appeal increased during the global financial crisis that began in the USA in September 2008 as he made measured and intelligent statements about the economy. In contrast, the volatile McCain desperately accused his opponent of being responsible for the nation's economic plight.

Therefore, Obama presented himself as a force to purify the 'American Democratic Experiment' by mediating between the darkness of a sullied past and the light of a bright future. Consequently, his candidacy was perched on the 'very hinge of history' and his heroic status was mediated through the iconic 'Hope' poster designed

Figure 4.1 Yes we can: Chicago uses Shepard Fairey 'Hope' poster to congratulate its most famous adopted son

by artist Shepard Fairey (Alexander 2010a: 68; Kellner 2009: 725). Obama appeared as a visionary leader who could face the troubles confronting America (Redmond 2010: 87). Moreover, he prevailed because he embodied many of the messages he was preaching. For instance, Obama spoke on race in March 2008 to allay fears that the campaign would be framed by racial division and emphasized the common hopes of the nation (Anstead and Straw 2009: 1).

Obama's rhetoric focused upon a communitarian response to the fear-inducing terrors of the modern age and was framed by media spectacle. Therefore, his campaign managers employed a series of must-see events and urged their candidate to make well-received speeches which were globally televised to heighten his public profile. Douglas Kellner contends that Obama became a 'super celebrity' to win the presidency: 'Spectacles are media constructs that are out of the ordinary and habitual daily routine which become popular media events, capturing the attention of the media and the public. They involve an aesthetic dimension and often are dramatic . . . and they feature compelling images, montage and stories' (Kellner 2009: 716).

Jeffrey C. Alexander has commented that Obama's acceptance speech for the Democratic nomination at the Mile High Stadium in Denver, Colorado, was on one level a highly stage-managed celebration of the rise of a black statesman.[2] However, it also offered an idealistic exchange of values between the candidate and the US citizenry (Alexander 2010a: 22–3). Paul M. Green describes the experience in quasi-religious tones, stating that 'there were people in the hot sun who at 2,500 feet above sea level were prepared to risk sunburn or sunstroke to see him and four hours before his speech in the stadium there was a two-and-a-half-mile queue to get in!' (Green 2011).

A similar experience would occur when Obama took the audacious decision to go on a week-long tour in the summer of 2008, visiting Afghanistan, Iraq, Israel, Germany, France and Britain. In the trip's most breathtaking moment, he was met by a crowd of 200,000 people at Berlin's Brandenburg Gate where the 'hunger for new American leadership was palpable' (Plouffe 2009: 278). In drawing enormous and enthusiastic crowds to these rallies, Obama had made politics and government 'sexy and appealing again' (Wilbekin 2008).

Later on, he would provide the same sense of political intoxication at his victory celebration in Grant Park in Chicago on 4 November 2008 and at his star-studded presidential inauguration concert, 'We are One', in January 2009. As these events attracted stadium-sized crowds and were littered with African-American celebrities, such as Spike Lee, and black leaders, including Jesse Jackson, they were covered by the global media so that Obama became a 'world celebrity superstar' (Kellner 2009: 730). His speeches were stage-managed television spectacles that were defined by visual editorial patterns which rhythmically intercut Obama with shots of the adoring crowd. These ritualized events suggested that he spoke with an authenticity to convey important truths to the nation (Redmond 2010: 87). In addition, he enhanced his CP1 role through his campaign team's 'ground-war' orchestration of an army of activists for fund-raising purposes and electoral support through new information technologies (Alexander 2010a: 59):

> The spectacle of Obama did not simply emerge, however, through such hyper-iconic images, broadcast live or tracked in news bulletins, and written about in the mainstream media. Obama's spectacular campaign colonized the internet and social networking sites and interfaces such as YouTube, Facebook, My Space and Twitter, and it sent [around the world] live text messages and updates to subscribers/devotees via their mobile phones, about upcoming speeches, rallies or as a call for donations or active support. (Redmond 2010: 87)

Mybarackobama.com – creating a grass-roots movement with 'avatar' Obama

Obama came into his own as a CP1 via his team's orchestration of a revolutionary 'citizen-initiated campaign' with the formation of MyBo (Gibson 2010: 1). Accordingly, he enhanced his celebrity status through social media networks to mobilize an army of 5 million grass-roots activists in order to raise monies from small contributors and to propagate his campaign. A significant change in political campaign management occurred as Obama realized that, while it remained necessary to ensure spectacle, it was further necessary to facilitate a 'shift . . . toward a looser "hybrid" mode of operation that incorporated the network tactics of protest movements' (ibid.: 5).

In part, this incorporation of information technology was driven by the larger amounts of dollars that could be raised online to fund the campaign. This meant that Obama decided to forgo the publicly available forms of party funding as he benefited from non-regulated private contributions. To this end, the social media focused on building a critical mass of small donors who could contribute sums of US$200 or less. Subsequently, the MyBo web site was transformed into a networking zone with a strong component of donations. Consequently, US$35 million was raised online, although this only accounted for 6 per cent of the total of US$729 million Obama raised in campaign funds (Green 2011; Straw 2010: 43).[3]

More importantly, Obama fused together this employment of new technologies with his previous experience as a community organizer. After a straightforward registration on MyBo, the site offered users a wide degree of involvement in an online political community. It facilitated local associations, invariably drawn from youth groups, college students and non-traditional political actors, to organize as grass-roots activists, thereby working in an inclusive and relational manner (Bang 2009: 132). This meant that Obama's network of campaign teams placed themselves at the centre of a movement composed of activist groups and lay people (Cogburn and Espinoza-Vasquez 2011: 201). The social capital that was drawn from Obama's online supporters became a pressing concern for Hillary Clinton in the primaries as: 'She worried that Obama seemed to be building some kind of movement in the cornfields. "Movement" was the word [Hillary] kept hearing from Maggie Williams, who told her it was easy to run against a man, but devilishly hard to run against a cause' (Heilemann and Halperin 2010: 52).

In addition, Obama popularized his appeal through a variety of podcasts, YouTube speeches and Blackberry messages. He was frequently shown to be using SMS/texting to remain informed and to mobilize support. The Obama campaign targeted e-mail messages which appeared to be 'sent' from the candidate to members of the electorate at key periods of the election (Cogburn and Espinoza-Vasquez 2011: 202). The wide number of 'social' portals meant that he defined a political image founded on reciprocity to encourage the popular scrutiny of his ideas. Therefore, the often disaffected 'mobile youth' gravitated towards him and his messages of change, hope and identity (Redmond 2010: 92): 'Obama's political speeches were the most popular speeches on YouTube for months and they were long speeches, sometimes 40 minutes. People definitely could not get enough of him' (Zaleski 2008).

Thus, as a 'liquid celebrity', Obama communicated with those American citizens who had become disenfranchised by machine politics (Redmond 2010: 82). He formed linkages with non-traditional activists by being a 'charismatic authority figure who promised . . . solidity yet stream[ed] in and out of material view, [as he did not] . . . fix or . . . propagate . . . [a] communion [with the public] beyond triumphant spectacularism' (ibid.: 81). Sean Redmond has defined this development as 'avatar Obama' in which the liquidity of his celebrity performance was established through a multiplicity of identities that allowed him to connect with the American electorate (ibid.: 83).

In this respect, Obama's team learned lessons drawn from the Democratic senator Howard Dean's 2004 Democratic Primary campaign. Dean had used social media to raise significant monies, but his candidacy had collapsed through a lack of connection with his support base. Alternatively, Obama's campaign benefited from the input of one of the co-founders of Facebook, Chris Hughes, who developed internet software which focused on real-world organizing with the electorate. Across the battleground states, Obama's utilization of social networking technologies enabled his campaign organization to swell to 1.5 million community organizers.

To aid their door-to-door canvassing, volunteers accessed constantly updated databases through field offices and via MyBo to obtain information about potential voters' political leanings (Lai Stirland 2008). Additionally, Obama activists were issued with an eighty-page instruction manual to illustrate the organizational focus of the campaign. They were assigned as team and data coordinators to lead cadre operations in particular states. This blend of volunteering, gumshoe canvassing and information processing became the hallmark of the Obama campaign as it:

> [built, tweaked and tinkered] with its technology and organizational infrastructure since it kicked off in February 2007 and [developed] the most sophisticated organizing apparatus of any presidential campaign in history . . . [It was] the first [campaign] to successfully integrate technology with a revamped model of political organization that stresses volunteer participation and feedback on a massive scale, erecting a vast, intricate machine [that fuelled] an unprecedented get-out-the-vote drive in the final days of [the campaign]. (Lai Stirland 2008)

However, Obama's team realized there needed to be some latitude in its blend of legwork and information technology. They allowed activists a greater degree of autonomy in rooting out the opinions of non-specifically targeted members of the electorate. For instance, a Florida campaign worker, Jeanette Scanlon, was encouraged to canvass her neighbourhood and utilized MyBo to explain the differences to wary locals between Obama's and McCain's tax policies (ibid.). The campaign spread its message virally by emphasizing the horizontal linkage of a range of non-traditional political actors. For instance, there was the user-generated YouTube video in which a young woman, Amber Lee Ettinger (the 'Obama Girl'), sang 'I've got a crush on Obama' interspersed with images drawn from his speeches. This proved to be one of the site's most popular items when it received five million hits (Kellner 2009: 4).

In turn, these participants were invited to solve common challenges and to scrutinize Obama's response to the range of problems that Americans faced, thereby enabling them to organize 'in new political communities for the exercise of good governance' (Bang 2009: 133). Through these inclusive techniques, Obama remained in constant touch with his core support and attracted online activists who experienced his celebrity in both a public and private sense:

> Obama articulated an image of himself as an inspiring political authority who does not expect a 'blind' or rationally motivated form of obedience . . . He spoke about authority as a reciprocal and communicative two-way power relationship . . . in order to get people with different . . . identities and projects freely to accept cooperation across all conventional boundaries (ibid.: 132).

Although several factors may explain Obama's landslide victory (the financial crisis engendered by the collapse of Lehman Brothers Bank, the coat-tails of President Bush's negative ratings and McCain's poor performance in the national election), he ushered in a new phase of celebrity politics. Obama constructed a popular narrative which combined two vital aspects of a CP1's performance – the formation of a credible persona with the orchestration of a political movement. Through the social media, he enhanced his image to become a mythological figure: 'When Bob Dylan spoke to the London *Times* in April 2009, just a few months after Obama's election, the legendary singer-poet gave voice to the mythical idea of Obama as not entirely of this earth: "He's like a fictional character, but he's real" . . . This is the stuff of which heroes are made' (Alexander 2010a: 314).

The 2010 UK general election – celebrity political leadership

British politicians looked across the Atlantic to see how they could import CP1 techniques into their own electoral practices. While UK party systems contrast with those in America, the media focused on the leaders' performance in the 2010 general election. In Britain, a CP1's success was determined by how far his or her political communication machinery could effectively target the section of the electorate known as 'Middle England'. As they were influenced by rational choice forms of political marketing, the parties remained 'electoral-professional' rather than 'citizen-initiated' (Davis 2010b; Lees-Marshment 2008; Newman 1999; Scammell 1995).

Although the Labour, Conservative and Liberal Democrat parties operated an extensive 'ground war' campaign by utilizing the information technologies, the UK general election was characterized by 'air war' techniques in the conventional media (Gaber 2011: 274). While blogs, tweets and web sites had a bearing on the campaign, they proved to be add-ons rather than key tools for mobilizing political support. Indeed, the social media of Web 2.0 were most effective when they were wrapped around television news stories and 'sharing thoughts and opinions' about the leadership debates (Newman 2010: 3).[4]

Similarly, there was considerable speculation that Gordon Brown's and David Cameron's respective wives, Sarah and Samantha, would be important figures in attracting voters. Again, while Sarah Brown's tweets received attention, the leaders' wives and families remained of marginal interest. Instead, the political elite focused on developing narratives, creating spectacle and determining the status of the party leaders (Boulton and Roberts 2011: 33; Dale 2010; Snow 2010). Consequently, this meant that the campaign effort was largely contained within the mainstream media of television, radio and newspapers.[5]

With varying degrees of success, CP1s including Brown, Cameron and Nick Clegg used their fame to promote their leadership qualities. In the run-up to the election, Labour spin doctors were concerned about Brown's toxicity with the electorate. Subsequently, he was forced to engage in several excruciating attempts to reconcile his austere capabilities as an economist with a more personalized form of leadership. In 2006, when he was still the Chancellor, Brown informed the public that he was a fan of the Arctic Monkeys. Later, in 2008, it was reported, even more bizarrely, that Brown loved the Bee Gees and listened to their disco classics on a daily basis! Further, he tried to employ the user-generated web site YouTube to speak to young people about his vision for the country. However, these online broadcasts were undermined by his poor demeanour. These manic attempts by Brown to popularize himself where ridiculed by Lord Prescott who noted that the then prime minister had 'the worst bloody smile in the world' (Summers 2009).

Brown agreed to be interviewed by the celebrity journalist Piers Morgan in front of a live audience in a one-hour programme which was shown on Independent Television (ITV) on Valentine's Day, 2010. In preparation for the show, he spoke to television presenter Fiona Philips about his grief in coming to terms with his mother's death (Philips 2010). Within the televised interview, Brown emphasized the kindness of his personality, his passions outside of politics and his love for his wife and two sons. Despite achieving an impressive audience of 4.2 million viewers, the show hurt Brown's chances because:

> Love him or loathe him, regardless of his strengths and failings, Gordon Brown has one great asset. He is a serious man in an era where the voters have grown cynical about presentational skills. Yet his handlers have decided we need to be persuaded that Brown can do it too. He can't . . . and no amount of life storytelling with Piers Morgan would have helped that. Last night's interview was a disaster. (Perkins 2010)

On the other hand, Cameron was far more comfortable in exposing his populist instincts to the media. He made capital from the pregnancy of his photogenic wife, Samantha, and defined himself as a compassionate Conservative who advocated the principles of the 'Big Society'. He simultaneously and ruthlessly criticized Labour's economic policies and Brown's poor leadership. But if Cameron had a weakness, it lay in his privileged Old Etonian background. When guesting on *Desert Island Discs*, he attempted to make light

Figure 4.2 'Dave' Cameron versus the 'Iron Frau': G20 leaders watching the 2012 Champions League penalty shoot-out

of his upbringing by picking the Jam's class warrior anthem, *Eton Rifles* (1979). Cameron had been warned that his open disdain towards Brown during the weekly parliamentary Prime Minister's Question Time (PMQ) was counterproductive. Inadvertently, it created public sympathy for Brown while Cameron was compared to the infamous public school bully 'Flashman' from *Tom Brown's Schooldays* (1857). Therefore, he tried to play down his 'toff' image, despite stories emerging about his student membership of the exclusive and notorious Oxford University's Bullingdon Club (Parsons 2008).

Instead, his media minders, led by the former *News of the World* (1843–2011) editor Andy Coulson (see chapter 5), placed the emphasis on Cameron's image as a family man. As 'Dave' Cameron, he was a more genial figure who altruistically believed that societal ills could be overcome by 'hugging a hoodie'. In many ways, Cameron benefited from his earlier experience in public relations when he worked as the head of communications for Carlton Television between 1994 and 2001. This meant that he realized the importance of presentation, and it enabled him to develop relationships with marketers, most notably Steve Hilton who went on to become his 'blue-sky' thinker (Robinson and Teather 2010).

In the run-up to the election, the Liberal Democrat leader Nick Clegg suffered from a lack of visibility (Drake and Higgins 2012: 379). When he did receive media attention, he proved to be a reasonably effective performer, most especially during the House of Commons' expenses controversy. Yet the Liberal Democrats' poor media coverage between elections and their failure to make a breakthrough in the 2005 general election meant that Clegg remained a peripheral figure. Moreover, he stood in the shadows of his deputy and 'Grand Financial Wizard' Vince Cable who performed ably in the financial crisis. If Clegg registered in the public consciousness, it was as a Cameron-lite clone because of his public school education and affluent background.

Indeed, before the election, Clegg had achieved greatest prominence when he foolishly agreed to be interviewed in *GQ* (1957 onwards) by Piers Morgan, where his answers about his sexual prowess had earned him the nickname of 'Nick Clegg-over' (Jones 2008: 5). However, his status was to change dramatically with the introduction of the 2010 general election's major innovation – the three televised prime ministerial debates between Brown, Cameron and Clegg:

> An episode of the topical comedy panel show, *Have I Got News for You* . . . included several jokes that were premised on Clegg's anonymity and the panellists' own reluctance to spend time on the third party's campaign. But their mockery would soon appear outdated. Clegg's securing of equal billing in the debates ensured his participation in what became the centrepiece of the election campaign. (Parry and Richardson 2011: 476)

The leadership debates and the celebrity politics 'X-factor'

Previously, UK prime ministers had shied away from televised debates as 'every party politician that expects to lose tries that trick of debates and every politician who expects to win says no' (Major 2011). In 2010, as each leader had to overcome a perceived weakness, the debates offered them a chance to gain significant leverage over the electorate. For Brown, it was felt that he could overcome his toxic personal image. For Cameron, it appeared to be a good opportunity to dispense with his aristocratic bearing. Moreover, despite the Conservative's leading position in the polls, he had 'nailed his colours so firmly to the debates . . . that retreat would be difficult, if not impossible' (Bailey 2011: 14). For Clegg, the debates provided him with a greater degree of visibility, thereby removing the perception that he was 'Cameron-lite'. Further, all three were fighting their first election campaign as leaders of their respective parties (Wring 2011: 1).

After several months of detailed negotiations, it was agreed that the leaders would appear in three prime-time ninety-minute debates. They were held across England in the north-west, the south-west and the Midlands and were covered by ITV, British-Sky-Broadcasting (BSkyB) and the British Broadcasting Corporation (BBC). The party managers were concerned about the composition of the studio audiences, the generation of the questions, their moderation and how each leader would be positioned on the platform (Harrison 2010: 265). Consequently, many commentators suggested that the debates' impact would be mitigated by the detailed rules that had been negotiated.

Initially, the debates were mocked, notably without any sense of self-irony, by television presenter Richard Madeley, who proclaimed 'we've been living in the age of celebrity for quite a long time now . . . so the moment that the [the reality talent show] the "X-Factor" met politics, live on ITV One television – vvvvooom!' (Richardson, Parry and Corner 2011: 309). Elsewhere, Andrew Gimson wrote that the politicians had 'descended to the level of some celebrity talent shows' (Gimson 2010). However, the first debate attracted an average audience of 9.4 million, the second brought the subscription satellite channel Sky News its largest-ever viewing figures of 4.1 million and the final one averaged 8.1 million viewers. Moreover, the debates enabled voters to see how the political leaders could explain themselves at a greater-than-sound-bite length, unmediated by spin doctors (Harrison 2010: 266).

The debates became a media spectacle as pollsters speculated on who had won and who had lost them. Indeed, after the first debate, each party spun a line on the success of their leaders. For instance, the former Labour Party home secretary Alan Johnson was employed to emphasize Brown's lack of televisual skills as a virtue by comparison with the 'slick' Cameron and the inexperienced Clegg. In truth, Brown's poor communication skills hindered his ability to act effectively as a CP1. They later reached a nadir when a mobile microphone attached to his suit was inadvertently left on so his private comments to an aide about the 'bigotry' of Rochdale pensioner Gillian Duffy were broadcast live by Sky News.

Brown's failure to project an effective televisual style, his poorly timed jokes and his constant refrain that 'I agree with Nick' did little to overcome his presentational shortcomings. His inability to act as a celebrity politician existed at a deeper level than mere rhetoric.

It meant that he suffered by comparison with Cameron and even more with Clegg in his attempts to generate any form of folksy charm (quite possibly an oxymoron in Brown's case), to trade insults (comparing the feuding Cameron and Clegg to his two young sons), to make negative attacks or, more profoundly, to defend his government's record during the global financial crisis (IPSOS MORI 2010: 2–3).

Ironically, while Brown was expected to have difficulties in expressing himself, the chief loser during the first two debates appeared to be Cameron. In agreeing to a three-way debate, it was felt that Cameron had been deflected from his attack on Brown and had underestimated Clegg's skills as a CP1. In the first debate, he tried to work the room rather than express himself through the camera. Similarly, he was thrown by the moderator Alastair Stewart's vigorous interruptions and by Clegg's ability to connect with the audience. In trying to overcome this handicap, Cameron suffered by being 'too negative' in his calls on Clegg to 'get real' and received public disapprobation in his attempts to emphasize his personal relations with nurses and 'ordinary' folk (ibid.: 3). Instead, Cameron only revitalized himself as a CP1 in the third debate by expressing a more populist agenda to public sector waste, the capping of immigration and the sacking of recalcitrant members of parliament involved in the previous year's expenses scandal.

The chief benefactor of the first two debates was Clegg, whose CP1 status was enhanced by the public's perception of him as an 'outsider' of established politics. His constant mantra of introducing a 'new politics' to emphasize his freshness and his attacks on the other leaders in the light of their parties' roles in the expenses scandal were well received. He appeared to be more personable than his rivals, particularly in relation to the dour Brown (ibid.: 3). Clegg's performance had been honed by hours of practice in pre-debate rehearsals, wherein he had learned to look into the camera and be comfortable with the format. Additionally, he made a point of responding to audience members by name. Further, Clegg received a positive response when he suggested that the public should be allowed to sack unpopular MPs. Conversely, the former Labour MP for Sunderland, Chris Mullin, cynically commented:

> Nick Clegg is widely reckoned to have been the clear winner of last night's debate. Ironic considering that, for his all his fluency and utter self-confidence, he is easily the biggest charlatan of the lot. Who would guess, listening to him prattling piously about the MPs' expenses that

> he was a maximum claimer? Or that six months ago, when it was flavour of the hour, he was demanding 'bold and savage cuts' in public spending, a subject on which he is now silent. (Mullin 2010: 442)

Clegg's triumphal performance in the first debate was reflected in a YouGov poll which put the Liberal Democrats on 30 per cent, Labour on 28 per cent and the Conservatives down to 33 per cent (ibid.: 442). Thus, the Conservative Party was forced to reconfigure its campaign: as a result of the 'spectacle' of the debates, Clegg had become a serious candidate and should be denounced accordingly (in Clegg's case, this led to attacks by the Conservative Party's media on his nationality and authenticity as a political leader).

Therefore, the prime ministerial debates tied in with a 'permanent' general election campaign which focused on the leaders' political celebrity. They made conspicuous the respective abilities of Brown, Cameron and Clegg to employ CP1 attributes for effective political capital. For Brown, the debates reconfirmed his disastrous inability to perform across the media. For Cameron, their effect was double-edged. While his performance improved, his stilted behaviour had taken the shine off his leadership. Moreover, Cameron's failure to define an effective campaign narrative would be reflected in the Conservative's inability to win the election outright.

Clegg was the most successful leader in delineating his political story and, in the resulting 'Cleggmania', he rose from 'zero to hero'. However, his performance was mitigated by the Liberal Democrats' failure to translate this success into an increased proportion of the vote. Yet, due to the extraordinary nature of the 2010 election result in which no one party attained a majority, they held the balance of power. Therefore, Clegg's CP1 performance launched him onto the national stage as a creditable political leader who would broker the agreements necessary to effect the Conservative–Liberal Democrat coalition. In turn, the Liberal Democrats would nevertheless achieve political visibility, however compromised and controversial, when Clegg became the deputy prime minister: 'We were like that mousy girl who goes to the proms in films, takes off her glasses, and shakes her hair and suddenly realizes how beautiful she is' (Liberal Democrat aide, quoted in Kavanagh and Cowley 2010: 331).

Once the coalition had been agreed, Cameron and Clegg emerged for a press conference on the Rose Garden lawn behind No. 10 Downing Street on 12 May 2010 as a CP1 dream team. However, Conservative MP (and Cameron's leadership rival in 2005) David Davis presented their 'marriage of convenience' in homoerotic terms, calling it the 'Brokeback Coalition' in reference to the romance which existed between the two homosexual cowboys in the western *Brokeback Mountain* (2005) (Parry and Richardson 2011: 485).

Clegg's personal popularity quickly evaporated, most especially in relation to his U-turn over university tuition fees. Moreover, the hubris that the Liberal Democrats displayed at their 2010 Conference as the junior partner within the coalition meant that they took the brunt of public disapprobation in the light of the UK government cuts agenda. However, with regard to British political life, the genie was let out of the bottle when the televised debates became a key fixture in the general election campaign. Further, the use of CP1 techniques brought about a renewed focus on those criticisms that suggested that the political classes had relied on style rather than substance when seeking to mobilize public opinion.

Barack Obama as 'the One' and 'Celeb': John McCain's negative employment of CP1 politics

While US presidential candidates have previously attacked each other in terms of policy or probity, the 2008 Republican nominee Senator John McCain (who had seen his previous position as a popular maverick erode) decided to turn Obama's celebrity against him. As Obama basked in the public adulation of his international tour in July 2008, McCain's campaign counter-programmed a series of web and cable promotions which presented the Democratic nominee as a self-important lightweight (Kenski, Hardy and Jamieson 2010: 77). Through this tactic, the Republican political strategist Steve Schmidt believed that Obama could be knocked off course if it was shown that he was aloof, hubristic and arrogant. In this manner, Obama's 'heroic image [would be separated] from his mundane person [thereby] making [him] seem fake and his performance staged' (Alexander 2010b: 412): 'Eventually, it was Schmidt who blurted out the epiphany concerning Obama. "Face it, gentlemen," he said. "He's being treated like a celebrity." The others grasped the concept – a celebrity like J-Lo! Or Britney! – and exultation overtook the room' (Draper 2008: 52).

The Republicans produced two negative political broadcasts entitled 'The One' and 'Celeb' to accuse Obama of inexperience and shallowness. In the first of these, McCain's team used Obama's own quasi-religious phrases against him by comparing him to Charlton Heston's Moses in *The Ten Commandments* (1956). The broadcast ended by asking the public, 'Barack Obama may be the one, but is he ready to lead?' The idea was to demonstrate that Obama was no more than an empty shell.

In the follow-up broadcast, 'Celeb', a powerful, if slightly blurred, tracking shot showed the enormous German crowd that gathered for Obama's speech in Berlin. A few seconds later, muffled chants of 'O-ba-ma! O-ba-ma! O-ba-ma!' began to roll ominously across the screen. As the chanting continued, flash bulbs popped brightly as the pop star Britney Spears and the socialite Paris Hilton were glimpsed in their famous poses. They were intercut with shots of a grinning Obama standing in front of a tilting Berlin Victory Arch. Over this deliberately grainy image, a voice-over gravely intoned, 'He's the biggest celebrity in the world, but is he ready to lead?' (Alexander 2010b: 413).

The idea of the 'the One' and 'Celeb' was to show Obama as a hypocrite who was out of touch with the requirements of the nation. These negative broadcasts were accompanied by an e-mail written by Fred Davis, McCain's leading advertising consultant, to social networkers that stated: 'Only celebrities like Barack Obama go to the gym three times a day, demand "MET-Rx chocolate roasted-peanut protein bars and bottles of hard-to-find organic brew – Black Forest Berry Honest" – and worry about the price of arugula' (Heilemann and Halperin 2010: 337). The message was straightforward: wealthy and self-absorbed celebrities such as Obama did not have to deal with the problems that faced average American families (Morini 2011: 33). The broadcasts were seen by a wide audience across the web and the conventional media. In the short term, they helped McCain's campaign to achieve an equal poll rating with Obama of 44 per cent.

However, when the Obama campaign team suggested that they reflected an unspoken racism, these attack broadcasts were castigated by the media. Further, they had little real long-term impact on the US electorate's beliefs about Obama's trustworthiness. Indeed, if anything, the broadcasts backfired on McCain. American voters saw them as being 'irrelevant, childish and pointless' and they undermined the perception that McCain was a non-typical politician (Plouffe 2009: 280). Elsewhere, some commentators suggested that, as a Vietnam veteran who had survived the notorious 'Hanoi hotel', McCain should have made greater political capital from his military history (Green 2011). Further as Kellner comments: 'Quite obviously, the Republicans did not understand that Obama's rising celebrity status was helping him become more popular, getting him more attention, support and, eventually, votes from a population that is generally attracted by celebrity status and culture' (Kellner 2009: 722).

Yet, the employment of celebrity metaphor demonstrated how far the cultural capital drawn from CP1 behaviour had become an integral part of modern campaigning. It created a new playing field upon which the US electorate had to decide whether they wanted to elect the 'biggest celebrity in the world' or 'an American military hero' (Alexander 2010a: 190). Therefore, for a short period of time, these negative forms of campaigning made conspicuous the criticisms that had arisen concerning the integration of celebrity politics with the political mainstream. However, in a further irony, it would be McCain who received disapprobation when he chose to nominate the little-known governor of Alaska, Sarah Palin, as his vice-presidential (VP) running mate.

The Hockey Mom – lipstick on a pit bull or a pig?: the rise and fall of Sarah Palin

> When [Fred] Davis, who was in charge of McCain's VP process, . . . stumbled upon a video of [Sarah] Palin appearing on *Charlie Rose*, [he] was bowled over. And so was [Steve] Schmidt, who screened the clip and proclaimed, 'She's a star!'
>
> Heilemann and Halperin (2010: 359)

McCain's decision to pick the obscure Palin as the Republican VP nominee was initially hailed as an audacious gamble that had destabilized the Obama campaign. His spin doctors had aimed to make the naming of the VP candidate a 'shock to the world' as they hoped it would prove to be a 'game changer' (ibid.: 354). Throughout the summer of 2008, they had courted McCain's Congressional ally, the Democratic senator and former VP nominee Joe Lieberman, as a potential running mate. However, the partisan difficulties associated with such a nomination proved to be too wide a gulf to breach. Simultaneously, McCain's strategists had considered many other more well-known Republican candidates for the vice-presidency and Palin's name had originally only appeared very low down on the 'longest of a long list of names' (ibid.: 358). Therefore, as Lieberman's nomination proved untenable, Schmidt and Davis changed their attitude towards the governor of Alaska as they were impressed by her outstanding 80 per cent approval rating (ibid.: 358–9) and decided that as:

> Few knew much about [her] . . . [Palin would be] a genuinely surprising pick. . . . One might think this is all pretty ridiculous, but American elections are often won on image and spectacle, and obviously . . . Palin provided good spectacle. Republicans . . . hoped that she would draw in Hillary Clinton supporters and other female voters because she was herself a woman (Kellner 2009: 723).

In the short term, McCain's decision boosted his campaign ratings when Palin's introduction to the population was orchestrated through her well-received Republican National Convention (RNC) acceptance speech on 3 September 2008, which was watched by 40 million Americans. The forty-four-year-old made an instant connection with the right-wing sections of the electorate who had been ambivalent about McCain as he represented the more liberal end of the Republican Party. Her youth counterbalanced McCain's age of seventy-two to allay fears that if he won he would be the oldest president in US history. Moreover, Palin's low-income background meant that she represented the 'real America [as] against some putatively other one' (Alexander 2010a: 198) to offset the image of conservatives as wealthy people who did not care about those living on modest incomes.

As a pin-up for the far right, she advocated state rights, was a pro-life anti-abortionist, against stem-cell treatment, and expressed her doubts about environmentalism. Indeed, during her twenty months as governor of Alaska, Palin had enthusiastically welcomed petrochemical companies to further their exploration for oil within the state. Moreover, she was a Christian fundamentalist whose small-town religious, ethical and patriotic values played out well in the Republican section of the electoral map (Alexander 2010a: 198).

Further, Palin was a photogenic candidate: she had been a former beauty queen who had achieved third place in the competition for Miss Alaska. The unusual nature of her 'updo' hair style was distinctive and her hairdresser in her home town of Wasilla commented that Palin took a considerable interest in her appearance.[6] Yet while displaying some extraordinary qualities to demarcate her CP1 status, she simultaneously emphasized her normality as an all-American 'hockey mom'. Palin's husband Todd was known as the 'first Dude' and she was a mother to a family of five children, including a son in the armed forces and a newborn baby with Downs syndrome. In her acceptance speech at the RNC, Palin emphasized the 'ordinariness' of her female identity when she blushingly deferred to McCain's military and foreign policy experience: 'As the mother of one of those troops, [McCain] is exactly the man I want as commander-in-chief. I'm just one of the many moms who will say a prayer every night for our sons and daughters, our men in uniform' (Palin 2008).

Elsewhere she continued to exhibit her difference, most especially with regard to her vigorous membership of the National Rifle Association (NRA). Palin enthused about her moose-hunting exploits and was filmed endlessly firing off rifles. Consequently, she tapped into the mythology of the 'taming of the frontier' of which the tundra of Alaska was the last outpost. Notably, a photograph of Palin in a 'Teddy Roosevelt' pose standing over a dead moose made the rounds of the news media and the blogosphere. Therefore, she provided endless photo opportunities (including a shopping trip with McCain's wife, Cyndi) and good copy, while appealing to the average US citizen: 'Mrs Palin is history in a dress. And her script is straight out of Hollywood – like those teen movies with the clichéd ending featuring the female valedictorian delivering the speech of a lifetime projecting a bold and transformative future with an independent-minded woman in charge. The future is now' (Brietbart 2008).

Most (in)famously, Palin commented that the only difference between a committed mother and a pit bull dog was lipstick! In response, Obama noted that you could apply lipstick to a pig, but it remained a pig. These remarks were seized upon by Palin's supporters to demonstrate that Obama was a 'sophisticated beltway insider' whose snobbishness stood at odds with mainstream US values. Further, the McCain team accused Obama of being sexist in referring to Palin as a 'pig'. Despite the ridiculous nature of the story, Obama modified his response since an out-and-out attack on Palin risked alienating a sizeable section of the female electorate. Instead, he used his political communications machinery to focus on McCain's shortcomings while waiting for Palin to make a mistake (Alexander 2010a: 209).

The Obama team proved to be prescient in its analysis that the gaffe-prone Palin would be no more than a short-term gimmick. Her exposure in the national media demonstrated her failings, not least due to her lack of basic political knowledge. Despite the McCain team limiting Palin's media appearances and her attempts to cram information through index cards, her televised performances proved to be disastrous. When quizzed about US foreign policy by Charlie Gibson of American Broadcasting Corporation (ABC) News, she stumbled over whether she agreed with the 'Bush Doctrine' by countering 'in what respects, Charlie?' (Heilemann and Halperin 2010: 397).

Further, she informed the bemused Gibson that she was an expert on the Russians as 'they're our next-door neighbours, and you can actually see Russia from land here in Alaska' (ibid.: 397). These problems would be exacerbated in a more brutal encounter with Katie Couric on the Columbia Broadcasting System's (CBS) News, in which Palin's poor performance resulted in a drastic decline in her approval ratings. In turn, she appeared to be ignorant of the existence of news and current affairs magazines such as *Time* and *Newsweek*. Palin's incompetence led to the film star Matt Damon castigating her candidacy as being a 'bad Disney movie'. She provided satirists with a field day, most especially the comedienne Tina Fey who performed a withering caricature of the Republican VP candidate on *Saturday Night Live* (SNL) (1975 onwards) which was televised on 13 September 2008. In this parody, Fey mocked Palin with the line, 'I can see Russia from my house!' (ibid.: 398).

Subsequently, Palin's candidacy was compared to that of the incompetent vice-president Dan Quayle, George H. W. Bush' running mate in 1988 and 1992, who had unwisely attacked the moral ethics of television situation comedy *Murphy Brown* (1988–98) when the fictional lead character had a baby out of wedlock. Vice-President Dick Cheney told his friends that McCain had made a 'reckless choice' based on his gut instinct (Heilemann and Halperin 2010: 368). It was felt by Democrats and Republicans alike that McCain's team should have properly vetted Palin before deciding upon her as the VP nominee. Most especially, as the US public saw more of Palin, her inexperience came increasingly to the fore.

Even more damagingly, she had become involved in several scandals. For instance, it came to light that her unmarried teenage daughter Bristol had become pregnant. This created a debate about whether Palin should have submitted her family to the inevitable media scrutiny that her candidacy would entail. Further, as she became the focus of attention, harmful information emerged about her tumultuous period in office as governor of Alaska. News stories circulated indicating that Palin had dismissed public officials who did not agree with her policies and that she had appointed former schoolfriends into key positions to do her bidding. These accusations of political malfeasance reached a crescendo during the so-called 'Trooper-gate' affair wherein Palin had dismissed Alaska's public safety commissioner Walter Moneghan as he had refused to sack her former brother-in-law and state trooper Michael Wooten (Kellner 2009: 723). Other reports suggested that she had also been a member of the secessionist Alaska Independence Party (AIP).

As her poor performances, media investigations and family pressures mounted, Palin's health and mental faculties suffered. Despite achieving a creditable second in the VP debate against Obama's running mate Joe Biden, McCain's media minders became concerned that Palin was an irrational control freak and that she was becoming a liability to the campaign. In a desperate attempt to quell the criticisms, she agreed to appear on SNL with her tormenter Fey. However:

> By the time she went on *SNL*, the definitional war over her had ended. She retained the ardour and loyalty of her fans, who continued to turn out for her, and defend her. But in the eyes of the broader public – and even more so those of the national media and political establishments – any traces of her image as a maverick reformer was erased. For them, Palin has been reduced to nothing more than a hick on a high wire. (Heilemann and Halperin 2010: 411)

Conclusion

This chapter has shown that CP1s have utilized various types of 'performance' to demonstrate their legitimacy when seeking electoral office. Celebrity politicians have appropriated image-making techniques taken from packaged campaigns to blur the lines between politics and entertainment. Therefore, modern leaders have honed their telegenic attributes to connect with the electorate. Moreover, Web 2.0 forms of social networking have been used to enhance the linkages between CP1s and the public. This demonstrates how popular political discourses have placed an emphasis on the CP1s' employment of fame, renown and fortitude.

Consequently, there has been a transformation from a personalization of politics into the celebritization of a politician's candidacy (Stanyer 2007: 73). In modern democracies, charismatic leaders with likeable yet unique personas have contested election campaigns. Thus, CP1 attributes have emerged as a result of permanent campaigns, the rise of the politician as an entertainer and electoral success. In such a manner, they have sought to attract untapped constituencies of support by making political capital from their celebritization of politics.

Barack Obama's candidacy was founded upon a blend of American virtues with the values of world citizenship. In creating this political narrative, he made reference to his unique upbringing as a child of mixed-race parentage who had lived in Indonesia and Hawaii, employed long-term strategies drawn from his background as a community organizer, demonstrated a cool intellect in relation to his scholarship and employed the 'common touch' which he had learned in previous campaigns. Throughout the 2008 presidential election, he concentrated upon building up the extraordinary nature of his celebrity while seeking to connect with the electorate through strong emotive appeal.

Further, Obama's campaign was orchestrated through the incorporation of must-see events into the social media to establish a political movement in which activists became intrinsic to the democratic process. Therefore, Bang has argued, Obama's victory marked a sea change in the reciprocal relations which existed between the candidate and the electorate (Bang 2009). Most especially, it may be contended that the Democratic nominee constructed a liquid form of celebrity which allowed him to project a vision of hope that meant he:

> [w]on the presidency because of his effectiveness at mobilizing media spectacle, whether on the campaign trail, traditional media publicity or through the internet, such as YouTube videos . . . as well as the circulation of [his] speeches, which were complemented by other videos made by Obama's often young supporters. Clearly, by the end of the long presidential campaign, Obama emerged as a celebrity of the highest order. (Kellner 2010a: 121)

These CP1 techniques have been transferred to other modern democracies, leading to specific political outcomes. In the 2010 UK general election, the party leaders came under the public spotlight and media scrutiny.[7] Most especially, the introduction of the televised debates between Gordon Brown, David Cameron and Nick Clegg meant that celebrity politics occupied a central position in the campaign. Each leader's performance was subject to intense media coverage in which their every gesture was minutely studied. The debates proved to be outstanding spectacles which revitalized public interest in politics by reflecting the respective leaders' effectiveness in matching their celebrity personas to their political ability. Thus, television audiences could see how Brown, Cameron and Clegg, unmediated by political spin, responded to questions from the public, which had sufficient time to consider the credibility of their performances.

Undoubtedly, questions about CP1 behaviour and political representation raise key concerns about the democratic worth of these developments:

> With new forms of entertainment, new sources of news, and a new digital age to deliver them . . . now we have politicians who have turned themselves into celebrities . . . . At their best, these politicians-turned-celebrities . . . could . . . [help] to educate and expand the electorate. Yet it would be naive not to believe that [they] . . . can just as easily trivialize complex issues and do more harm than good. (Ross 2011: 416)

In particular, these matters were made conspicuous in the 2008 presidential campaign when the Republican nominee, John McCain, employed a form of celebrity metaphor to attack Obama's legitimacy. However, due to public response to the negative campaign broadcasts 'the One' and 'Celeb', the McCain team's bluff was called when they drastically underestimated the worth of Obama's celebritization to US voters. Being a CP1 meant that Obama connected with previously disaffected and unregistered members of the electorate and enhanced his appeal.

Conversely, McCain's decision to nominate Sarah Palin as his VP running mate proved to be a disastrous usage of celebrity politics. After an initial surge in her popularity, Palin was undermined by her basic lack of political skills and the impression that she was wildly out of her depth. Later, in her reality television programmes such as *Sarah Palin's Alaska* (2010–11), she connected with the anti-statist Tea Party which employed celebrity metaphors of its own in the formation of a social movement. Moreover, as Obama's presidency became mired in the compromises of office and the failure of his economic policies, his reliance on CP1 techniques was questioned.

Therefore, the CP1's utilization of political aesthetics had both positive and negative outcomes. This account has shown how new forms of identification have affected the relations between politicians, the media and the public. It has demonstrated that CP1 techniques have become commonplace in modern election campaigns and will continue to be deployed in modern democratic politics. While there are undoubted problems associated with these forms of behaviour, the renewed focus on leadership has required political elites to find ways to reconnect with the public as there has been a reconfiguration of the polity in democratic societies.

Questions

- How did Barack Obama construct a celebrity persona through the conventional and social media?

- To what extent did the UK general election leadership debates focus on the construction of celebrity leaders?
- How has celebrity been used as a political weapon and what did Sarah Palin's rise and fall demonstrate about the politics of illusion?

Further reading

Alexander, J. C. 2010a: *The Performance of Politics: Obama's Victory and the Democratic Study for Power*. Oxford, New York: Oxford University Press.

Heilemann J. and Halperin, M. 2010. *Race of a Lifetime: How Obama Won the White House*. New York: Viking Penguin.

Kavanagh D. and Cowley, P. 2010: *The British General Election of 2010*. Basingstoke: Palgrave Macmillan.

Parry, K. and Richardson, K. 2011: Political imagery in the British General Election of 2010: The curious case of 'Nick Clegg'. *British Journal of Politics and International Relations* 13(4): 474–89.

Plouffe, D. 2009: *The Audacity to Win: How Obama Won and How We Can Beat the Party of Limbaugh, Beck and Palin*. London: Penguin.

Wring, D., Mortimore, R. and Atkinson, S. (eds) 2011: *Political Communication in Britain: The Leaders' Debates, the Campaign and the Media in the 2010 General Election*. Basingstoke: Palgrave MacMillan.

5

Politicized Celebrities: Agency and Activism

This chapter considers how politicized celebrities (CP2s) have become important figures in modern political communications. In recent years, CP2s have been positioned at the interface of causal-based activity, social engagement and cultural practice. Moreover, as the social media has grown exponentially; film, music and television stars have used their fame to mediate 'a more expansive conception of political capital' (Coleman 2007: 15). Consequently, CP2s have raised public awareness concerning campaigns that have existed outside the purview of partisan-based politics.

Therefore, this chapter employs John Street's (with apologies to Colin Hay) usage of a 'differentiated yet inclusive definition of politics' to analyse these 'types' of CP2 activity (Hay 2007: 65; Street 2011: 7). According to Street, smaller-scale power relations, which had been previously conceived as being marginal to representations of public life, should be recognized as legitimate forms of political agency (Street 2011: 7). Politicized celebrities have provided credibility for issue-driven campaigns within policy agendas: 'It is important to note that these practices are not confined to political parties. Interest groups and social movements also deploy [politicized celebrities]; [and] . . . [as] they are among the most skilled practitioners of 'branding' . . . they [have become exploiters] of celebrities to promote political causes' (Street 2010: 241).

This analysis will begin by considering how the branding of film, television and sports stars has created points of public identification with specific campaigns. It will look at national examples within the United States (US) and United Kingdom (UK). In the USA, CP2s have become patrons, advocates and fund-raisers for a multitude of causes, including injustice, the environmental movement, public health and reform of education systems. They have lobbied Congress and state legislatures or engaged in direct action to bring attention to social movements. As UK celebrity culture has grown, there has been an accompanying rise in star activism in public health, residence rights and fund-raising campaigns.

Secondly, this greater political consciousness has led to celebrities standing for electoral office in their own right.[1] Ronald Reagan's ascendancy from a 'B-list' actor to American president (1981–9) represented a career trajectory which had been instituted by the former Hollywood song and dance man George Murphy when he became the Republican senator of California in 1964 (Ross 2011: 163–70). Other US celebrities, including Clint Eastwood, Jesse Ventura, Arnold Schwarzenegger, Sonny Bono, Fred Thompson and Al Franken, have won mayoral, gubernatorial, congressional and senatorial elections. This has become an international phenomenon in states as diverse as India, Pakistan, Haiti, Liberia and Lithuania (Imran Khan, Wyclef Jean, George Weah).

Finally, the chapter will consider how the blurring of the entertainment and news media has defined how celebrities influence political agendas (Inthorn and Street 2011: 1). For example, many of the unethical practices that had been endemic within Rupert Murdoch's now-defunct *News of the World* were made conspicuous by the 'Hacked Off' campaign, fronted by aggrieved celebrities, including Hugh Grant and Steve Coogan. However, CP2 activities have been praised and condemned in equal measures. Many questions remain about politicized celebrities' effects in shaping public opinion, political agendas and policy outcomes (Brockington 2009: 9). In particular, celebrity activism has either been seen to be worthwhile or a shallow expression of a consumer-led culture. Therefore, the chapter will reflect on whether celebrity activists can reinvigorate politics against the fears that they will erode political culture.

Politicized celebrities: political advocates, branding and changing cultural expectations

> Celebrities are supposed to use their celebrity to pull focus to issues . . . that's our function.
>
> Dreyfuss (2000)

As Richard Dreyfuss comments, politicized celebrities have realized that they may draw public attention to a range of causes. Stephen

Huddart has explained how CP2s have 'performed' as patrons, advocates and fund-raisers for social movements (Huddart 2005: 40). For example, a patron refers to those celebrities who allow an organization to cite their name, thereby affording credibility to external publics and validation to internal audiences. In tandem, a spokesperson or endorser is a celebrity who is identified with a charity and makes statements on its behalf. Through their participation in a public service announcement, the writing of an opinion piece or an appearance at a public rally, celebrities can attract visibility to a cause. Consequently, CP2 participation has shifted from partisan endorsement to causal-based activism (ibid.: 8).

This reflects how stars have become 'brands' such as the 'likeable action hero' (Bruce Willis), the 'all-American boy' (Tom Cruise) and the 'girl' (Sandra Bullock) or the 'pretty woman' (Julia Roberts) next door. They have achieved this status through establishing a star iconography and by negotiating modern public relations systems. In the political realm, star appeal has been determined by the replacement of older mechanisms of party campaign machinery with more individualist processes associated with a candidate's leadership status (Rabidoux 2009: 79). Thus, CP2s have utilized their 'brand identity' when lending their support to causes. For example, Sam Waterson's persona as New York District Attorney Jack McCoy in *Law and Order* (1993–2010) provided an image of integrity when he advertised the liberal magazine *The Nation*. Similarly, Arnold Schwarzenegger altered his image from a Reagan-era action hero to a more sensitive family hero to conform with changes in the Republican Zeitgeist during George H. W. Bush's (Bush Sr) one-term presidency (1989–1993) (Ross 2011: 365).

Consequently, stars have achieved autonomous power in the political arena when seeking to influence public opinion (Rabidoux 2009: 79). Ellis Cashmore has noted that there has been a major cultural shift in which celebrities have assumed a moral authority among target audiences which was 'once associated with sages or charismatic leaders' (Cashmore 2006: 218). While celebrities were politically active in the past, their fans demonstrated little or no desire to see their favourite actors, musicians and performers in a political guise. With the growing demand from audiences for authentic forms of celebrity engagement, transformative CP2s have realized their value as advocates for a wide range of causes. Therefore '[c]elebrities must create a political persona that invokes their own credibility and authority, which then gets conferred onto the cause to which they are associated. . . . They must use these resources to demonstrate authenticity in order to get the attention and sympathy of the audiences they seek, and to protect themselves from retribution should they alienate audiences' (Collins 2007: 186).

US celebrity activism: fund-raising, public awareness, advocacy and adding controversy to campaigns

For many years, American celebrities have been involved in fund-raising campaigns. From 1952 to 2011, the film, television and nightclub comedian Jerry Lewis was the national chairman of the US Muscular Dystrophy Association (MDA). In this capacity, he hosted an annual MDA telethon from 1966 to 2010 which raised a total of US$2.6 billion. Such activity was apparent when the 'outlaw' country and western star Willie Nelson, along with Neil Young and John Mellencamp, founded *Farm Aid* in 1985. This organization's annual concerts have raised millions of dollars to support US farmers. In 1986, Barbra Streisand established the Streisand Foundation, which supports campaigns concerning nuclear disarmament, the preservation of the environment, educational rights, women's rights, AIDS research, voter education and civil liberties.

More recently, Hollywood CP2s, including George Clooney, Brad Pitt, Tim Robbins, Sean Penn, Danny Glover, Susan Sarandon, Jessica Lange, Sally Field, Sissy Spacek, Angelina Jolie, Natalie Portman, Rosie O'Donnell, Ashley Judd, Alec Baldwin and Martin Sheen, have brought awareness to pro-choice rights concerning abortion, lobbied for agricultural reforms, led projects to shield the homeless, promoted gender and sexual minority rights, criticized the American justice system and explored anti-globalization causes. Hispanic actresses Eva Longoria and Rosario Dawson have crusaded for reforms to US immigration laws. Further, US celebrities have engaged in the *Free Nelson Mandela* concerts, rock musicians have lent their support to initiatives such as Music Television's (MTV) *Rock the Vote* (2001) and the activist-performer Steve Earle has campaigned against capital punishment.

George Clooney has emerged as the most forceful liberal voice in Hollywood. Initially, this occurred shortly after 9/11 when he became the prime organizer of the victims' families telecast *America: A Tribute to Heroes*. This programme included many stars, including Clooney, Tom Hanks, Will Smith, Jim Carrey, Sarah Jessica Parker, Tom Cruise, Julia Roberts and Chris Rock, and raised US$129 million for the United Way charity. Subsequently, he campaigned for his father

Figure 5.1 George Clooney: Hollywood 'A-lister' and its most credible liberal political activist

Nick, a Cincinnati television news anchor, who ran for a Democratic congressional seat in Kentucky in 2004.

As Clooney became more involved in politics, his image changed from being a lightweight film star to a figure of political substance. This was literally the case when he put on the pounds during his Academy Award-winning turn in the Middle-Eastern political thriller *Syriana* (2005). Moreover, he co-wrote, produced, directed and appeared in *Good Night and Good Luck* (2005) which told the cautionary tale of the Columbia Broadcasting System (CBS) reporter Edward R. Murrow's battle against McCarthyism. These films, along with Clooney's high-profile role in campaigning against the atrocities in Darfur (see chapter 6), have resulted in him becoming a powerful advocate for social reforms.

Hollywood stars have most visibly attached themselves to the causes of conservation and environmentalism. Such activity has resulted in raising awareness, the setting up of foundations, the production of documentaries and direct action. For instance, the television actress Stephanie Powers has been a long-standing organizer of the late William Holden's foundation for the conservation of wildlife in Kenya. Accordingly, Sigourney Weaver became an advocate for the protection of gorillas when she appeared in *Gorillas in the Mist* (1988) as the zoologist Dian Fossey who was murdered because of her opposition to the hunting trade (Brockington 2009: 30).

In 1999, Woody Harrelson joined protesters who mounted the Golden Gate Bridge to the irritation of passing motorists, and he briefly owned an oxygen bar 'O2' in Los Angeles. In May 2004, the National Resources Defence Council (NRDC) received contributions totalling US$3 million at a Brentwood fund-raiser which included Tom Hanks, Leonardo DiCaprio, Rob Reiner, Martin Short, Michelle Pfeiffer, Tobey Maguire, Steve Bing and Ray Romano. It was overseen by Laurie David, a former television producer turned full-time activist, and then wife of *Curb Your Enthusiasm* (1999 onwards) star Larry David. In turn, Streisand has been one of many celebrities who have donated a total of US$20 million to a range of national environmental organizations (Dickenson 2003).

Harrison Ford had his chest-hair painfully removed by a waxing cloth to make the point: 'It hurts [when] every bit of rainforest . . . get ripped out over there' (Brockington 2009: 25). Former US Vice-President Al Gore was awarded a share of the 2007 Nobel Peace Prize due to his Oscar-winning film *An Inconvenient Truth* (2006) and his campaigning against anthropogenic climate change. Glamorous celebrities, such as Pamela Anderson, Eva Mendes and Christy Turlington have posed nude for the People for the Ethical Treatment of Animals (PETA) videos exposing the fur trade. Alec Baldwin provided the commentary for PETA's documentary *Meet your Meat* (2003) which led to the fast-food chain Burger King cutting its links with slaughterhouses that did not meet governmental standards. Consequently:

> Single issue advocates continue to seek to network with and identify stars, who . . . can shine the public spotlight on their cause. Savvy . . . politicos . . . are well aware that [celebrities] can attract a lot of heat or publicity to a cause. If such publicity is then managed skillfully, it can lead to change or reform down the road. (Rabidoux 2009: 77)

Increasingly, US CP2s have attracted attention due to their ability to generate controversy. A tradition of outspoken politicized celebrities emerged in the 1960s and 1970s, as in the cases of Jane Fonda and Harry Belafonte (see chapter 2). After being blackened as 'Hanoi Jane', Fonda turned her attention to feminist and gender equality causes. In the 1980s, she was a founder member of the Hollywood Women's Political Committee (HWPC). With her then husband, Californian state senator Tom Hayden, Fonda established the Network, comprised of younger stars including Tom Cruise and Rob Lowe, to lobby for nuclear disarmament and other causes. However, despite growing public standing, she continued to be vilified by the conservative right. In tandem, Belafonte has remained a divisive figure, declaring President George W. Bush (Bush Jr) to be a war criminal and then Secretary of State Colin Powell and National Security Advisor Condoleezza Rice to be 'field hands'. More recently, he has been critical of Barack Obama's presidency, claiming 'I find nothing in his policies . . . that speaks to the issues of the disenfranchised' (Ross 2011: 225).

Similarly, Matt Damon expressed his disappointment with Obama's presidency when he claimed that 'You know, a one-term president with some balls who actually got stuff done would have been . . . much better' (Elmhirst 2012: 27). In August 2011, his liberal political credentials were enhanced when he addressed thousands of teachers in Washington DC who were protesting against standardized testing. He informed them that, as the son of a teacher, he had flown across the country as he 'needed to tell you all, in person, that I think you are *awesome*' (ibid.: 27). Damon has also set up the H20 Africa Foundation for the provision of clean water in poverty-stricken states and narrated *American Teacher* (2008) which he co-produced with the author Dave Eggers.

When Michael J. Fox was diagnosed with Parkinson's disease, along with heavyweight boxing legend Muhammad Ali, he became a lobbyist for research funding for the illness. He donated his royalties from *Lucky Man* (2002), the bestselling book he wrote about his degenerative illness, to the Michael J. Fox Foundation for Parkinson's Research which has raised a total of US$200 million. In 2006, Fox appeared, shaking uncontrollably, in a campaign broadcast for the successful Democratic senatorial candidate for Missouri, Claire McCaskill, who supported stem-cell research. The promotion was attacked by the conservative radio talk show host Rush Limbaugh who accused Fox of being a Democratic Party stooge who had exaggerated the effects of his illness, but this criticism backfired.

More controversially, Sean Penn has visited Iran and Cuba and befriended the Venezuelan President Hugo Chavez while appearing on platforms with the Green Party's Ralph Nader. His causes have ranged from opposition to the 2003 Iraq invasion to support for gay rights. In the wake of the 2005 Hurricane Katrina and the 2010 Haiti earthquake, Penn engaged in reconstruction efforts in New Orleans and Port-au-Prince respectively to aid thousands of displaced people. He became a cause célèbre as ambassador-at-large for the Haitian government when he argued that Britain had engaged in a form of neocolonialism against Argentina when Prince William had been deployed to the Falklands Islands as a Royal Navy helicopter pilot. Through his efforts, Penn has shown that he prefers direct action over the lobbying of Congress or making appearances at campaign rallies. Therefore, his influence comes more from his personal engagement with gritty challenges, rather than engaging in vanguard political pronouncements.

Access to the powerful: interest groups, social movements and CP2 lobbying

US interest groups have received CP2 participation and support. On the right, the National Rifle Association (NRA) included its former president Charlton Heston and board member Tom Selleck. On the Centre-Left, celebrities including Rob Reiner, Aaron Sorkin and Moby have been active in lobbying organizations, including MoveOn.org. Moreover, CP2s, such as Tim Daly, Joe Pantoliano, Anne Hathaway and Barry Levinson, have been key figures in the Creative Coalition which was formed in 1989 by Ron Silver and Christopher Reeve. This is a 501(c)(3) non-profit and non-partisan group whose purpose is to bring together celebrities to tackle issues including First Amendment rights, public funding for the arts and arts education in the public schools. Creative Coalition members have testified before Congress, sponsored awareness-building events and participated at Democratic and Republican conventions.

Concurrently, as the political classes have realized how celebrities can bring public attention to social movements, they have understood that sharing the spotlight with CP2s invariably provides good publicity. Thus, they have made time in their schedules 'to meet with [a] Jessica Lange or Sally Field about farm policy [rather] than with another lobbyist or policy expert' (Meyer and Gamson 1995: 186). In this manner, politicized celebrities may provide grass-roots activists with an entry into policy circles that would otherwise be closed to them. Further: '[Celebrities] teach us how to think and act politically. . . . Speaking . . . about the relative importance of Washington and Hollywood in the public mind, former-Republican-turned-Democratic Senator Arlen Specter remarked, "Quite candidly, when Hollywood speaks, the world listens. Sometimes when Washington speaks, the world snoozes"' (Ross 2011: 5).

As CP2s have influenced policy agendas they have become exemplars of US political leadership. In 2006, *Time* magazine cited twenty-five leading celebrities as part of its 100 'people who shape our world'. These comprised 'Leaders and Revolutionaries', including Oprah Winfrey, Paul Simon and Angelina Jolie, along with Sean

'P. Diddy' Combs as a 'Builder and Titan'. In addition, leadership scholar Warren Bennis cited musician Herb Alpert and the late film director Sydney Pollack as entertainment leaders who were worthy of emulation (Bennis and Nanus 2003): 'Our [the US] political system has been transformed into one dominated by "celebrity politics." . . . We [do not] aspire to having a political system of philosopher-kings because today we have the "celebrity king and queen" in our star-laden politics' (West and Orman 2003: 1–2).

UK CP2s and public campaigns – the Alternative Vote Referendum, Jamie Oliver's Feed Me Better campaign, Joanna Lumley and the gurkhas, and Comic Relief

These forms of CP2 behaviour have taken root in modern British politics. In 2011, British comedians, actors, musicians sports personalities and poets, including Eddie Izzard, Stephen Fry, Chris Addison, David Schneider, Jonathan Ross, Helena Bonham Carter, Joanna Lumley, Nicholas Hoult, Colin Firth, Billy Bragg, Kris Akabussi and Benjamin Zephaniah, were invited to the launch of the Alternative Vote (AV) Referendum campaign. Further, their endorsements were included in mailshots to voters' home addresses.

However, despite such high-profile celebrity participation, the AV referendum aroused little public interest and the vote was lost. As with UK partisan CP2 endorsements (see chapter 3), the lines of demarcation between the political and entertainment realms have remained more fixed in British politics. This reflects the nature of the parliamentary system in which insider-lobbying groups have had access to government and causal groups, including Citizens UK, Greenpeace, Shelter and Friends of the Earth, have preferred to use grass-roots or direct forms of activism to popularize themselves.

Although UK CP2 activities have increased in relation to social movements and global activities, they have attracted limited attention in the mainstream of British politics. Invariably, politicized celebrities have preferred to engage in charitable activities; for example, Lord Brian Rix retired from acting in 1980 to become the president of the Royal Mencap Society. Elsewhere, a number of UK performers and sports figures have joined the ranks of the 'great and the good' to sit on public bodies, regulators, arts organizations and university boards. For instance, Lord Richard Attenborough was the chairman of the British Film Institute (BFI) from 1982 to 1992 and remains the honorary president of the film and television industries' trade lobby, the

British Screen Advisory Council (BSAC). Similarly, Olympic gold medallist and television presenter Jonathan Edwards was appointed as a member of the Office of Communications (OfCom) Content Board in 2003.

Yet, as British celebrity culture has exponentially grown, CP2s have used their fame in a more instrumental manner to mobilize public interest in campaigns. In 2005, the television chef Jamie Oliver's *Feed Me Better* campaign placed the improvement of nutritional values of school dinners on the policy agenda. This occurred as a result of his documentary series for Channel Four, *Jamie's School Dinners*, which was designed to educate the public about children's eating habits and the dangers of teenage obesity. Due to the programme's popularity and the public's support for the campaign, then Prime Minister Tony Blair promised to improve school meals shortly after it was aired. Moreover, on 30 March 2005, Oliver met with education ministers and delivered to Downing Street 271,677 signatures drawn from an online petition on the *Feed Me Better* web site. Subsequently, with varying degrees of success and opposition from recalcitrant parents, Oliver has used his status to promote healthier diets for children.

The stage and television actress Joanna Lumley became the public face for the Gurkha Justice campaign in 2008. She argued that those Nepalese Gurkha veterans who had served in the British army before 1997 should be allowed to settle in the UK once they had retired. The British government had extended this offer to all Gurkhas who had been in the regiment after that date. Lumley contended that this was a gross injustice to a body of men who had provided 200 years of distinguished service to the British army. Therefore, on 20 November 2008, she delivered a petition of 250,000 names calling for all Gurkhas to have the right of settlement. However, despite all-party parliamentary support, the UK minister for immigration Phil Woolas informed five veterans who had applied for UK residency that their appeals had been rejected.

As a result of this betrayal, Lumley confronted Woolas at the BBC's Westminster studios where they held an impromptu press conference at which she pressured him into agreeing to further talks on the issue. Consequently, as a result of Lumley's campaigning skills, then Home Secretary Jackie Smith agreed that all Gurkha veterans who had served four years or more in the British army before 1997 would be allowed to settle in Britain. In July 2009, on her arrival at Tribhuvran airport in Kathmandu, Lumley was hailed as a 'daughter of Nepal' by the crowds of fans. Further, in August 2010, she cooperated with the British food company Sharwoods to develop a limited edition of

Figure 5.2 Having supported the Gurkhas, Joanna Lumley takes on the Liberal Democrats!

mango chutney with Kashmiri chilli for which ten pence from each jar sold would be donated to the Gurkha Welfare Trust.

Such linkage between celebrity activism and commercial interest has been evident in the orchestration of the biannual UK charity telethon *Comic Relief*. This event began as a small-scale response to enduring African poverty and was launched by the comedian Lenny Henry and the comedy writer Richard Curtis. In its early years, 'Red Nose Day' was constructed in an ad hoc manner and there was no lasting certainty it would be repeated. However, as the level of its fund-raising increased, *Comic Relief*'s board of trustees realized that a greater professionalism was required to more effectively deploy the monies raised.

Comic Relief (along with the accompanying *Sport Relief*) was further institutionalized when the British Broadcasting Corporation (BBC) agreed to broadcast a biannual spring telethon in 2000. The charity also benefited from the commercial sponsorship of the supermarket chain Sainsbury's and the telecommunications company British Telecom. This backing led to a dramatic increase in *Comic Relief*'s fund-raising activities so that the charity has raised a total sum of £750 million over the years (Brockington 2011: 13).[2] Henry and Curtis drew their inspiration from Bob Geldof's 1985 *Feed the World* campaign which marked a new phase in the cross-fertilization between a more conscious form of CP2 activity, commercial interest and the global media (see chapter 6). Thus, as the conscious use of fame to propagate causes has grown within the celebrity classes, the concurrent phenomenon of celebrities-turned-politicians has become more prevalent in modern democratic politics.

Celebrities turned politicians

A growing number of politicized celebrities have become candidates for electoral office and have taken up governmental positions. Bollywood film stars have become Indian members of parliament, the rapper Wyclef Jean tried to stand for president of Haiti and the former world footballer of the year George Weah became an active figure in Liberian politics. Since his retirement as Pakistan cricket captain, Imran Khan has campaigned against poverty and injustice. With regard to the role of celebrity politicians in the global South, a mixed picture has emerged. In part, such celebrities have challenged the democratic deficiencies of those societies. However, the voting for stars in some regions of India and the Philippines has highlighted the flaws of their political populism and inexperience. This became more apparent when the second largest party in Lithuania, comprised of television stars, singers and producers, took office as part of a coalition government in 2008. More recently, the former footballer Eric Cantona declared that he would put himself forward as an unlikely independent candidate in the 2012 French presidential election.

In Britain, a small number of thespians, such as the late Labour MP Andrew Faulds and the Member of the European Parliament (MEP) for the West Midlands Michael Cashman, have entered electoral politics. In fact, only one bona fide film, television and stage star, Glenda Jackson, became a minister of state in the Blair government. Yet Jackson made it clear that, once she had become a politician, any previous 'luvvie' affectation would be consigned to the dustbin! From 2000 to 2004, the comic actor and long-standing Labour Party member Tony Robinson was a member of the National Executive Committee (NEC). The comedian Eddie Izzard has also suggested that he intends to stand as London mayor, MP or a MEP in 2020 (Izzard 2011). Additionally, several actors have been made life peers, including Laurence Olivier, Richard Attenborough, Bernard Miles, Brian Rix and Julian Fellowes. The former British athletics champion Sebastian Coe was made a Conservative Lord when he worked as an advisor to then leader William Hague. Previously, from 1992–7, he had occupied a Conservative Party seat in the House of Commons for Falmouth and Cambourne.[3]

In addition, during the 1970s and 1980s, Vanessa Redgrave and her late brother Corin became involved in the Trotskyite politics of the Workers Revolutionary Party (WRP) with limited effect. In fact, Redgrave's radicalism led to her being blacklisted from Hollywood when she made an acceptance speech at the 1978 Academy Awards in support of the Palestine Liberation Organization (PLO) in which she condemned a 'bunch of Zionist hoodlums' who had campaigned against her nomination (Considine 1994: 343).[4] She claimed, 'I am misrepresented very often, but so is everyone who has got something to say' (Davidson 2012: 34). A similar absence of public enthusiasm was also evident when the television presenter Esther Rantzen unsuccessfully ran as an independent in Luton South (the seat of disgraced Labour MP Margaret Moran) in the 2010 general election. The most effective well-known figure to be elected was the news reporter Martin Bell who fought the 'cash for questions' Conservative MP Neil Hamilton to win the parliamentary seat at Tatton for one term in 1997.

Undoubtedly, this phenomenon has been most fully realized in the USA. In the 1930s, Helen Gahagan Douglas, the actress wife of film star Melvyn Douglas, transferred her acting skills into political ambition and became an advocate for the rural poor in California. She forged a close relationship with Eleanor Roosevelt and became a Democratic congresswoman in 1944. Later, she was castigated as 'the Pink Lady' when she stood as a candidate in the bitter 1950 California senatorial contest against Republican Richard 'Tricky Dick' Nixon (Mitchell 1998: 21–2).

Moreover, as US celebrity politicians (CP1s) have lent themselves to the promotion of image candidacy and personalized politics, there has been a cross-fertilization in the public mind between stardom and political activity. In turn, CP2 activity has demonstrated how a politicized star's persona has become associated with his or her real-life adherence to a cause. These dynamics have led to calls for CP2s to become serving politicians. In recent years, stars such as Warren Beatty, Martin Sheen, Matt Damon, Ben Affleck and George Clooney have been associated with Democratic politics or liberal causes.

In 1999, there was speculation that Beatty might run for the White House when he made several inscrutable comments in an article for the *New York Times* entitled 'Liberties: Will You, Warren?' (Dowd 1999: 5). However, while doing little to dispel these rumours, he preferred to use the publicity to promote *Bulworth* (1999), his satire on a corrupt senator who tells the truth about race relations and political greed through rap music. Sheen's image as the 'best President America has never had' (due to his portrayal of the commander-in-chief Josiah 'Jed' Bartlett in *The West Wing*) became indelibly incorporated into the American public mind and he was asked to be a running mate of the Green Party candidate Ralph Nader. He graciously declined, arguing that as an actor he would not have the emotional make-up to be a politician. Moreover, Sheen claimed that his appearance in the programme already provided him with a platform through which to articulate his political views:

> 'If Bartlett had been a Republican, you wouldn't see me sitting here, I promise you.' Long before his association with the series, Sheen professed that his activism was inextricably linked to his profession as an actor: 'I don't stop being an actor when I attend a demonstration. I don't stop being an activist when I go to work as an actor.' (Collins 2007: 201)

More recently, the agit-prop journalist Michael Moore promoted Matt Damon as a legitimate political candidate for the Democratic Party. Damon's best friend Ben Affleck was also mooted as a potential Democratic leader, due to his close affiliations with Al Gore's and John Kerry's presidential campaigns in 2000 and 2004. Further, George Clooney's activism has led to calls for him to stand for office, and he even directed himself as a flawed Democratic presidential candidate in *The Ides of March* (2011). Consequently, it is an irony that, while Hollywood remains a bastion of liberalism, its two most famous actors-turned-politicians have been Republicans – Ronald Reagan and Arnold Schwarzenegger.

Ronald Reagan's path from film star to president

According to Steven J. Ross, the election of the former Hollywood 'hoofer' George Murphy as senator for California in 1964, when he defeated John F. Kennedy's press officer Pierre Salinger, pioneered the transformation of conservative celebrity activism into electoral success (Ross 2011: 131–71). In this respect, Murphy's victory influenced his fellow conservative and friend Ronald Reagan's decision to run for the governorship of California in 1966. Moreover, as a consummate politician, Reagan used his presentational skills not only to propagate his right-wing values within the Sunshine State but to further his appeal to the US electorate on the national scene.

Reagan's path to the presidency took over forty years, during which he used his fame, oratory skills and personality to construct an effective right-wing identity which could be sold to the American electorate. In the 1940s, Reagan made his name as a 'B-player' at Warner Brothers, notably appearing in *Kings Row* (1942) wherein he delivered his most famous line, 'Where's the rest of me'? He would later stress how his values of individualism, family, community, Judeo-Christianity and the American way were shaped by the films he had appeared in as a Warner contract player (Vaughn 1994: 235–6). Subsequently, he was elected as a registered Democrat to the presidency of the Screen Actors Guild (SAG) in 1947. As an anti-communist trade unionist, Reagan appeared before the House Committee for Un-American Activities (HUAC) as a 'friendly' witness.

And his right-wing ideology became further intertwined with his communication skills when he became a spokesman, salesman and advertiser for the General Electric (GE) Corporation in the 1950s (Hopper 1965). During Reagan's 'GE years' (1954–1962), he met the corporation's public relations guru Lemuel Boulware, who refined Reagan's free-market vision when he appeared on several GE speaking tours across the USA. Boulware advised him to jettison his New Deal liberalism and to get in touch with the individualist and hawkish Cold War values which had been embraced by Middle-American voters. Consequently, while these tours ostensibly raised morale in the GE workforce, Reagan used them to articulate a patriotic conservatism that stood him in good stead when he sought electoral office (Evans 2008).

When Barry Goldwater fought the 1964 presidency campaign against Lyndon Johnson, the converted Republican Reagan (he registered as such in 1961) legitimized himself as a front runner in the Grand Old Party (GOP). Most especially, he delivered a well-received and nationally televised speech entitled 'A Time for Choosing' that not only demonstrated Reagan's support for Goldwater's nomination but illustrated his ambitions to run for office. In this address, Reagan skilfully presented his anti-statist views and anti-communist agenda while providing an appealing and likeable persona: 'The power of The Speech lay less in what Reagan said than how he said it. Like the best preachers, he won over his audience with a reassuring voice that mixed calm certainty with a passionate call for action' (Ross 2011:

172). This speech gave Reagan enough public credibility to receive support from the Southern Californian business community whose financial contributions enabled him to run for the governorship of California in 1966.

In Reagan's campaign against the incumbent governor Edmund 'Pat' Brown, he presented himself as an honest man uncorrupted by vices, thereby turning Democratic and indeed Hollywood's criticisms of his inexperience on its head. For instance, on hearing that Reagan was running for governor, movie mogul Jack Warner, who employed Reagan as a second-level leading man, had proclaimed 'No, no. Jimmy Stewart for Governor, Ronald Reagan for best friend!' (ibid.: 131).

Yet in spite of such dismissals and Brown's attacks on Reagan's Hollywood background, in which he stated that his opponent was 'only an actor and an actor killed Lincoln' (Brown 1966), Reagan won the election by using his celebrity to define an identifiable personality which would prove popular with the Californian electorate. He took advantage of television's growing importance in US politics by keeping his message simple and exhibiting a personable political character to make palatable his anti-statist agenda (Ross 2011: 174). In effect, Reagan had transformed his image to that of a candidate who entered 'the election as Barry Goldwater, but finished it as Nelson Rockefeller' (CBS Reports 1967).

Throughout his governorship (1967–1975), Reagan refined these skills and he contested the presidential primaries in 1968. His stardom attracted donors whose funds allowed him to buy airtime for spot-ads and press coverage. After leaving office, he remained in the national consciousness by making speeches, writing columns and seeking the Republican nomination in 1976. Consequently, by the time of the 1980 presidential election, when Reagan defeated Jimmy Carter, he had forged a political image in which his celebrity had been transformed into a folksy populism to mediate the radical reforms he would enact in the 1980s. As Reagan's son Ron notes: 'It took my father some time to get to the Presidency. He didn't just wander into the Presidency because he got a casting call. He had been preparing for quite some time' (BBC Storyville 2011).

Arnold Schwarzenegger – the Governator

Following on from Reagan, there has been a phenomenon of celebrities becoming politicians as the American political system exhibited partisan de-alignment and voter disengagement. This meant it became open to media representations, sophisticated political marketing and a huge increase in campaign costs. As a result, the film action hero Clint Eastwood became mayor of his local town, Carmel; the late Sonny Bono (of Sonny and Cher fame) became a Republican congressman; the actor Fred Thompson was senator for Tennessee and the former wrestler Jesse Ventura was elected as governor of Minnesota. In 2010, the comedian and political commentator Al Franken became a Democratic senator, also in Minnesota.

The most famous film star-turned-politician was Arnold Schwarzenegger, who successfully campaigned for the Californian governorship during the 2003 recall vote. Although Bush Sr had called him 'Conan the Republican' (West and Orman 2003: 69), unlike Reagan, the 'Governator' was a political neophyte. Schwarzenegger's experience was limited to being chairman of the Presidential Council for Physical Fitness and Sport in 1991. In 2002, he had also sponsored Proposition 49, a Californian state bill to provide after-school child care. But Schwarzenegger had remained more of a Republican political celebrity than an ideological activist like Reagan and Murphy (Ross 2011: 364).

In part, he achieved office through his connections. Schwarzenegger was married at the time to Maria Shriver, a television journalist and the daughter of George McGovern's running mate, Sargent Shriver. Crucially, her mother was John F. Kennedy's sister, Eunice Kennedy, so Schwarzenegger became associated through marriage with American political royalty. In turn, Eunice's uncle, Ted Kennedy, was a key advisor in his campaign. However, it was Schwarzenegger's fame that generated the voluminous media coverage and financial support that was necessary for a successful campaign (West 2003). He proved to be a shrewd communicator but, unlike Reagan, whose film career had been eclipsed, he remained an A-list star, appearing in *Terminator 3: The Rise of the Machines* (2003) shortly before announcing his candidacy on Jay Leno's *Tonight Show*.

Schwarzenegger's opportunity to run for office occurred in one of the most bizarre campaigns in modern American politics. In 2002, the Democratic governor Gray Davis, a colourless technocrat, was re-elected in a dirty election in which he concealed the economic crisis affecting the state. As California plunged into deficit, Davis slashed health, education, transport and policing budgets. Subsequently, a San Diego Republican congressman, Darrell Issa, devoted several million dollars to raise the signatures required for a recall petition against Davis, exploiting an obscure state law passed in 1849. This led to voters being asked two questions: first, should Davis be recalled and, second, who should replace him?

Therefore, along with Schwarzenegger, 135 candidates stood in the recall election. In the ensuing media circus, allegations surfaced about his promiscuity, harassment of women and father's membership of the Nazi party. However, Schwarzenegger offset these accusations by employing his fame to gain unprecedented national and international media exposure. He utilized his star status to make appearances on television talk shows, was interviewed by shock jocks and employed the internet to '[reverse] the usual media constellation by putting entertainment outlets at the centre of his campaign and pushed the usual news outlets to the margins. In a strategy meeting . . . he repeatedly told his advisors, "I'm a different kind of candidate . . . [and] I can't run a campaign like a traditional politician"' (Ross 2011: 395).

To sustain his message, Schwarzenegger's consultants orchestrated press conferences, public platforms, photo opportunities and sound bites, enabling him to attack the high levels of Californian taxation and the special interests in the state capital of Sacramento. He cited his background as an Austrian immigrant who became a champion body builder and movie superstar as a personal representation of 'the American dream'. Yet, along with fiscal conservatism and US mythology, he embraced a liberal agenda which promoted pro-choice and gay rights, demonstrating his independence from fundamentalist Republican thinking.

Marketing himself for the Californian electorate, he used his celebrity to gain widespread support. In the event, the Californians voted to recall Davis and Schwarzenegger won the second election with 48 per cent of the popular vote, benefiting from disenchanted voters who created an unusual opportunity for him to exploit his fame. In 2006, in the regular gubernatorial election, Schwarzenegger won a second term against the state treasurer, Phil Angelides, another dull technocratic Democrat.

Yet Schwarzenegger's inexperience as a politician remained a problem throughout his period in office. His celebrity did not correlate with an ability to govern and his populist attempts to castigate opponents as 'girlie men' led to him being viewed as an outsider by Democrats and Republicans alike. This undermined his influence with the Democratic-led state legislators and stymied many of his initiatives. Most damagingly, Schwarzenegger's failure to reform the ailing Californian economy meant that he left office with a mere 22 per cent approval rating. Ultimately, his governorship collapsed in personal acrimony when it was declared that he had fathered a child out of wedlock. Subsequently, his greatest asset, Shriver, divorced him shortly after the end of his tenure in office. His failure brought into question the legitimacy of celebrity within politics: 'When Arnold Schwarzenegger . . . won the gubernatorial elections for California in 2003, critics saw their worst fears confirmed: celebrity had become more important than political substance, and people voted on the basis of superficial Hollywood appeal rather than on a reasonable assessment of policy alternatives' (van Zoonen 2005: 70).

The critiques of celebrity political activism: divisions within the popular media and public opinion

A controversy has emerged in relation to those CP2s who have engaged in causal and other forms of political activism. For left-wing commentators such as George Monbiot, politicized celebrities have reinforced the prevailing order (Brockington 2009: 123–4). These writers have built upon Chris Rojek's academic critique in which celebrity has been presented as a corollary of a reward culture that favours monetary status to reinforce neoliberal values (Rojek 2001: 198). Thus, a polemical documentary by UK film-maker Chris Atkins, entitled *Starsuckers* (2009), suggested that celebrities and corporations had undermined the rights of citizens to perpetuate global consumerism and injustice (see chapter 6).

In a similar vein, an American web site, 'Citizens Against Celebrity Pundits', declared 'we don't believe [celebrities] have a clear understanding of how we live, what we fear, and what we support' (Street 2010: 248). This view has meant that CP2s are often seen to lack any political substance and this serves to undermine their claim to be representative (West and Orman 2003). Concurrently, the journalist Marina Hyde has contended that the modern obsession with celebrity has led to emotive rather than rational responses to complex issues: 'Celebrities tend to react emotionally to problems. . . . These are absolutely not qualities you'd look for in a public intellectual. Complex problems like the humanitarian fallout from counter-insurgencies need to be approached analytically not emotionally' (Hyde 2009: 115).

Hyde believes celebrities are narcissistic personalities with an almost pathological desire to be liked. Therefore, she questions how truly altruistic such CP2 activity is: celebrities not only want to raise public awareness but to promote themselves in the process (ibid.:

114). Such criticisms were made by the Conservative MP Gerald Howarth in the wake of Joanna Lumley's pursuit of the Gurkhas' UK residential rights. Howarth, who represents the Aldershot constituency where many of the regiment's Nepalese soldiers resettled in 2009, complained that Lumley had not thought out the consequences for resourcing such an 'influx' of immigrants or their impact on the local community (Hollingshead 2011).

From the perspective of the right-wing US media, it is often suggested that overpaid celebrities should keep clear of making political statements because of their sanctimonious trivialization of issues. Most especially, the *Fox News* pundit Bill O'Reilly and the right-wing radio shock jock Rush Limbaugh have criticized CP2s as being 'out of touch' with popular sentiment. O'Reilly saved his venom for George Clooney, whom he damned for appearing on celebrity-driven fund-raisers concerning 9/11 and the 2004 tsunami victims. The conservative presenter claimed that the monies raised from these telethons did not go to their intended charities and he blamed celebrity do-gooders for misleading the public about the effect of their contributions. Conversely, Clooney took O'Reilly to task by claiming that he had lied about the misappropriation of funds and that as 'a celebrity . . . (he) should "ante up", and "put your considerable money where your considerable mouth is . . . rather than simply stand on the sidelines and cast stones"' (Rabidoux 2009: 162).

Such criticisms have led to fears among stars that they can destroy their careers by becoming too political. For instance, when the liberal film star William Baldwin tried to recruit new members to the Creative Coalition, he commented, 'I can't tell you how many famous stars came up to me and said . . . I'm happy to write you a check . . . but I can't appear on stage representing your organization [as] it might endanger my career' (Ross 2011: 5). Moreover, for some celebrities a close involvement with the political classes has been deemed counterproductive. Sir Mick Jagger felt he would become a 'political football' if he attended an event organized by Prime Minister David Cameron at the Davos economic summit in January 2012. Despite spending his post-1960s career eschewing any form of political involvement, Jagger's prospective attendance had been interpreted as demonstrating his support for the Conservative Party. This inspired tabloid headlines satirizing old Stone tracks such as 'Sympathy for the Dave-il' and 'Paint it Blue'! Jagger was also annoyed by the hubris expressed by some governmental spin doctors: 'Mick . . . was invited over to Davos to support British enterprise and industry . . . But as soon as he found out that his presence was being paraded by the Tories as a publicity coup, he packed his bags and left. He just feels exploited' (Lyons 2012).

Therefore, many controversies have emerged about the worth and the willingness of CP2s to engage in politics. More specifically, two opposing clichés have competed in the public imagination. On the one hand, there is the celebrity as 'superhero' and on the other there is the celebrity as the 'screw up'. Consequently, this means that while some celebrities have been successful in fronting campaigns, others have failed to be effective communicators or have a negative public persona which is out of keeping with the issues. Moreover, while some celebrities are well briefed, other celebrities have gone vehemently off-message. This has created a love/hate relationship between the public and famous people (Harris 2011: 82). Further, as Michael Buerk has asked, does CP2 behaviour facilitate a 'sense of social conscience in us all, or have we sacrificed content on the altar of celebrity and . . . is celebrity activism good for our democratic process?' (Buerk 2011). In many respects, the duality between the veneration of stars and the questioning of their influence became conspicuous in the US media's responses to CP2 activities during the 2003 invasion of Iraq.

Operation Iraqi Freedom and the Bush Doctrine: CP2 responses and defences of their activism

Certain action stars, such as Bruce Willis, provided an unquestioning patriotic response to the war in Iraq (2003–11). Indeed, Willis visited Iraq in 2003 when he made a United Services Organization (USO) appearance in front of US troops with his band the Accelerators. It was suggested that Willis had intended to enlist in the military but was deterred by his age, and there were unsubstantiated reports that he would make a pro-Iraq war film in 2005. Moreover, there was the spectacle of actor Jon Voight, the former liberal activist (and father of humanitarian star Angelina Jolie), becoming a vociferous advocate for Bush Jr's supremacist foreign policy doctrine. Voight renounced his previous liberalism, became an active Zionist and was a fervent supporter of the Bush administration's neo-con realist agenda.

However, despite such super-patriotism, many CP2s were critical of President Bush's intervention in Iraq. The anti-war movement was supported by a range of musicians and bands, including Lou Reed and Massive Attack. In particular, the Armenian-American thrash metal band System of a Down's song 'Boom!' (2002) provided the soundtrack for the movement.[5] Elsewhere, Tim Robbins castigated US forces for indiscriminate bombing, war-mongering and destabilizing democracies when he wrote the play *Embedded* (2004), satirizing Donald Rumsfeld, Richard Perle and Paul Wolfowitz as neo-con plotters taking over the world. At the 2003 Oscars, Robbins and his then wife Susan Sarandon made peace signals to the crowds outside the Kodak Theatre. Sarandon had been one of the main speakers at an anti-Iraqi war rally in New York where she claimed Bush had 'hijacked our losses and our fears' (Bergman Rosamond 2011: 74). She pleaded for the rights of Iraqi civilians and against the needless waste of the lives when asking 'for more dialogue . . . and arriving at other solutions than force to resolve disputes between states' (ibid.: 74). For her pains, she was labelled an unpatriotic 'bin Laden lover' (CBS News 2009).

However, their actions were as nothing compared to the leftist polemicist Michael Moore. Notably, when he received an Oscar for his anti-gun documentary *Bowling for Columbine* (2003), his speech closed with 'We are against the war, Mr Bush . . . shame on you, shame on you, shame on you' (Dickenson 2003). Subsequently, Moore directed *Fahrenheit 9/11* (2004), a blistering attack on Bush Jr's foreign policy and the use of America's underclass as cannon fodder. In publicizing his documentary, Moore accused Disney Studios of cowardice because it refused to distribute the film, despite its winning the Palme d'Or at the 2004 Cannes Film Festival. Thus, he became a national figure who was both feted and demonized: 'Ultimately, Michael Moore is an American original, combining the crusading idealism of JFK liberalism with left-wing anticorporate populism, and the comic antics of the Yippies and the performance orientated Left, still visible in the anticorporate globalization movement. He is highly controversial, intensely polarizing and extremely partisan' (Kellner 2010c: 101).

In response, many reactionary radio shock jocks and web sites damned US celebrities for their anti-Americanism. When the country and western band the Dixie Chicks' singer Natalie Maines voiced opposition to the Bush Doctrine, they were banned from Clear Channel's one thousand or more radio channels. In turn, Robbins and Sarandon were disinvited to the Baseball Hall of Fame's celebration to commemorate the 15th anniversary of *Bull Durham* (1989) in which they had played leading roles (Anthony 2004: 14). Similarly, Sean Penn received vehement denouncements from the US Right when he visited Iraq in 2003 to highlight the human rights abuses that had been conducted by American forces.

When O'Reilly accused Martin Sheen of being a 'traitor' because of his defiant opposition to the Iraq war, the film and television star was physically accosted and received 'an avalanche of hate mail' from the US Right (Rabidoux 2009: 195). Sheen's passionate opposition led him into a confrontation with the National Broadcasting Company (NBC) at the height of the *West Wing*'s popularity in 2003. In particular, NBC executives were concerned that his attacks on President Bush could negatively impact on the show's ratings. Yet Sheen remained defiant, asserting that the chief executive was a 'moron' who surrounded himself with war criminals! Further, Sheen (whose real name is Ramon Estevez and is the son of a Galician immigrant) has been arrested on numerous occasions when protesting on behalf of Hispanic civil rights, free assembly, gay marriages and taking a stance against the death penalty. Consequently, as Sheen does not flinch from advocating difficult positions that he believes to be worthy, he gained respect from the Centre-Left. Moreover, the 'inter-textual' nature of Sheen's fictional representation of being a courageous liberal president with his own more radical activism accorded him mythological status in the US political psyche:

> If Sheen's activist life were turned into a movie script, is there any young star on the rise one could imagine convincingly playing the legendary actor? Better yet, is there any rising star ready, willing and able to follow the real-life path of the social and political activism the elder Sheen has blazed over the course of his long career? Now, there's a tough casting call. (Rabidoux 2009: 198)[6]

Elsewhere, politicized stars, such as the Creative Coalition's Tim Daly and the film director Barry Levinson, have accused the news media of distorting CP2 forms of behaviour. Levinson contends that there has been a demonization of celebrities when they claim their rights to act as citizens. This means that CP2s are often presented as being elitist or out of touch with common people. However, Levinson demonstrated in his documentary *Poliwood* (2009a) that there was a significant degree of commonality between celebrities and the public. He contends that the divisions between CP2s and the public have been manufactured 'because the media seeks to polarize positions so there is more conflict, because it makes better television. . . . if someone was to say something and the other person agreed, "that's a good point," it wouldn't work; it is more entertaining to disagree' (Levinson 2009b). In turn, related critiques of unfair representations of celebrities reached a peak in the UK phone-hacking scandal during the summer of 2011.

Hacked off – Hugh Grant, Steve Coogan and celebrity campaigners against privacy intrusion: the 2011 phone-hacking scandal and the Leveson Inquiry

The controversy surrounding the unscrupulous use of phone-hacking practices by journalists led to an unprecedented public revulsion at Rupert Murdoch's tabloid newspapers. In 2005, Murdoch's the *News of the World* (NOTW) Royal Correspondent Clive Goodman was accused of using the private investigator Glenn Mulcaire to tap Prince William's mobile phone voice-messaging service. Subsequently, Goodman and Mulcaire were given custodial sentences when they were found guilty of phone-hacking.

Both News International (the UK newspaper division of Murdoch's global media empire News Corporation) and the Metropolitan Police investigators claimed that the Goodman case was a one-off. Yet, the hacking allegations refused to go away when the Professional Footballers' Association (PFA) Chairman Gordon Taylor and the actress Sienna Miller discovered that they too had been subject to phone-hacking. As more celebrities, politicians and sportspeople realized they had been victims of such privacy intrusion, it became clear that hacking had occurred on an industrial scale.

However, the tipping point occurred when the investigative journalist Nick Davies reported in the *Guardian* in July 2011 that Mulcaire had listened into murder victim Milly Dowler's mobile phone voicemails and allegedly deleted several of these so more messages could be left.[7] This intrusion had cruelly given the Dowler family a renewed but false hope that their daughter might still be alive. In the wake of these allegations, a devastating public scandal engulfed Murdoch's News International papers. Subsequently, Murdoch flew in from the USA and apologized to the Dowler family.

Shortly afterwards, the proprietor announced that he would close his flagship tabloid *NOTW* but refused to take any editorial blame. He was required to appear with his son James before the UK Parliamentary Culture, Media and Sport Select Committee to respond to the accusations that his managerial ethics had inculcated an immoral culture at his newspapers. The scandal brought into question the relationship between the press and Metropolitan Police officers who had been illegally paid to pass on information to the tabloids, leading to the resignation of Chief Constable Sir Paul Stephenson.

The controversy scuppered Murdoch's ambition to take complete control of the UK satellite broadcaster BSkyB which had been approved by Jeremy Hunt, the then Department of Culture, Media and Sport (DCMS) secretary of state. In the ensuing parliamentary debates and within the 163 pages of e-mails and texts released by News Corporation to Lord Justice Brian Leveson's inquiry into media ethics (2011–12), the deal was seen to be reflective of the close proximity of Prime Minister David Cameron to senior Murdoch executives, including Rebekah Brooks, as part of the so-called 'Chipping Norton set'. The Labour Party leader Ed Miliband questioned the unwarranted power of Murdoch over the political establishment, Cameron's judgement in employing former editor of the *NOTW* Andy Coulson as his director of communications and Hunt's complicity with News Corporation.[8] Coulson and Brooks were arrested, although the extent of their involvement in the phone-hacking scandal remains subject to potential criminal prosecution.

Throughout these remarkable events, the British film star Hugh Grant had become the public face of 'Hacked Off', a campaigning organization which stood against press intrusion. Grant, along with fellow tabloid victims who included the former Formula One motor-racing boss Max Mosley (who had placed his considerable wealth behind the campaign), the comedian Steve Coogan and the Labour MP Tom Watson (a member of the Select Committee and ardent critic of Murdoch's influence in UK politics), was one of the key spokesmen propagating the charges of illicit phone-hacking.[9] Indeed, he had become a cause célèbre when he secretly recorded the former *NOTW* features editor, Paul McMullan, bragging about the range of illegal practices that the tabloid had employed to gain scoops. The unrepentant McMullan claimed that the *NOTW* reporters had bribed Metropolitan Police officers on a regular basis and, on Coulson's watch, phone-hacking was endemic. He also argued that celebrities were fair game as they had courted the media to become famous, although he expressed limited regret for the victimization of private individuals.

Grant made effective appearances on the BBC news and current affairs programme *Newsnight* (1981 onwards) where he appeared with the dishevelled McMullan to question him about the morality of phone-hacking. Moreover, he was highly critical of Cameron's close links with Brooks, Coulson and Murdoch. Grant also appeared on *Question Time* (1980 onwards) where he claimed that Murdoch exhibited 'power' without 'responsibility', which undermined the health of UK democracy. He accused his fellow panellist and Murdoch apologist, Jon Gaunt, of being 'cheap and pathetic' when the shock jock brought up Grant's arrest in Los Angeles for consorting with prostitute Divine Brown in 1995. In tandem, Steve Coogan was also involved in an altercation with McMullan on a *Newsnight* programme, suggesting:

> I think you are a walking PR disaster for the tabloids, because you don't come across in a sympathetic way. You come across as a risible individual who is symptomatic of everything that is wrong. . . . You are not uncovering corruption, you are not bringing down institutions that are inherently corrupt. You are just trying to find out who is sleeping with who. It is about selling newspapers. (Thorpe 2011)

Thus, Grant and Coogan used their celebrity status to make a stand against privacy intrusion, despite the risk of becoming 'red-top' targets. They appeared as star witnesses for the Leveson Inquiry in December 2011. However, their involvement remained controversial, not least when Grant suspected that the *Daily Mail* had hacked his phone to run a story that he had cheated on his former partner, Jemima Khan, with a 'plummy-voiced' woman. Further, he believed that his voicemails had been hacked when the paper declared that he had fathered a child with a former girlfriend. He accused the paper's editor, Paul Dacre, of 'trashing his reputation' because he had opposed the *Mail*. An unrepentant Dacre, in front of Leveson, renewed his accusations that Grant had made 'mendacious smears' about the paper. The antagonism between celebrities and the media will doubtless continue to be played out within the UK courts, public inquiries and British political communications for some considerable time to come.

Conclusion

This chapter has considered how celebrity activists have popularized campaigns as they have provided credibility for political agendas among target audiences. It has demonstrated how CP2s have orchestrated fund-raising for causes, have brought attention to policy debates and have attracted public support for social movements. In addition, the audience's capacity to consume celebrity activities has increased due to the collapse of trust in the political classes. This politicization of celebrities has reflected how celebrity culture has expanded in western democracies, especially in the USA and the UK. Consequently, there has been a 'push' in audience demand for celebrity activism, along with an accompanying 'pull' from transformative CP2s who have realized their value as 'politicians-without-office' or as elected politicians (Cashmore 2006: 218).

While the phenomenon of celebrities becoming politicians has occurred across many democracies, it has been most pronounced in the USA. The iconographic status of film, television and pop stars has cross-fertilized with real-life political interests to establish effective CP2 personas that have entered the public imagination. Therefore, many liberal film stars like Warren Beatty, Martin Sheen and George Clooney have been asked to cross the Rubicon from activism to politics. However, only a few have made this transition and America's most successful actors-turned-politicians have been conservatives – Reagan and Schwarzenegger. Both demonstrated a mastery of imagery and symbolism to communicate their messages to the electorate. However, while Reagan's career followed a more standard trajectory, Schwarzenegger's fame remained his principal asset though he proved unsuccessful in office.

Schwarzenegger's failure made conspicuous the criticisms concerning the legitimacy of CP2 forms of activism. Left- and right-wing polemicists have contended that the use of celebrity in politics has led to the electorate becoming unduly influenced by the merging of imagery, glamour and ideology. Moreover, when American stars opposed President George W. Bush's war in Iraq, they were castigated as being naive at best or traitorous at worst. This led to conservative pundits claiming that cosseted stars were 'out of touch' with public thinking. Conversely, CP2s have argued that it has been the media which has sought to falsely polarize opinions between celebrities and the public. In reality, they contend that there are many areas of shared interest and this has meant that celebrity-led campaigns have received popular support.

A duality has emerged in which CP2 activism has been praised and vilified. These controversies tie in with the wider debate about celebrity and democracy in which politicized celebrities have either renewed public interest in political affairs or have been condemned for undermining proper forms of representation. Undoubtedly, there have been examples of good, bad and indifferent CP2 activity. These debates have been further amplified as celebrity activism has expanded from national to global arenas. And the next chapter will consider how transnational forms of 'celebrity diplomacy' have occurred in the wake of the activities conducted by controversial CP2 humanitarians such as Bob Geldof and Bono.

Questions

- How far do celebrity activists use their fame to bring attention to grass-roots campaigns?
- What are the pros and cons of celebrity activism?
- To what degree has the UK phone-hacking case been dictated by the activities of celebrities such as Hugh Grant?

Further reading

Huddart, S. 2005 (2002): *Do We Need Another Hero? Understanding Celebrities' Roles in Advancing Social Causes*. Montreal, Canada: McGill University.

Hyde, M. 2009: *Celebrity: How Entertainers Took Over the World and Why We Need an Exit Strategy*. London: Harvill Secker.

Kellner, D. 2010: Michael Moore and the aesthetics and politics of contemporary documentary film. In M. H. Bernstein (ed.), *Michael Moore: Filmmaker, Newsmaker, Cultural Icon*. Ann Arbor: University of Michigan Press, pp. 79–104.

Ross, S. J. 2011: *Hollywood Left and Right: How Movie Stars Shaped American Politics*. Oxford, New York: Oxford University Press.

West, D. M. and Orman, J. 2003: *Celebrity Politics*. Upper Saddle River, NJ: Prentice Hall.

Wheeler, M. 2006: *Hollywood: Politics and Society*. London: British Film Institute.

6

Transnational Celebrity Activism: Advocacy and Diplomacy

This chapter will examine the rise of transnational forms of celebrity advocacy and diplomacy. These phenomena have emerged through the transition from state-centric to public types of diplomatic initiatives. In this respect, a new 'currency' of public diplomacy has evolved in which emotion and rhetoric have shaped the outcome of international affairs. Moreover, with the rise of 24/7 news programming and social media, there has been a decentralization and fragmentation of opinion that challenges the traditional orthodoxies of global power. Thus politicized celebrities (CP2s) have made dramatic interventions in international campaigns and diplomatic arenas.

In recent years, celebrity philanthropists such as Bob Geldof, Bono, Angelina Jolie, George Clooney, Bill Gates and Jeffrey Sachs have orchestrated globally televised benefit concerts, fund-raisers and public campaigns such as *Live Aid*, *Live 8*, the *One Campaign*, Product RED and Not on Our Watch. Moreover, governments have employed celebrities as cultural diplomats, and the United Nations (UN) has had a long-standing tradition of goodwill ambassadors. In turn, non-governmental organizations (NGOs), such as the Red Cross, Oxfam and Save the Children, have been represented by celebrities who include Pierce Brosnan, Gwyneth Paltrow and her husband Chris Martin of the rock band Coldplay (Huliaris and Tzifakis 2011: 35).

This analysis will consider how transnational celebrity activism originated in the deployment of an American 'jazz diplomacy' in the 1950s and 1960s. This was accompanied by more fully realized star support for the UN. Within this institutional tradition, celebrities conformed to their perceived role as 'good international citizens' to propagate a cause or an issue. For instance, when Danny

Kaye became involved with the United Nations Children's Fund (UNICEF) in 1953, he publicized the agency's activities in alleviating the plight of children. Similarly, the glamorous film star Audrey Hepburn and the actor, writer and raconteur Peter Ustinov remained apolitical when promoting UNICEF.

However, as CP2s became more politically consciousness, transformative celebrity activists have raised concerns about the inequities of debt, conflict and injustice. These activities have been accompanied by an expansion in the scope of the UN goodwill ambassador schemes under the former secretary-general Kofi Annan, leading to the creation of 'Messengers of Peace'. In tandem, these expressions of celebrity diplomacy have been incorporated into NGO public relations techniques. For instance, well-known figures, such as the late Diana, Princess of Wales, have lent their support to the Mines Advisory Group (MAG). Yet, the archetypical celebrity humanitarians have been Sir Bob Geldof and Bono, who have been instrumental in bringing together celebrities, statesmen and corporations to facilitate the utilization of aid in developing societies.

The worth of such celebrity advocacy has been extensively debated in the popular media and the academy. Invariably, this use of CP2s has been presented as an anti-democratic phenomenon in which celebrities are 'bards of the powerful' (Monbiot 2005). Lisa Ann Richey and Stefano Ponte contend that celebrity activism has interfaced with a neoliberal corporate interest to effect a form of 'Brand Aid' which undermines aid initiatives (Richey and Ponte 2011). Conversely, Andrew F. Cooper has conceived 'celebrity diplomacy' as an alternative form of agency in which stars fill the void in public trust created by the political classes (Cooper 2008). He contends that the 'Bonoization' of diplomacy has led to new and valid ways in which stars may not only draw attention to a range of international activities but promote meaningful change.[1] Therefore, this chapter will consider the efficacy of celebrity diplomats as:

> We want to know whether [celebrity diplomacy] is a clever use of what is called 'soft power' . . . We also want to know whether we are investing our emotions, our time and our money in celebrity activities and whether this is a sound investment. The bottom-line question may well be: does celebrity diplomacy and celebrity activism help or harm? (Wiseman 2009: 5)

Celebrities as good international citizens: ad hoc relations, publicizing the cause and glamorous conformity

While celebrity involvement in international affairs has only been identified in recent years, a historical analysis of celebrity diplomacy offsets this apparent novelty. In the late 1950s and early 1960s, American jazz stars like Duke Ellington, Louie Armstrong, Dizzy Gillespie, Benny Goodman and Dave Brubeck were sent overseas to promote a positive image of the USA there during the height of the Cold War. For the USA, the artistic individuality of jazz musicians was a useful device with which to counter the collectivism of the Soviet Union. Thus, the State Department funded musical junkets by jazz masters as a form of soft power to popularize America's capitalist brand of democracy while easing bipolar political tensions (Davenport 2009).

However, such behaviour was most fully realized when celebrity relations were institutionalized within the UN. From its earliest days, the UN created a Department of Public Information (DPI) which was concerned to promote the work and purpose of the organization. Therefore, to publicize the UN's activities, the DPI commissioned film, radio and television programmes to propagate its message. Invariably, these early documentaries were narrated by Hollywood stars such as Henry Fonda and Melvyn Douglas. Concurrently, the UN Radio Services employed famous personalities to make conspicuous its position on collective security and human rights:

> The reason why we use these actors is that we have found that this does – after all . . . reach people . . . and . . . give them . . . the basis of an operation, its raison d'être, to explain the UN activities to them. We feel that if our audience increases because they know a certain actor is going to narrate a certain part or is going to be used in a certain programme, our purpose is served. People listen and . . . get the austere UN message, and their purpose is served because they get this message served with a sugar coating, as it were, of famous names or actors. (United Nations 1958: 38)

Furthermore, by appointing Danny Kaye as UNICEF's first goodwill ambassador, the UN began to employ celebrities to raise funds, affect diplomatic agendas and draw attention to development causes.

These forms of celebrity activism were brokered through the ad hoc relationships which had informally developed between film stars and UN officers. For instance, Kaye became involved with UNICEF through his accidental meeting with the agency's executive director,

Maurice Pate, on a near-calamitous aeroplane flight between London and New York which was forced to return to Shannon Airport. Pate, along with UN Secretary-General Dag Hammarskjold and the president of the UN General Assembly, Vijaya Lakshmi, arranged to meet Kaye at a lunch to propose to the film star that he act as a spokesperson for UNICEF. As Kaye was already planning a trip to Asia, he was asked if he could visit UNICEF's health and nutrition projects in the Far East to attract monies for the impoverished organization (Gottfried 1994: 207).

Kaye readily agreed and Pate made the star's association with UNICEF official by appointing him as its ambassador-at-large. Shortly afterwards, Kaye toured UNICEF projects in Myanmar, India, Indonesia, Korea, Thailand and Japan to publicize its activities in alleviating the plight of children. Hundreds of thousands of feet of film were shot of his trip and the footage was edited into an hour-long programme entitled *Assignment Children* (1954) which was underwritten by Paramount Pictures. The documentary was shown to an estimated audience of 100 million and its profits entered UNICEF's coffers. The award-winning film favourably identified UNICEF in the public mind with the cause of needy children to create an atmosphere of goodwill for the organization: 'For the film, *Assignment Children* by Danny Kaye, we arranged a Thai Royal Command performance – sponsored by the King and Queen two years ago and we had a packed house. It was shown . . . all over Asia. We had it in New Delhi, Bombay, Madras, Manila and Japan' (United Nations 1958: 27–8).

Kaye continued to focus attention on UNICEF's activities through a range of trips to war-torn or blighted areas. By remaining a newsworthy presence, he publicized the agency's programmes, notably when he performed an improvised victory ballet while accepting the Nobel Peace Prize for UNICEF in 1965: 'On the day Danny Kaye became a UNICEF Goodwill Ambassador, a new kind of star was born. The kind that shines its light on the hardship and injustices . . . [and] confronts us and melts away our indifference' (Annan 2003).

Following on from this model of celebrity involvement, Jack Ling, UNICEF's director of the Information Division in the 1960s, courted stars including Peter Ustinov, Elizabeth Taylor, Richard Burton, Eddie Albert, Muhammad Ali, Pele, Sacha Distel and Dinah Shore (Ling 1984). While not all of them would become goodwill ambassadors, they hosted fund-raising European gala events and fronted television appeals. One of the most successful was the appeal for the relief of Japanese child victims of the Osaka earthquake in 1970, for which UNICEF raised over US$200,000.

UNICEF strengthened its institutional links when it joined forces with George Harrison, Ravi Shankar and Harrison's business manager Allan Klein to stage two concerts on 1 August 1971 at Madison Square Gardens in front of a total of 40,000 people to raise monies for Bangladeshi children who had suffered in the Bhola cyclone. This natural disaster struck at a time of turmoil resulting from the Bangladesh war that had already created a tremendous refugee problem in West Bengal. When a range of superstars, including Harrison, Shankar, Eric Clapton, Ringo Starr and Bob Dylan, sang the song 'Bangla Desh', it demonstrated how their celebrity status could bring international attention to the country's plight. The success of the concerts and the subsequent album resulted in vast sums of monies for the cause.

With these factors in mind, in 1979 the Bee Gees, Robert Stigwood and David Frost organized a further fund-raising concert at the UN General Assembly called *The Music for UNICEF Concert: A Gift of Song*, which featured Abba, Kris Kristofferson, Olivia Newton-John, Donna Summer and Rod Stewart. For this concert, each star signed a parchment supporting UNICEF goals and pledging to donate their performance royalties and those from one of their songs to the agency's coffers. Throughout these celebrity trips, galas and concerts, the ad hoc relations were formalized as the extension of celebrity fund-raising meant greater institutional structuring was required.

Moreover, long-standing UNICEF goodwill ambassadors such as Kaye and Ustinov (1968–2004) conceived themselves as good international citizens who could engender a 'thick layer of goodwill for UNICEF' (Ling 1984: 9). They saw it as their role to promote UNICEF's activities. In 1968, Ustinov received a telegram from UNICEF, asking him to act as master of ceremonies for a concert to be held at the Theatre Nationale de l'Odeon in Paris. Impressed by the selfless work of UNICEF officials and the moral worth of the agency's activities, he also helped to put together other galas in Italy, Switzerland and Japan. His appointment as a goodwill ambassador appealed to him as a self-proclaimed 'world citizen' who had Russian, Swiss, French, Italian and even Ethiopian origins. He not only became a tireless worker for UNICEF but an advocate for the UN:

> It is so easy . . . to attack the United Nations as a fertile field for undemocratic or anti-democratic ideas, but such critics conveniently overlook the fact that it was constituted as a democratic forum, and

> that the ideas of the majority cannot be roughly pushed aside . . .The General Assembly and the Security Council are but the shop window . . . [but] within the shop . . . all is different. . . . Confronted with problems, Christian and Communist, Moslem and Socialist, Buddhist and Conservative do their best within the means at their disposal to solve them. This is a source of confidence even to the most jaded cynic. (Ustinov 1977: 329)

The celebrity who provided the template for this 'glamorous . . . conformity' (Cooper 2008: 18) was Audrey Hepburn. Although, she did not become a UNICEF goodwill ambassador until the 1980s, her reputation as international film star and fashion icon and her experiences in the Second World War meant she epitomized the credible use of politicized celebrity. She made visits to Ethiopia and Somalia with little fear for her personal safety, met African leaders and took causes to the US Senate. Hepburn used her fame for humanitarian causes and refused to take sides, insisting the worst violence in Africa was widespread poverty: 'Audrey Hepburn created a model of star power expressed via the UN organizational structure that other celebrities could – and did in quite large numbers – try to follow. It was a model that allowed celebrities to go global with their enthusiasms . . . In this model glamour worked to enhance a sense of commitment' (ibid.: 20).

Transformative celebrity diplomacy: rising political consciousness and a widening of activities within the organs of the United Nations

The increase in celebrity activity in the 1980s and 1990s reflected the extension of the employment of celebrities by UNICEF and other agencies, notably the Office of the United Nations High Commissioner for Refugees (UNHCR) and the World Health Organization (WHO), and led some celebrities to feel they should become more politically engaged. This transformative stage of celebrity activism can be traced to relations forged between UNICEF and Marlon Brando when the star raised funds for children affected by famines in India in 1966. In this capacity, Brando's involvement became a more polemically driven commitment to international conceptions of justice.

In 1978, UNICEF asked the Swedish actress Liv Ullman to become a goodwill ambassador. Ullman had previously visited Thailand to add weight to a Swedish mission dealing with refugees. During this trip, she was approached by Ling about working for UNICEF, and he accompanied Ullman on her first visit to Sri Lanka. Subsequently, Ullman became a more autonomous figure when representing Kampuchean refugees and the Vietnamese boat people (Ling 1984: 8). She demonstrated a greater political consciousness than her predecessors and used her status as a serious 'European' film actress to appear a creditable figure when representing UNICEF in US House and Senate hearings (ibid.: 8). Effectively, she reconceived the role of the goodwill ambassador by taking a clear stance on poverty: 'We must be so outraged. We mustn't wait and talk about making resolutions; we must urgently start acting now' (Ullman 1993).

In turn, several goodwill ambassadors criticized the moral stance of the UN. One of the more problematic cases is that of Richard Gere, who has represented the UN in world health/AIDS and ecological matters. As a devotee of the exiled Tibetan leader the Dalai Lama, he came into conflict with the UN over its non-recognition of Tibet. In the late 1990s, Gere, as chairman of the International Campaign for Tibet, made high-profile visits to the UN headquarters in New York to support Tibetan hunger strikers and backed the US resolution to the United Nations Human Rights Commission (UNHRC) criticizing China's human rights record. When the UNHRC voted to take no action, he accused it of being shamefully manipulated by the Chinese. More recently, he supported calls for the boycotting of the 2008 Beijing Olympics.

Thus, the UN's deployment of more politically engaged celebrities has proved problematic. In this transformative era of celebrity diplomacy, stars have felt they should use their fame to expose injustices. However, this deployment of celebrity diplomats has led to difficulties when politicized stars have fallen out with the UN. Another case was that of Mia Farrow, who was critical of the UN's inability to protect human rights when she visited Darfur as a UNICEF goodwill ambassador. Moreover, the positive and negative connotations of celebrity diplomacy have intensified with the escalation of the number of goodwill ambassadors and the creation of messengers of peace.

Embracing celebrity culture: Kofi Annan's public relations revolution – restructuring and reform

When Kofi Annan was appointed UN secretary-general on 1 January 1997, he engaged in the ubiquitous employment of goodwill ambassadors. At the time of his departure in 2007, there were over 400 UN goodwill ambassadors, including actors such as Vanessa Redgrave, Liam Neeson, Roger Moore and Ralph Fiennes, along with sports stars like Roger Federer and the singer Shakira. To promote the work of UNICEF, Redgrave and her son, Carlo Nero, made a documentary entitled *War on Want* (2006). In addition, former Secretary-General Annan established a new tier of celebrity diplomats known as messengers of peace. In many respects, this demonstrated how the growing culture of celebrity had permeated the diplomatic environment (Drezner 2007).

Annan believed that significant reforms were required to improve the UN's public profile and he oversaw the wider deployment of goodwill ambassadors. This was tied to the growth in the number of departments in the UN's local, regional and international offices with responsibilities for media and communications, celebrity relations and special events. In turn, the Celebrity Relations Department formalized three tiers for goodwill ambassadors – international, regional and national. International ambassadors are film, music or sports stars who have a wide degree of recognition from the world's media for their activities. Regional and national ambassadors are those celebrities whose impact is conditioned by more local forms of fame.

When a UNICEF goodwill ambassador makes a field visit, the agency's media and communications staff seek to maximize publicity through a variety of local, national and media outlets by arranging press conferences, video shoots and photo opportunities. To follow up, a press day or conference will be set up after the goodwill ambassador returns to his or her home country for consultation between the media section and the celebrity. This might take the form of an informal briefing, a press conference or one-on-one interviews and can take place in the headquarters' location or in a city near the celebrity's residence.

In addition, wherever feasible, a meeting will be arranged between the celebrity and the executive director or another member of senior management to discuss the impressions and outcomes of the field visit. Finally, a follow-up package must be sent immediately to the celebrity containing press coverage, a report on any funds raised as a result of the visit and a letter of thanks from the executive director or National Committee/field office senior staff person, explaining exactly how the trip has made an impact (UNICEF 2006).

Idealism and universalism: Annan's aims for goodwill ambassadors and messengers of peace

Annan's decision to escalate the number of goodwill ambassadors was designed to offset the international cynicism that had been directed towards the UN and to counterbalance the view that it was beholden to the USA's realist foreign policies (Cooper 2008: 28). In 2002, Annan hosted a conference called 'Celebrity Advocacy for the New Millennium' which included stars such as the Brazilian footballer Ronaldo, and declared 'he wanted celebrities to be the tools the UN would use to pressurize reluctant governments to take seriously the rhetorical pledges they make during every General Assembly' (Alleyne 2005: 179). He believed celebrities could influence international public opinion to support the UN's goals of idealism and universalism.

To enhance this process, Annan inaugurated the Messengers of Peace Programme in 1997 to identify nine individuals who would propagate the UN's mission across the global media. This group of 'distinguished men and women of talent and passion' are composed of those celebrities whose fame has been understood to provide a global focus for the 'noble aims of the UN Charter: a world without war, respect for human rights, international law and social and economic progress'(United Nations 2007). They are selected from the fields of art, literature, music and sports and serve as messengers of peace for an initial period of three years. Since the programme's inception, more than ten individuals have been honoured as messengers of peace and the current cohort includes Michael Douglas, Jane Goodall, Daniel Barenboim, George Clooney, Stevie Wonder and Charlize Theron.

In raising the UN's profile for liberal internationalism, the most spectacular success has been the film actress Angelina Jolie, whose image was transformed from Hollywood 'wild-child' to a credible celebrity diplomat. Her links with UNHCR were established over several years in which she 'auditioned' to become a goodwill ambassador. Jolie became acquainted with the plight of refugees through trips to West Africa. Undoubtedly, Jolie has demonstrated that her fame, looks and photogenic qualities can attract the attention of the world's media to the causes she advocates. Similarly, UNHCR has sought to place 'attractive' refugees in the camera frame next to her to provide an iconic representation of displacement.

However, she has effectively blended her personal and professional life when acting as a celebrity diplomat. This was evident when she gave birth in Namibia to her son, Shiloh, by her partner Brad Pitt and adopted children from Cambodia and Ethiopia. Yet these adoptions did not arouse the controversy associated with the pop star Madonna's attempts to adopt underprivileged children from Malawi. Instead, Jolie's role as an 'earth mother' was part of the greater package in which she placed herself in dangerous situations to promote humanitarian causes. Moreover, her emotive responses have been seen to be legitimate, particularly as her published diaries from her visits demonstrated her commitment to the needs of refugees.

Jolie's understanding of refugee conditions led to her writing an open editorial in the *Washington Post* about the crisis in Darfur in February 2007. Subsequently, in her press junket to promote her film, *A Mighty Heart*, she included interviews with *Foreign Policy*'s web site and a glowing profile in *Newsweek* which was immodestly titled 'Angelina Jolie Wants to Save the World.' In that story, former US Secretary of State Colin Powell described Jolie as 'absolutely serious, absolutely informed. . . . She studies the issues' (Smith 2007). Further, the cover of the July 2007 *Esquire* featured a sultry picture of Jolie with an attached story which suggested something even more provocative: 'In post-9/11 America, Angelina Jolie is the best woman in the world *because* she is the most famous woman in the world – because she is not like you or me' (Junod 2007).

Therefore, Jolie's activism epitomized Annan's belief that, through celebrity diplomacy, the UN's mission for universalism would be enhanced. The same could be said for George Clooney, who became a UN messenger of peace as a consequence of his support for NGO projects in war-torn Darfur. Like Jolie, Clooney became well acquainted with the issues and was effective in fronting a humanitarian campaign which was forged from a coalition of groups embracing political liberals, the African-American community and the Christian Right. In 2006, Clooney visited Darfur with his father, Nick, and shortly afterwards he appeared at a press conference with then Senator Barack Obama and Senator Sam Brownback.

Later, he addressed the UN to appeal to the international community to act against the genocidal atrocities committed in Darfur (Cheadle and Prendergast 2007: 150). Subsequently, in 2007, Clooney narrated and acted as executive producer for a documentary entitled *Sand and Sorrow*. In the same year, he co-founded a non-profit organization called Not on Our Watch with Pitt, Matt Damon, Don Cheadle and film producer Jerry Weintraub. This was designed to bring resolution to the conflict in Darfur and draw attention to other human rights abuses in Burma, Sudan and Zimbabwe (Weintraub with Cohen 2010: 231). Notably, in March 2012, after a trip to the war-torn Nuba Mountains, Clooney appeared before the US Senate and was arrested with his father at a protest outside the Sudanese Embassy in Washington staged to bring the global media's attention to the ongoing human rights abuses: '"I'm just trying to raise attention," Clooney told reporters as he was led away. With his hands tied behind his back, he addressed the plight of "innocent children" in Sudan. "Stop raping them and stop starving them," he said. "That's all that we ask."' (Devereaux 2012).

Transformative celebrity activism and NGOs

These forms of transnational star activism have moved beyond the institutional confines of the UN as NGOs have used global celebrities to publicize their activities and direct media attention to issues. For instance, Angelina Jolie has worked independently of the UN and has collaborated with rock singer Peter Gabriel in his Witness Programme. Similarly, the singer Annie Lennox has accompanied her role as a UNESCO goodwill ambassador with active support for Amnesty International, Greenpeace and Burma UK.

The American Red Cross utilizes a fifty-member Celebrity Cabinet that includes Jamie Lee Curtis, Jane Seymour, L. L. Cool J. and Jackie Chan. Concurrently, Save the Children employed CP2s such as David Bowie, Melanie Griffith and Antonio Banderas, while Oxfam America has used the UN model of 'ambassadors', such as Archbishop Desmond Tutu, Coldplay and actors Kristin Davis, Colin Firth and Scarlett Johansson to promote its cause. *Make Poverty History* produced its 'click' video which showed Geldof, Bono, Clooney, Pitt, Kate Moss and Kylie Minogue clicking their fingers to symbolize a child dying from extreme poverty every three seconds. And the celebrity philanthropist Bill Gates with his wife Melinda has set up the Gates Foundation which has raised funds and entered policy areas that had previously been the purview of the WHO.

For NGO communication managers, there are several groups that can be targeted by the use of celebrities. First, CP2s enable them to get their message across to major fund-raisers, while also being effective in attracting small donors and a younger audience of future donors. Second, celebrity diplomats can reach out to members of the public who otherwise would not be interested in the NGO, so their involvement may enhance recruitment. Third, celebrities can provide access to decision makers. As Donald Steinberg of International Crisis Group argues, 'It's going to be hard for a foreign government to say no to Nicole Kidman' (Traub 2008: 38).

In pairing up CP2s andNGOs, the 'fit' between the motivations of a celebrity and a charity is a priority. One of the most successful linkages occurred when the late Princess Diana became an advocate for the banning of landmines and agreed to endorse the Mines Advisory Group (MAG). She had become involved with MAG when representing UK Red Cross as part of her responsibilities as the wife of Prince Charles. However, she realized her image of 'glamour with compassion' could deliver a message with which she had a very personal concern. In making her trips to Angola and Bosnia to publicize the landmines issue, Diana enthusiastically commented: 'This is the type of format I've been looking for' (Cooper 2008: 26).

Yet events and media perceptions also shaped how the landmines message was publicized and received. Princess Diana was due to attend the first major meeting concerning the banning of landmines which occurred on the 1 September 1997. This was, of course, the day after she and Dodi Al-Fayed were killed in a car crash in Paris. However, she was so closely associated with the cause that her influence on the campaign proved instrumental even after her death. Several years earlier, in 1985, when they attended the opening of his *Live Aid* show, Bob Geldof had realized that the royal seal of approval from Prince Charles and Princess Diana was necessary to provide credibility for the entire enterprise: 'I thought it would be important that [Charles and Diana] came because at that time they were glamorous and there was excitement around their relationship. And they represented the country' (Geldof 2005).

'Saint' Bob Geldof: celebrity philanthropy and anti-diplomacy

Such transformative forms of celebrity behaviour increasingly emerged in the wake of Bob Geldof's *Feed the World* campaign (Cooper 2008). His globally televised *Live Aid* shows reconfigured the public's attitude towards charities by making them 'cool' and demonstrating that fund-raising could be chic. Further, *Live Aid* provided a template for subsequent CP2-fronted campaigns such as *Comic Relief*. And its spectacular impact could only have been achieved because transnational celebrity activism received widespread coverage in an entertainment-driven and globalized media.

On 24 October 1984, the *BBC News* showed correspondent Michael Buerk's devastating report on the widespread starvation of Ethiopian refugees due to famine in camps at Korem. In the resulting outpouring of public grief, the horrified Geldof, the frontman of a fading post-punk band, the Boomtown Rats (named in honour of Woody Guthrie's *Bound for Glory*), became an unlikely celebrity humanitarian. Geldof cajoled forty-five UK pop stars, including Bono, George Michael and Sting, to form *Band Aid*, which recorded a charity single, 'Do They Know It's Christmas?' (1984) that he had co-written and produced with fellow musician Midge Ure. As a result of the success of the record, millions of pounds were raised; this led to another celebrity-fronted single for the Ethiopian cause, 'We Are the World' (1985), which was recorded by American pop stars, including black superstars Lionel Ritchie and Michael Jackson (Lynskey 2010: 482–3).

However, it was Geldof's enraged commitment that caught the public imagination, not least when he visited Ethiopia in January 1985. Notably, he called the Ethiopian dictator Mengistu Haile Mariam a 'prize c**t' and lectured Thatcher on the failings of international aid. In turn, as the 'People's Champion', he bullied celebrities such as David Bowie, Paul McCartney, Mick Jagger, Lionel Ritchie and Elton John, along with the bands Dire Straits, Queen, U2 and the Who, into performing at the *Live Aid* concerts held simultaneously in London and Philadelphia on 13 July 1985. As Geldof secured fifty-eight major acts to contribute to his 'global jukebox', other countries bought the rights to the British and American shows.

Geldof, along with promoter Harvey Goldsmith, faced many organizational difficulties in a venture which had been perceived as foolhardy. They had to overcome an attempted boycott by US artists and had a major fallout with the legendary US music entrepreneur Bill Graham, who actively undermined the Philadelphia show that he was meant to be promoting. Moreover, while Geldof and Goldsmith built on the foundations of previous charity events, such as Harrison's UNICEF concerts, the global nature and unprecedented sixteen hours of live television coverage massively enlarged the scale and pace of this type of activity. For instance, the Genesis singer/drummer Phil Collins, having performed at Wembley Stadium, was required to take a Concorde flight to appear alongside Led Zeppelin at the John F. Kennedy (JFK) Stadium in Philadelphia.

The global spectacle brought the plight of the starving Ethiopians to the attention of two billion viewers across 160 countries and challenged them to contribute to the cause, not least due to Geldof's impatience. As the BBC had failed to effectively advertise the phone lines which had been opened for public donations, only a relatively small amount of money had been raised. Consequently, *Live Aid* is remembered for Geldof's (in)famous outburst on a pre-watershed channel which has inaccurately gone down in folklore as 'Give us your fucking money!' To this end, *Live Aid* raised a global total of £50 million and Geldof's indignant behaviour was seen as crucial to its success: 'A combination of [Geldof] being a horrible stroppy bastard and being incredibly aggressive and forceful, along with having an enormous will and drive were the things that made this happen. If he had been rather nice, self-effacing and self-deprecating, he could not have possibly have put this project together' (Gray 2005).

On the twentieth anniversary of *Live Aid* in 2005, Geldof, with Bono and Richard Curtis, produced another series of globally televised celebrity concerts for *Live 8* on 2 July at Hyde Park in London and on 5 July at Murrayfield Stadium in Edinburgh. These events were designed to mobilize support for the *One Campaign* to deal with international debt and were timed to coincide with the G8 Gleneagles Summit. However, at *Live 8* Geldof was keen to incorporate Tony Blair, George W. Bush and the other G8 leaders as the focus of his campaign. On the delivery of the G8's pronouncements for combating debt and poverty, he appeared at a press conference to provide a 'mission accomplished' communiqué where he gave the G8 marks for the doubling of aid and debt relief.

Geldof's anger at the world has been a key determinant in his approach to international relations. Cooper has contended that he is an 'anti-diplomat' who has smashed through the niceties of diplomacy to achieve his goals (Cooper 2008: 52). His verbal belligerence and desire for personal recognition has been countered by his genuine sense of compassion, organizational skills and realization of the power of public spectacle. It has been noted that Geldof, whatever responses he arouses, has demonstrated a long-term commitment to his endeavours. However, his approach has often led to his being treated as an outsider by the diplomatic classes while he is simultaneously accused by the aid community of being a pawn of those very same decision makers: 'Having branded himself as a provocative anti-diplomat since the 1980s, buying into a more orthodox script contained dangers . . . Echoes of support for official diplomacy came at a cost. Other campaigners said that Geldof had become too close to the decision-makers to make an objective view of what has been achieved at this summit' (Vallely 2009).

Figure 6.1 'Unexpected bedfellows, that's what we do': Bono (the U2 singer), Blair, Putin and Geldof join forces at the 2001 Genoa World Trade Organization summit

Moreover, a duality has emerged in attitudes to CP2 activity as politicized celebrities have been seen to be either self-interested or populist diluters of complex issues. The lessons of *Live Aid* and *Live 8* were not lost on some of its participatory acts, including Queen, U2, Sting and a reformed Pink Floyd, whose careers, as well as their status, received a vital shot in the arm. As Roger Taylor, the drummer in Queen, noted, their performance revitalized their position as a global rock act in front of an audience of two billion people. U2 became a major international act on the back of their appearance in the globally televised spectacle and their frontman Bono, akin to Geldof, has utilized his fame to break down the barriers between entertainment and global advocacy to become a spokesman on human rights. However, both celebrity activists have been accused of making their causes apolitical, thereby perpetuating a risk-averse approach to the protest movement.

The 'Bonoization' of celebrity advocacy and diplomacy

Bono has been responsible for tilting much of the focus of celebrity advocacy towards poverty in the southern states of the global economy.[2] He has edited special editions of national newspapers such as the *Independent* and *Liberation*, along with magazines such as *Vanity Fair*, to publicize concerns about international debt and economic justice. Bono has placed an emphasis on direct action and the building of effective institutions, while using his fame to access the inside track to lobby governments. The rock singer is the co-founder and the public face of the *One Campaign* and DATA (Debt, AIDS, Trade, Africa) which advocates the ending of extreme poverty and the AIDS pandemic and promotes international debt relief. He was also instrumental, along with Jeffrey Sachs and Paul Farmer, in the construction of Product RED which combined celebrity activism with corporate social responsibility (Nike, Apple, Gap) to support the Global Fund in its fight to stem the spread of HIV/AIDS, tuberculosis and malaria in Africa.

As a regular speaker at the G8, the Davos World Economic Forum and World Bank meetings, Bono's views on aid and debt relief for developing nations have garnered the attention of world leaders, senior policy makers, NGOs, the media and the public. To this end, he has combined his charismatic abilities as a rock star with a detailed knowledge of the issues:

> Here is a multi-millionaire global rock star, but instead of doing what a good many civic-minded celebrities do – that is, add their names to a benefit, send a check and do a public announcement – Bono shows up. He is there in person. He personally tugs at the lapels of public officials whose advocacy and power are necessary to flesh out the programmes into which Bono invests his time, his energy, and his presence. . . . He knows what he is talking about. He doesn't need aides around him whispering facts in his ear or passing him talking points (Valenti 2007: 408–9).

Consequently, Bono has utilized his central position as a global performer to bring politicians and corporate executives together (Jackson 2008: 218). Undoubtedly, he has demonstrated tenacity in establishing political alliances not only with liberal figures such as Bill Clinton and Bill Gates but also with George W. Bush and Jesse Helms, the late arch-conservative senator from North Carolina. In this manner, Bono has achieved cross-party consensus for the Jubilee 2000 debt relief alliance in Africa and placed the issue firmly on the political agenda in Washington. As a result, Bono topped both the Republican and Democratic Parties' lists as the world's most effective celebrity advocate in the *National Journal of Republican and Democratic Political Insiders*.

Bono has also been instrumental in mobilizing other celebrities to build a 'superhighway between Africa and Hollywood' (Traub 2008: 38). In 2004, he was invited by Pitt to address Tom Hanks, Sean Penn, Julia Roberts, Justin Timberlake and the architect Frank Gehry so that they would lend their support to the *One Campaign*. Further, Bono recruited Clooney for the campaign and the film star has made explicit reference to his influence in the diffusion of other CP2 forms of activism:

> 'Bono's model really worked,' Clooney says. 'There is more attention on celebrity than ever before – and there is a use for that besides selling products.' Stars like Brad Pitt (Katrina), Ben Affleck (Congo), and Sean Penn (Haiti) followed suit. 'A lot of the young actors I see coming up in the industry are not just involved, but knowledgeable on a subject and then sharing that with fans,' says Clooney. No one's just a 'peace activist' anymore – they have a specialty. (Avlon 2011: 16)

Cooper has noted how Bono has become a successful celebrity diplomat who has used his fame to place matters of human rights and global inequity on the international agenda (Cooper 2008: 38). He has gained access to the corridors of power to make effective interventions by appealing to the fascination that modern leaders, such as Blair and Clinton, have with popular culture, and his charismatic egotism matches that of the political classes. Bono has been prepared to attend Republican as well as Democratic national conventions to extend his message and mobilize support for his causes. Such political expedience has been necessary to achieve the greater good of aid reform.

Yet as Bono has willingly engaged with compromised political leaders such as Bush, Blair and Gordon Brown, as well as 'despots' such as Vladimir Putin, his activism has been divisive. From the point of view of the Debt and Development Coalition Ireland (DDCI) and UK Art Uncut, he is a hypocritical self-publicist who has engaged in tax avoidance schemes while simultaneously lecturing western governments on how they should deal with international debt. At the 2011 Glastonbury Festival, UK Art Uncut unfurled a twenty-foot inflatable banner emblazoned with the legend 'U pay your tax 2'. In turn, the anarchist band Chumbawumba wore 'Bono Pay Your Tax' T-shirts when they appeared at the festival and have criticized the U2 singer's close relations with the powerful. Notably, their first album was entitled *Pictures of Starving Children Sell Records* (1986) (Lynskey 2010: 485). John Cooper Clarke, too, parodied the rock star in his poem 'Who Stole Bongo's Trousers' (2011) in which the U2 singer 'Bongo' (sic) has his Stetson hat, designer sunglasses and leather trousers stolen. When he is forced to dress in a lounge suit, no one (including guitarist 'The Hedge') recognizes him: 'He can't save the planet dressed like that!'

Others have suggested that Bono's proclamations at his concerts have been a good way of selling tickets for his band and easing consumer guilt. In particular, Richey and Ponte have maintained that Bono, along with Sachs and Farmer, has constructed a form of 'compassionate consumption' in the wake of Product RED. They argue that there has been a de-linking of the relations which existed between capitalist exploitation and global poverty (Richey and Ponte 2011: 179). Consequently, with the increase in celebrity diplomacy, the value of such activism has been questioned and its impact on cultural and political practices has become more controversial.

The critiques of celebrity advocacy and diplomacy: trivialization, neoliberalism, neocolonialism and the betrayal of the global South

Therefore, as the gap between the expectation and resolution of human rights has widened, celebrities have been criticized for their simplistic or moralistic responses to the complexity of these issues (Brockington 2009). Furthermore, the media's focus on the individual celebrity often means that the cause becomes an afterthought. Celebrity advocates have been accused of debasing the quality of international debate, diverting attention from worthy causes to those which are 'sexy', and failing to represent the disenfranchised. They have been seen to be superficial and to remain unaccountable.

Consequently, concerns have been raised that goodwill ambassadors have trivialized the UN's mission. Infamously, Sophia Loren arrived at a UNHCR meeting in aid of starving Somali refugees in a brown Rolls-Royce and dressed in a fur coat. When criticized by a journalist, without any hint of irony Loren commented, 'When someone asks a question like this I don't know why you should be in this place. This is something very serious' (Naughton 1992). In the case of Sarah Ferguson, her financial collapse caused by her divorce from Prince Andrew meant she could not afford to perform *pro bono* tasks for the UN. As for Geri Halliwell (Ginger Spice), her inability to perform her tasks as an advocate for family planning and her decline in fame meant she did not stand the test of a comparatively short period of time (Cooper 2008: 30).[3]

Mark D. Alleyne argues that the UN's deployment of goodwill ambassadors has been elitist and ethnocentric. He maintains that the employment of celebrities was part of a general malaise in which a desperate UN incorporated public relations techniques into its marketing so that the international media would provide it with favourable coverage (Alleyne 2005: 176). Essentially, Alleyne argues, this placed a 'happy', but ultimately impotent, face on the UN to cover serious shortcomings in its values, conduct and credibility. This was a shallow approach to solving crises, reinforced ethnic stereotypes by perpetuating an imbalanced view of need and offered 'a primarily meliorative approach, giving succour to the incapacitated rather than hope for a better life through programmes of education, consciousness-raising and cultural affirmation' (William Over, quoted in Alleyne 2003: 77). These views were reinforced by reports that a UNICEF officer had been infuriated by the organization's obsession with celebrity:

> 'It's bad enough having to accommodate celebrities and their entourage in the aftermath of every major humanitarian disaster,' she said. 'But when most people think of the UN now they think of Angelina Jolie on a crusade, not the work that goes on in the field after humanitarian disasters or on a long-term preventive level. Celebrity is at the heart of every UNICEF campaign these days and the association is being sold incredibly cheaply.' (McDougall 2006)

Further criticisms contend that compliant CP2s have reinforced the economic inequalities between the global North and South to replicate the 'obscenities' of capitalist exploitation (Kapoor 2011). Following *Live Aid*, Richey and Ponte maintain that a 'fourth wave' of celebrity activism has occurred. Principally, Band Aid was commoditized into 'Brand Aid' so that major corporations and celebrities combined to support charities aimed at alleviating African poverty. Thus, as these apparently ethical forms of behaviour sell 'suffering' to the public, Riche and Ponte argue that aid causes have become 'brands' to be bought and sold in the global marketplace. Most prominently, Product RED marked the point at which there was a fusion of consumption and social causes:

> The primary goal of RED is not to push governments to do their part, but to push consumers to do theirs through exercising their choices. The contemporary era of celebrity activism will be more eclectic, with different kinds of celebrities holding power in various realms and with shifting alliances between various kinds of celebrities holding sway over diverse constituencies. (Richey and Ponte 2011: 33–4)

Consequently, Richey and Ponte outline the development of aid 'celebritariats' who not only appeal to the consumers but also to the international aid community. It is argued that these celebrities have filled the void that has been left by those institutional actors who have failed to coordinate the effective provision of economic relief for the global underclass. While these authors do not make light of the celebrity activists' impulse to 'do good' globally, they contend that there are inherent dangers in conceiving that stars, philanthropists and corporate executives can effect solutions to global crises.

In addition, they maintain that this apparent altruism provides another means by which corporations may market themselves in relation to the growing concerns with lifestyle, culture and identity. Thus, corporations gain from developing 'responsible practices' so that they can then brand themselves for a wider consumer base. However, by focusing public attention on the plight of 'distant others', they deflect the focus away from their own dubious behaviour in exploiting developing states. In this respect, celebrities lend credence to and validate such 'ethical' corporate behavior.

Within this schema, Chris Atkins's *Starsuckers* (2009) suggests that celebrities and media corporations had conspired to manipulate global public opinion. In tandem, Ilan Kapoor contends that the ideological underpinnings of celebrity advocacy are not so much about humanitarianism as self-promotion, brand marketing and elite-centred politics (Kapoor 2011). Thus, Geldof and Bono's involvement in *Live 8* has been criticized for sloganizing poverty, deflecting the public's attention away from the viability of aid and being co-opted by the political classes. Concurrently, anti-poverty campaigners such as Making Poverty History have claimed that *Live 8* wilfully undermined their message of 'justice not charity', stole the media agenda and depoliticized the cause through its construction of a dependency culture:

> Anyone with a grasp of development politics who had read and understood the ministers' statement could see that the conditions it contains – enforced liberalization and privatization – are as onerous as the debts it relieves. But Bob Geldof praised it as 'a victory for the millions of people in the campaigns around the world' and Bono pronounced it 'a little piece of history.' Like many of those who have been trying to highlight the harm done by such conditions . . . I feel betrayed by these statements. (Monbiot 2005)

This has meant, then, that popular culture has inaccurately mythologized Geldof and Bono as humane philanthropists because in reality they have reinforced the West's neocolonial rule over the global South. According to Andrew Darnton and Martin Kirk the 'Live Aid legacy' has established an inequitable relationship between 'powerful givers' and 'grateful receivers' (Darnton and Kirk 2011: 6). This dominant paradigm has meant that the real causes of poverty are ignored; instead it is suggested that aid will 'magically' release the 'victims' from their shackles in southern societies. Within this apparently benevolent narrative, the focus on indigenous peoples' needs rather than the facilitation of their creativity has been used to 'police' the boundaries of the public's imagination (Dieter and Kumar 2008; Yrjölä 2011: 187).

Such criticisms suggest that this cluster of celebrity activists remain North-centric actors. Celebrity advocacy, however, will only reach representational authenticity when more stars from the global South are elevated to the same stature as Bono and Jolie. However, the current forms of CP2 transnational activism have been seen to reinforce these cultural precepts. For instance, Geldof's concerts have been accused of failing to provide a platform for African and other multicultural artists.

More profoundly, Jemima Repo and Riina Yrjölä maintain that the values of celebrity advocacy preserve global stereotypes. Principally, Bono, Geldof, Clooney and Jolie are represented as selfless western crusaders, dedicated to alleviating the suffering of Africans who exist outside the 'civilized' processes of development, progress, peace and human security. Therefore, celebrities and 'Africa' operate under assumed roles which are presented as part of a wider discourse about the natural order of world politics (Repo and Yrjölä 2011: 57). Consequently, celebrity diplomacy indicates an underlying cultural imperialism which has abused 'the Third World [so that] the latter becomes [a stage] for First World self-promotion and hero-worship, and [the] dumping ground for humanitarian ideals and fantasies' (Kapoor 2011).

Celebrity advocacy and diplomacy: globalism, public space, agency and soft power

Throughout these analyses of celebrity advocacy, transnational CP2 activism has been presented as propagating powerful economic, social and political interests. Invariably, this means that celebrity advocates, corporate executives, political leaders and media elites have been seen to collude with one another to undermine the rights of the exploited in order to reinforce capitalist relations. However, despite these accusations of star complicity, celebrities have effected successful interventions within international policy circles. These developments have been tied to a democratization of foreign policy in which global concerns have been placed on the popular agenda: 'Celebrity activists . . . operate within the framework of *globalism*, cultivating the potential for shifting concerns of politics away from traditional struggles of sovereignty towards issues of mutual concern. Celebrities provide and represent *cosmopolitanism* to audiences, constructing the identity of global citizenship and solidarity' (Tsaliki, Huliaras and Frangonikolopoulos 2011: 299).

Thus, Lisa Tsaliki, Christos A. Frangonikolopoulos and Asteris Huliaras argue that celebrity activists can 'bridge' the gap between western audiences and faraway tragedies by using their fame to publicize international events (ibid.: 299). Further, they may complement the work of NGOs by using their charismatic authority to establish an equitable discourse within global civil society concerning the value of an organization's work. For instance, Liv Ullman became a public advocate for UNICEF's long-term programmes which dealt with health care, education and the autonomous rights of peoples. In particular, she highlighted the benefits of aid development which could be used to facilitate indigenous productive capabilities:

> The interesting programmes are . . . like women getting job opportunities by [having] a sewing machine that enables them to create cloth and then sell [it] on the market; like fish ponds so you can start having your own place of finding food. . . . Give the tool, don't give the fish. Give the net, and the first fish, and that will just prosper. (Long 2006: 139)

Moreover, CP2s can provide an effective lead 'through the "non-confrontational" reordering of political and economic forces in the service of global goals' (Tsaliki, Huliaras and Frangonikolopoulos 2011: 300). Therefore, Geldof's *Live Aid* and *Live 8* campaigns demonstrated the skilful linkage of pop music with famine imagery to generate philanthropic activity amongst the public. In a similar vein, Bono's Product RED makes conspicuous how American Express, Motorola, Armani and Microsoft can be used profitably (in both senses of the word) to effect real material change to avert poverty. According to Julie Wilson, cosmopolitan stars represent 'global governmentality . . . [as] . . . they . . . bring media audiences, primarily those in the western world, into alignment with the international aims and programmes of global governing' (Wilson 2011: 59).

In turn, Cooper argues that celebrity diplomacy creates a new 'space' in which stars provide a conduit between foreign affairs and the public to overcome the traditional 'disconnect' which has occurred as official diplomats have sought to husband information rather than share it (Cooper 2008: 113–14). Celebrity advocacy contrasts with diplomatic traditions in which there has been a coordination of state interests with broader conceptions of collective security and economic power. Previously, the mechanisms of bargaining, interest and cooperation have operated as a diplomatic 'currency' for insider groups, including British Foreign Office mandarins, ambassadors and US State Department officials. This has been presented as being part of a realist discourse on international issues in which matters of ethics, emotion and public opinion have been balanced against the complexities of the international state system. However, the normative values of the Westphalian diplomatic order are being challenged by celebrity diplomacy's appeal to the new currencies of 'emotional commitment' and an engagement with public opinion to facilitate a democratic arena for political change: 'If diplomacy is wedded to everyday activity along a wide continuum and a robust and open-ended version of individual agency, the normative claims of traditional state-centric diplomacy are eroded' (ibid.: 2).

Therefore, Cooper contends that as celebrity advocates have innovated unofficial forms of public diplomacy to raise levels of expectation, they have initiated new diplomatic mechanisms to facilitate a counter-consensus to the issues (ibid.: 13). For example, Cooper notes that Geldof and Bono have not only drawn public attention to major causes by creating a media buzz, but have employed their fame and rhetorical power to intervene at the centres of global power (ibid.: 119–20). He argues that Geldof's abrasive style at the Gleneagles Summit allowed him to play 'bad cop' to Bono's 'good cop' (ibid.: 121; Vallely 2009). This has meant that they have gained extended face-time with national leaders in which there is a two-way attraction since politicians can cultivate a populist legitimacy with celebrities who can simultaneously advance their causes.

As a result, Geldof was free to express the problems with the G8 compromise in terms of it being a 'total farce', whereas Bono could make the more technical critiques. This double act was further enacted as Geldof cajoled the political classes, enabling Bono to 'play key leaders off each other, balancing intense involvement with an eye for keeping the boundaries of access open to as many decision makers as possible' (ibid.: 122). Thus, autonomous celebrity diplomacy has occurred wherein points of public identification have combined with diplomatic skills to move on international policy agendas.

In terms of agency, celebrity diplomacy's adaptive possibilities have been personified by the continued rise of Angelina Jolie. She has

Figure 6.2 Former United Nations Secretary General Kofi Annan links up with 'Brangelina' at the World Economic Forum

mixed her art with real life by starring in exotically located films while becoming educated in the complexities of global governance. This form of personal growth has been complemented by an appreciation of how she can employ her fame to become a credible participant in promoting the rights of refugees and oppressed peoples (ibid.: 116). However, Jolie's activism is not representative of an untrammelled individual autonomy as it requires significant organizational backup and support. For instance, when she appeared on a two-hour special edition of *Anderson Cooper 360*, Jolie's remarks had been prepared by her international advisor Trevor Nielson, who had worked for DATA and the Gates Foundation. This meant she was attuned to the issues in a legitimate manner and could demonstrate her long-term commitment to the cause of refugees.

Other celebrities, including Virgin chairman Sir Richard Branson, have also performed effectively in advocating causes when they have been briefed by NGOs such as MAG. The amount of time it takes to prepare, brief and engage with celebrities to make their involvement viable, valid and workable should not be underestimated. Such a liaison between celebrities and NGO officers demonstrates how CP2s have learned to take advice from campaign professionals who are conversant in raising appropriate issues to mobilize public interest.

Furthermore, the lobbying power of celebrity diplomats is 'dependent on the extent to which they work within networks and coalitions and elaborate pragmatic goals' (Huliaris and Tzifakis 2011: 40). Bono has become the quintessential 'outsider-insider' as he has combined his public appeal as a political brand with the requisite networking skill in order to access the powerful (Cooper 2008: 42–4). Consequently, the 'Bonoization' of diplomacy has demonstrated how celebrity activism operates as a form of political capital: 'Has a celebrity ever accumulated more political influence than Bono? No one has ever really come close [and he] . . . has made himself the fulcrum of an extraordinary global network of political leaders, philanthropists, development experts, and celebrities dedicated to relieving poverty in the developing world, particularly Africa' (Brownstein 2011).

Finally, celebrity diplomacy accords with Joseph Nye's concept of 'soft power' which refers to the ability to effect change through the rules of attraction rather than coercion or payment (Nye 2004). In terms of nation-states, this power derives from the legitimacy of a society's culture, political ideals and policies towards other countries. At the more individualist level, Cooper has contended that celebrity diplomats have utilized the 'politics of attraction' to legitimize their space in the global public sphere and to access influential networks of power (Cooper 2009: 10). This 'soft power' potential has meant CP2s have lent weight to transnational campaigns in a commercially driven global news media. In this manner, they have provided a definable focus for public engagement and have employed their star power to put pressure on diplomats, international policy makers and national leaders. Thus, celebrities have promoted new or alternative discourses and, by occupying a diplomatic space, have brought about credible interventions throughout the international community.

Conclusion

This chapter has analysed the development of the celebritization of international politics. In the early stages of UNICEF activity, celebrity diplomats such as Danny Kaye, Peter Ustinov and Audrey Hepburn defined themselves as 'good international citizens' whose activism was conformist. In an era of transformative celebrity diplomacy, the goodwill ambassadors' behaviour was epitomized by more politicized celebrities who came into greater focus during former UN Secretary-General Kofi Annan's intensification of celebrity involvement. The success of film stars such as Jolie and Clooney may be seen to indicate that Annan's vision of politicized celebrities advancing the UN's idealist values across the world's media has been realized.

There has been an expansion of celebrity advocacy across the UN and throughout the NGO international community. Consequently, a range of charities and aid organizations have cooperated with celebrity activists such as Geldof and Bono who, in turn, have become major humanitarian figures. Most specifically, *Live Aid* exponentially expanded the reach and impact of previous forms of international CP2 behaviour and provided a template for other forms of celebrity activity. Subsequently, in the modern phase of celebrity diplomacy, there has been a recalibration of fame within an ever-increasing range of global media and social media resources. This range of portals has been matched by more sophisticated forms of political marketing to raise the public profile of transnational causes.

However, such activism has been controversial. Not least, celebrity advocates such as Bono and Geldof have been divisive figures who have been praised and condemned in equal measure. On the one hand, several NGO communication managers suggest that CP2s have popularized issues which would not otherwise receive a public hearing. Moreover, their fame has been vital in achieving access to influential circles of diplomatic power. On the other hand, they have been criticized for their trivialization of the issues and simplistic emotional responses to the complexities of state-centric power. Even in the case of Jolie, it can be argued that her response to thorny international problems has been framed in 'terms of a scenario, in which, once certain key scenes are linked . . . the plot will proceed inexorably to an upbeat fade' (Dideon 1998: 519). Thus, Jolie has accelerated the process of star power but may be seen to have made some naive interventions in which her activities have been indulged by a compliant media (Cooper 2008: 34–5).

The gulf between celebrity and diplomacy has shown how populist 'narratives' have uncomfortably clashed with realist forms of international power. It has led to criticisms that while star power has brought attention to international affairs, it has created little in the way of real change. Moreover, within the academy, celebrity advocates have been accused of reinforcing global capitalist interests and exacerbating global stereotypes. Kapoor contends that apparently humanitarian celebrities are beholden to a massive corporate 'celebrity cultural machine' which has made international audiences passive and de-politicized (Kapoor 2012). In one of the most sophisticated critiques of celebrity humanitarianism, Rinna Yrjölä argues that Bono and Geldof's moral 'war against poverty' has been rooted in: 'the foundational superior morality of the west and its grand histories of progress. . . . Reflecting colonial rescue narratives, cloaked with religious language of crusades and inscriptions of western self-mastery, "Africa" becomes located, through these interpretations, outside western modernity, freedom and civilization, rendering the continent as a central battleground between good and evil' (Yrjölä 2012).

Despite the validity of these criticisms, a more nuanced approach to celebrity diplomacy is required. For instance, in a commercially dictated global media, the escalation of UN goodwill ambassadors was one of the few realistic responses open to Annan and his successor Ban Ki-Moon, along with NGOs, to promote the international community's activities (Kellner 2010a: 123).[4] Undoubtedly, some celebrity diplomats have been beyond parody (Loren, Halliwell). However, the ability of celebrity advocates like Jolie and Clooney to bring focus to international campaigns, to impact on diplomatic agendas and to advocate the global principles has been of significant worth in a period of international conflict.

Cooper has shown how this phenomenon has brought about a new form of engagement which has indicated a transformation from state-centric to more populist approaches to international relations. These reforms have taken place within a construct of global collaboration so that networks of institutional and ideological power facilitate diplomatic reforms. Thus, in 'soft power' terms, the politics of attraction within celebrity-led campaigns such as *Make Poverty History* and Product RED have constructed greater forms of agency to alleviate global suffering. As a consequence, the celebritization of politics should not be dismissed as an erosion of diplomatic culture but can be understood within the framework of a change in global political activism from which there will be both positive and negative outcomes.

Questions

- How effective has the 'Bonoization' of diplomacy been?
- How did Bob Geldof organize *Live Aid* and *Live 8*?
- Does celebrity humanitarianism represent an alternative type of political agency or is it another form of capitalist power?

Further reading

Alleyne, M. D. 2005: The United Nations' celebrity diplomacy. *SAIS Review*, Baltimore: The Johns Hopkins University Press.

Cooper, A. F. 2008: *Celebrity Diplomacy*. Boulder, London: Paradigm Publishers.

Kapoor, I. 2012: *Celebrity Humanitarianism: The Ideology of Global Charity*. London and New York: Routledge.

Richey, L. A. and Ponte, S. 2011: *Brand Aid: Shopping Well to Save the World*. Minneapolis, London: University of Minnesota Press.

Tsaliki L., Huliaras, A. and Frangonikolopoulos, C. A. (eds) 2011: *Transnational Celebrity Activism in Global Politics: Changing the World?* Bristol: Intellect.

Wheeler, M. 2011: Celebrity diplomacy: United Nations' Goodwill Ambassadors and Messengers of Peace. *Celebrity Studies: Special Edition on Celebrity and the Transnational*. 2(1): 6–18.

Conclusion

Throughout this book's analysis of celebrity politics, several concerns have emerged about whether such activities have devalued or enhanced opportunities for democratic engagement. It has been noted that celebrities have become more politically conscious in an era of global mediation of communications. At the same time, politicians have incorporated the value of celebrity within the forms of political imagery they have developed. Thus, such a celebritization of politics has brought about alternative forms of political engagement which indicate cultural changes in the concepts of citizenship and participation.

Undoubtedly, some of the activities of celebrity politicians and activists have been problematic. Yet, a more nuanced understanding of star power needs to be attained in relation to the broader employment of film, music and sports personalities. In commercially dictated global media, the mass escalation of celebrity politics may indicate a realistic means through which to promote political engagement. The dialogue between celebrity politicians and the public has allowed for new opportunities for political participation. This has reflected a growing willingness within the audience to accept celebrities as authentic political figures because of a decline in trust in the political classes and the public's greater identification with stars, brought about by the celebritization of popular culture.

Therefore, this analysis suggests that the traditional academic paradigms accounting for the rise of celebrity and decline of political rationality need to be critically re-evaluated. This does not mean that it unconditionally accepts the validity of celebrity politicians or political celebrities, as their democratic worth remains contested. However, it suggests that the cynicism expressed in parts of the popular media and some of the functionalist accounts within the academy should be replaced with a more intellectually curious critique of celebrity politics.

John Street's arguments that celebrity politics has given a greater expression to the representation of democratic behaviour are persuasive. In particular, Street asks whether celebrities can reinvigorate politics with an aggregated form of political agency. He is concerned about the connection celebrities can make with the public through their ability to be 'in touch' with popular sentiment. This has been mediated through 'fandom' in which an 'intimacy with distant others' can be understood as the basis of political representation. Street contends that such a representational relationship is established by the 'affective capacity' of the celebrities and modern politicians' cultural performances. As celebrities and image candidates assume the authority to promote political agendas, they have become significant actors in election campaigns, policy agendas and activism.

These concerns segue into a wider debate about the dynamics that are shaping post-democratic societies. Here, it is contended that traditional civic duties are being replaced by alternative forms of virtuous participation. Within this new political environment, different types of agency, such as celebrity politics, have become centrifugal forces for public engagement. In this respect, celebrity politics can be linked to Henrik Bang's arguments that new forms of political capital are emerging as 'everyday makers' utilize community based narratives to engage with one another. Similarly, John Keane's concept of 'monitory democracy' has considered how consumer-led changes to the matters of 'voice' and 'output' have reformed democratic practices.

Yet for celebrity politics to have a democratic worth, it must enhance civic virtues through the mechanisms of input and agency, as much as providing openings for voice and output. Therefore, celebrity politicians and politicized celebrities need to demonstrate ideological substance and provide clarity in establishing a fixed range of meanings through which people may achieve a real sense of connection with political causes. Consequently, such forms of activity should provide the basis for citizens to act in terms of their own political efficacy to define a wider sense of the common good. It has been this work's intention to make a contribution to these debates.

Finally, this analysis looks forward to further research designed to consider the impact on the celebritization of politics of the growth in social media and questions of public efficacy. Moreover, Street contends that relatively little work has been carried out with reference to celebrities' involvement in the delivery of policy (Street 2012: 3–4). Therefore, the study of celebrity politics remains pertinent and this book has outlined some of the directions in which this phenomenon may continue to be analysed.

Notes

Introduction

1 Street has included a new chapter reflecting upon celebrity politics in his second edition of *Mass Media, Politics and Democracy*. See Street (2010: 244–60).

Chapter 1 Celebrity Politics in an Era of Late Modernity

1 Elsewhere, Kellner has talked about the notion of 'progressive' spectacle. See Kellner (2009: 715–41).
2 These questions concerning the political authenticity of celebrities are debated by Sue Collins who considers how Bourdieu's concepts of cultural capital can be utilized to discuss whether celebrities are forms of capitalization or cultural resistance. For further details, see Collins (2007: 180–211).
3 In this respect, van Zoonen's analysis shares some of the values defined by Franceso Alberoni, who argued that, as paraphrased by Herminio Martins, 'the lives of the celebrities . . . symbolise the ubiquity and permanence of certain common-human problems; they are "like us" after all, and reassure us as to a basic uniformity in the major dilemmas of life, just because they are otherwise remote, and enjoy a unique degree of freedom from social control and opportunities which the fan lacks' (Martins 1964).
4 In this respect, Boykoff and Goodman's work accords with Thomas Meyer's analysis of the rules of the media, which includes factors of time, news values, 'media stage management', personalization and parasitic publicity. For further details, see Meyer with Hinchman (2002).

Chapter 2 A Historical Analysis of Celebrity Politics: The American Experience

1 Several writers have argued that there was an essential distinction between fame in the pre-modern and modern societies. In the earlier period, fame went beyond charisma to mediate the supremacy of emperors, kings, religious and political leaders. For further details, see Pleios (2011: 251–2).
2 In 1902, Teddy Roosevelt (TR) was reported as having refused to kill an injured and tied-up bear. This incident became part of TR's legend and toy manufacturers produced 'teddy bears' which became a national craze. Later in TR's second term, Edwin S. Porter produced a thirteen-minute short entitled *The 'Teddy Bears'* (1907). For further details, see Greenberg (2011).
3 Throughout the 1920s and 1930s, radio popularized Huey Long, the governor of Louisiana, and the right-wing Father Charles Coughlin.
4 Eisenhower was coached by the actor Robert Montgomery for his televised spot adverts.
5 Kennedy's facade of a healthy demeanour covered up his acute back problems and medical conditions brought on by his contraction of Addison's disease.
6 The link between entertainment and politics was evident in the use of US presidential campaign songs drawn from the era of Thomas Jefferson and John Adams.
7 After his falling out with the Kennedys, Sinatra switched allegiance from the Democrats to the Republicans and became an avid support of Richard M. Nixon and Ronald Reagan. For further details, see Schroeder (2004).
8 HUAC had been established in the 1930s and had investigated Hollywood in 1938 under the reactionary Chairmanship of Congressman Martin Dies. See Wheeler (2006: 86–7).
9 Buckley appeared with the comedian Woody Allen in the *Kraft Music Hall Look at 1967*. In a question and answer session, when asked what he understood to be the meaning of liberal, Allen commented: 'Liberal, you got me on this . . . If a girl will neck with me she's liberal! If Mr Buckley will neck with me he's very liberal!' (Allen 1967).

Chapter 3 The Mediatization of Celebrity Politics in Modern Partisan Affairs within the United States and the United Kingdom

1 Galloway's controversial behaviour was evident in the 2006 version of *Celebrity Big Brother* where he pretended to be a cat licking milk from actress Rula Lenska's hands and appeared in a leotard, dancing with the transsexual pop star Pete Burns. As a standing MP, he was accused of bringing parliament into disrepute. He further appeared as a presenter on the Talk Sport radio station and the Iranian government-funded Press

TV. Galloway's fame was seen as being crucial in his electoral victory in Bethnal Green and Bow in 2005, but his career appeared to be declining after poor results in the 2010 general election for the neighbouring East London seat of Poplar and in 2011 for the Scottish Parliament. However, in a Lazarus-like resurrection, Galloway won as the Respect candidate in Bradford West on 29 March 2012, where he gained a 36 per cent swing of the vote to win with 18,341 votes (55.9 per cent). He claimed that his victory represented a 'Bradford Spring' in which Labour 'must stop imagining that working people and poor people have no option but to support them if they hate the Tory and Liberal Democrat coalition partners'. For further details, see Robinson (2012) and Pidd (2012).

2 Clinton's love affair with Hollywood became less tenable in his second term, not least as it was felt that he had let down the entertainment community's many minority constituencies (ethnic, gender, sexual). For instance, the Hollywood Women's Political Committee (HWPC) formed by Barbara Streisand, Jane Fonda, Lily Tomlin and Paula Weinstein in 1984, which was run by a seasoned political activist Marge Tabankin and had access to funding from its wealthy constituency, could not compete with the special interest groups when Clinton signed the Welfare Repeal Bill. When the Democratic National Committee increased the HWPC 1997 gala's ticket prices to US$2,500, Tabankin decided to fold the political action committee for good. For further details, see Dickenson 2006 and Wheeler 2012.

3 Thatcher had been given the epithet of 'the Iron Lady' by the Soviet Union in 1976 due to her aggressive anti-communist rhetoric.

4 Earlier in the 1987 general election, the film director Hugh Hudson made *Kinnock: The Movie*, a Labour Party PEB which focused directly on Neil Kinnock's political leadership and finished with a call to 'Vote Kinnock' rather than 'Vote Labour'.

5 When performing their hit 'Tubthumping' at the 1998 Brits, due to New Labour's failure to support the 1996 Liverpool dockworkers' strike, Chumbawumba included the lyric 'New Labour sold out the dockers, just like they'll sell out the rest of us.'

6 Shortly after the 1997 election, the Blair government appointed Alan McGee to sit on a task force for creativity and young people. The Creation Records' boss objected to the plan for young musicians to be forced to find work. This created a dispute with fellow Blair supporter Mick Hucknall, lead singer of the band Simply Red, who accused McGee of shallowness. Conversely, McGee responded that Hucknall was a sycophant who 'had his tongue so far up Tony Blair's arse . . . because he wanted to receive an OBE'!

7 The film was directed by Jesse Dylan, son of Bob.

8 There have been several American CP2s who have sided with the Republicans, particularly in 'red' states where country singers such as Garth Brooks have been popular among GOP candidates. Hollywood

has had its share of supporters of both George H.W. Bush and George W. Bush, including Bruce Willis, Kelsey Grammer and Sylvester Stallone.

Chapter 4 Celebrity Politicians as the Stars of Modern Election Campaigns

1 Paul M. Green suggests that Obama beat McCain by a whisker except among one group of US voters – young voters, where he dominated at a rate of two to one (interview with the author 1.8.11).
2 The US actor Tim Daly (*Diner*, *The Sopranos)* commented on the 2008 party conventions, 'the contrast that was really stark was how it was like going to the twenty-first century with the Democratic convention and with the Republicans it was akin to the nineteenth century.'
3 As Green notes, 'it is a myth that Obama received all his money from US$20 contributors or from guys in the street with paper coffee cups saving their quarters. The money raised through MyBo was only a small percentage of the overall campaign funds' (interview with the author 1.8.11).
4 Rachel Gibson et al. contend that while the UK parties' employment of information technologies did not directly replicate the practices within US campaign politics, the British parties did extensively integrate the internet into their political marketing and advertising practices. For further details, see Gibson, Williamson and Ward (2010).
5 Elsewhere, Ivor Gaber noted that the use of Twitter, Blackberry and iPhones proved to be instrumental in reshaping the orchestration of the media's coverage of the campaign. He comments that this led to the demise of the press conference and press releases. See Gaber (2011: 263).
6 Palin's candidacy was associated with the production of dolls manufactured in her image. Further, Hustler produced a pornographic film entitled *Who's Nailin' Paylin?* (2008) in which a porn star, Lee Ann, played a character called 'Serra Paylin' who was based on the Republican VP running mate.
7 The UK general election's focus on the leaders' celebrity had been predated by the London mayoral election in 2008 between the Conservative candidate Boris Johnson and Labour Party incumbent Ken Livingstone. While Livingstone had a long-standing tradition as a left-wing leader of the Greater London Council (GLC) in the 1980s and as an (originally) independent mayor, Johnson had many of the attributes of a CP1 as a nationally televised figure, journalist and personality politician. According to Johnson's biographer, Sonia Purnell, 'Boris's evident cross-party appeal in London has been built on personality, jokes and cycling . . . His unique personality showed how celebrity can help a Tory candidate rise above politics and win over thousands of Labour supporters' (Purnell 2011). A similar situation occurred in a rematch in May 2012, when Johnson's and Livingstone's personalities and enmities came into greater

focus and Johnson managed to narrowly retain the mayorship, despite a national collapse in the Tory vote at the local level.

Chapter 5 Politicized Celebrities: Agency and Activism

1 Under Street's definitions of a politicized celebrity (CP2), they do not use their fame to become electable. However, for the purposes of this analysis, CP2 behaviour will be inclusive of the phenomenon of celebrities-turned-politicians.
2 American comedians including Robin Williams, Billy Crystal and Whoopi Goldberg established a US version of *Comic Relief*. While this body engages in continuous charitable activities, its events and televised shows are held in a more irregular pattern and are usually shown on the pay-TV station Home Box Office (HBO).
3 Sebastian Coe would later head up the successful bid for the 2012 UK Olympics and hold the chair of the event's organizing committee.
4 Redgrave's anti-Zionist tirade was rebuffed by the American Jewish scriptwriter Paddy Chayefsky who later in the 1978 Oscar ceremony commented, 'I would like to say . . . that I am sick and tired of people exploiting the Academy Awards for the propagation of their own personal propaganda . . . I would like to suggest to Miss Redgrave that her winning the Academy Award is not a pivotal moment in history . . . and a simple "Thank you" would have sufficed.' For further details, see Considine (1994: 342–6).'
5 The anti-war video for 'Boom!' was directed by Michael Moore. System of a Down have also written songs such as 'Holy Mountains' (2005) and 'P.L.U.C.K.' (1998) and have been significant advocates for pressuring the US Senate to officially recognize the Armenian genocide of 1915–23, carried out by the remnants of the Ottoman empire and the succeeding Kemalist nationalists.
6 For further details of the merging of Martin Sheen's real-life activism with his fictional political person, see Collins (2007).
7 A considerable controversy ensued about whether it was Mulcaire, acting on behalf of the *NOTW*, or the voicemail system on Milly Dowler's mobile phone that had deleted the messages.
8 Jeremy Hunt had declared himself on his web site a 'champion' for News Corporation. His position at the DCMS became more problematic when his special advisor, Adam Smith, resigned due to improper conduct in relation to the BSkyB takeover deal.
9 Tom Watson is the co-author of *Dial M for Murdoch* (2012) and controversially used his position in the Parliamentary Media Select Committee to insert in its report that Rupert Murdoch was 'not fit' to run a global media corporation.

Chapter 6 Transnational Celebrity Activism: Advocacy and Diplomacy

1 While Cooper is broadly positive about celebrity interventions in diplomacy, he remains critical of certain defects such as the deflection of public attention away from more serious diplomatic efforts, amateurism, the discrediting of causes and the focus on North-centric rather than southern celebrities. However, his argument is targeted against the prevailing academic 'one-image-fits-all perspective' which he claims has missed the complexity and benefits of celebrity diplomacy (Cooper 2008: 13).

2 Previously, Bono had been vocal in his opposition to the 'Troubles' in Northern Ireland and wrote the song 'Sunday Bloody Sunday' (1983). U2 would also record 'Pride (In the Name of Love)' (1984) in honour of Martin Luther King.

3 In 2003, the UN Secretary-General issued the first-ever 'Guidelines for the Designation of Goodwill Ambassadors and Messengers of Peace' to specify the conditions of services and termination of contracts with celebrity diplomats. This marked a desire to control the escalating use of stars and led to a significant rationalization in goodwill ambassadors, greater quality mechanisms, self-generated funds for travel and finite periods of operation (Fall and Tang 2006: 2).

4 These initiatives have continued to be carried out by the current UN Secretary-General Ban Ki-Moon who visited Hollywood to negotiate for favourable representations of the UN in feature films as part of the Creative Community Outreach Initiative run by Eric Falt, the director of the Outreach Division of the Department of Public Information.

References

Alberoni, F. 1972: 'The powerless elite', in D. McQuail (ed.), *Sociology of Mass Communications*. Harmondsworth: Penguin.

Alexander, J. C. 2010a: *The Performance of Politics: Obama's Victory and the Democratic Study for Power*. Oxford, New York: Oxford University Press.

Alexander, J. C. 2010b: Barack Obama meets celebrity metaphor. *Society* 47(5): 410–18.

Allen, W. 1967: *The Kraft Music Hall: Woody Allen Looks at 1967*. National Broadcasting Corporation.

Alleyne, M. D. 2003: *Global Lies? Propaganda, the UN and the World Order*. Basingstoke: Palgrave Macmillan.

Alleyne, M. D. 2005: The United Nations' celebrity diplomacy. *SAIS Review*, Baltimore: The Johns Hopkins University Press.

Annan, K. 2003: Secretary-General praises celebrity advocates as 'new kind of star', shining light on hardship, injustice, in remarks at UNICEF gala. UN Press Release SG/SM/9049/ICEF/1863, 4 December. www.unis.unvienna.org/unis/pressrels/2003/sgsm9049.html (accessed 12.9.10).

Anstead, N. and Straw, W. (eds) 2009: *The Change We Need: What Britain Can Learn from Obama's Victory*. London: Fabian Society.

Anthony, A. 2004: Acting up: Why Tim Robbins won't be silenced. The *Observer Magazine*, 29 August: 14–17.

Atkins, C. 2009: *Starsuckers*. S2S Productions.

Avlon, J. 2011: A 21st-century statesman. *Newsweek*, 28 February: 16.

Bai, M. 2010: Internet populism buffets politics. In *New York Times* articles selected by the *Observer*, 7 November: 1–4.

Bailey, R. 2011: What took so long? The late arrival of TV debates in the UK General Election of 2010. In D. Wring, R. Mortimore and S. Atkinson (eds), *Political Communication in Britain: The Leaders' Debates, the Campaign and the Media in 2010 General Election*. Basingstoke: Palgrave Macmillan.

Bang, H. P. (ed.) 2003: *Governance as Social and Political Communication*. Manchester: Manchester University Press.

Bang, H. P. 2004: Cultural governance: governing reflexive modernity. *Public Administration* 82(1): 159–90.

Bang, H. P. 2009: 'Yes we can': identity politics and project politics for a late-modern world. *Urban Research & Practice* 2(2): 117–37.

Baum, M. A. 2005: Talking the vote: why presidential candidates hit the talk show circuit. *American Journal of Political Science* 49: 213–34.

Bauman, Z. 2000: *Liquid Modernity*. Cambridge: Polity.

BBC Storyville 2011: American idol: Reagan. Broadcast on BBC4 9.6.11.

Beck, U. 1992: *Risk Society*. London, Thousand Oaks, New Delhi: Sage Publications.

Bennett, J. 2011: Celebrity and politics. *Celebrity Studies: Special Edition on Celebrity and the Transnational* 2(1): 86–7.

Bennis, W. and Nanus, B. 2003: *Leaders: Strategies for Taking Charge*. New York: Harpers Collins Business Essentials.

Bergman Rosamond, A. 2011: The cosmopolitan–communitarian divide and celebrity anti-war activism. In L. Tsaliki, A. Huliaras and C. A. Frangonikolopoulos (eds), *Transnational Celebrity Activism in Global Politics: Changing the World?* Bristol: Intellect.

Bernstein, M. H. (ed.) 2010: *Michael Moore: Filmmaker, Newsmaker, Cultural Icon*. Ann Arbor: University of Michigan Press.

Biskind, P. 2010: *Star: How Warren Beatty Seduced America*. London, New York, Sydney, Toronto: Simon and Schuster.

Blair, T. 2010: *A Journey*. London: Hutchinson.

Boorstin, D. 1971: *The Image: A Guide to Pseudo-Events in America*. New York: Atheneum.

Boulton, A. and Roberts, T. C. 2011: The election debates: Sky News' perspectives on their genesis and impact on media coverage. In D. Wring, R. Mortimore and S. Atkinson (eds), *Political Communication in Britain: The Leaders' Debates, the Campaign and the Media in the 2010 General Election*. Basingstoke: Palgrave Macmillan.

Bourdieu, P. 1991: *Language and Symbolic Power*. Cambridge, MA: Harvard University Press.

Boykoff, M. and Goodman, M. 2009: Conspicuous redemption? Reflections on the promises and perils of the 'celebritization' of climate change. *Geoforum* 40(3): 395–406.

Braudy, L. 1997: *The Frenzy of Renown: Fame and Its History*. New York: Vintage Books.

Bretherton, L. 2011: *Defending Populism against the Tea Party Movement*, ABC Religion and Ethics. www.abc.net.au/religion/articles/2011/01/12/3111126.htm (accessed 2.2.11).

Brietbart, A. 2008: Say it ain't So, O. *Real Clear Politics*, 8 Sept. www.realclearpolitics.com/articles/2008/09/Say_it_aint_so_o.html (accessed 7.3.2013)

Brockington, D. 2009: *Celebrity and the Environment: Fame, Wealth and Power in Conservation*. London and New York: Zed Books.

Brockington, D. 2011: A history of celebrity and development. Unpublished paper. University of Manchester.

Brown, E. 1966: Campaign commercial: man versus actor. National Museum of Television and Radio, Beverly Hills, CA.

Brownstein, R. 1990: *The Power and the Glitter: The Hollywood–Washington Connection*. New York: Vintage Press.

Brownstein, R. 2000: Interview. In Kenneth Bowser, *Hollywood DC: A Tale of Two Cities*. Fremantle Corporation.

Brownstein, R. 2011: The NJ 20: The most politically effective celebrities of all time. *National Journal*, 28 April. http://nationaljournal.com/magazine/the-nj-20-the-most-politically-effective-celebrities-of-all-time-20110428?page=1 (accessed 19.1.13).

Bruck, C. 2004: *When Hollywood had a King: The Reign of Lew Wasserman, who Leveraged Talent into Power and Influence*. New York: Random House.

Buerk, M. 2011: Moral maze: celebrity activism. British Broadcasting Corporation, 20 April. www.bbc.co.uk/iplayer/episode/b010drkx/Moral_Maze_Celebrity_Activism (accessed 7.2.11).

Calcutt, A. 2005: *Celebrity Politics and the Politics of Celebrity*. Unpublished paper presented at the annual conference of the Association for Journalism Education, University of Westminster, London, 9 September.

Cashmore, E. 2006: *Celebrity/Culture*. London and New York: Routledge.

CBS News 2009: Sarandon got death threats over Iraq, 11 February www.cbsnews.com/2100-207_162-1561644.html (accessed 7.3.2011).

CBS Reports 1967: What about Ronald Reagan? CBS Reports take a look at Ronald Reagan's first run for president in this 1967 report. www.cbsnews.com/video/watch/?id=2996948n (accessed 12.9.11).

Ceplair, L. and Englund. S. 2003: *The Inquisition in Hollywood: Politics in the Film Community, 1930–60*. Urbana and Chicago: University of Illinois Press.

Cheadle, D. and Prendergast, J. 2007: *Not On Our Watch: The Mission to End Genocide in Darfur and Beyond*. New York: Hyperion.

Coburn, M. L. 2008: Oprah unbound. *Chicago Magazine* 22 Dec. www.chicagomag.com/Chicago-Magazine/December 2008/Oprah-Unbound (accessed 7.3.13)

Cogburn, D. L. and Espinoza-Vasquez, F. K. 2011: From networked nominee to networked nation: examining the impact of Web 2.0 and social media on political participation and civic engagement in the 2008 Obama campaign. *Journal of Political Marketing* 10(1–2): 189–213.

Coleman, S. 2007: *Beyond the West(minster) Wing: The Depiction of British Politicians and Politics Beyond Soaps*. Research Report, Institute of Communications Studies, University of Leeds.

Collins, S. 2007: Traversing authenticities: *The West Wing* president and the activist Sheen. In K. Riegart (ed.), *Politicotainment: Television's Take on the Real*. New York, Washington DC/Baltimore, Bern, Frankfurt am Main, Berlin, Brussels, Vienna, Oxford: Peter Lang, pp. 181–211.

Columbia Broadcasting System (CBS) Reports. 1967: *What About Ronald Reagan?* CBS System, 12 December.

Considine, S. 1994: *Mad as Hell: The Life and Work of Paddy Chayefsky*. New York: Random House.

Cooper, A. F. 2008: *Celebrity Diplomacy*. Boulder, London: Paradigm Publishers.

Cooper, A. F. 2009: Celebrity diplomacy: The effectiveness and value of celebrity diplomacy. An edited transcript of a Panel Discussion at the USC Center on Public Diplomacy at the Annenberg School, Norman Lear Center, 21 April.

Corner, J. 2000: Mediated persona and political culture: dimensions of structure and process. *European Journal of Cultural Studies* 3(3): 389–405.

Corner, J. 2003: Mediated persona and political culture. In J. Corner and D. Pels (eds), *The Media and the Restyling of Politics*. London, Thousand Oaks, New Delhi: Sage Publications.

Corner, J. and Pels, D. 2003: Introduction: The restyling of politics. In J. Corner and D. Pels (eds), *Media and the Restyling of Politics: Consumerism, Celebrity and Cynicism*. London, Thousand Oaks, New Delhi: Sage Publications.

Couldry, N. and Markham, T. 2007: Celebrity Culture and Public Connection: Bridge or Chasm? *International Journal of Cultural Studies* 10: 403–21.

Critchlow, D. T. and Raymond, E. 2009: *Hollywood and Politics: A Sourcebook*. New York and London: Routledge Taylor & Francis Group.

Crouch, C. 2004: *Post-Democracy*. Cambridge: Polity.

Dahlgren, P. 2009: *Media and Political Engagement: Citizens, Communication and Democracy*. Cambridge: Cambridge University Press.

Dale, I. 2010: This was meant to be the internet election – so what happened? The *Daily Telegraph*, 27 April. www.telegraph.co.uk/news/election-2010/7640143/General-Election-2010-This-was-meant-to-be-the-internet-election.-So-what-happened.html (accessed 1.10.11).

Darnton, A. and Kirk, M. 2011: *Finding Frames: New Ways to Engage the UK Public in Global Poverty*. London: Oxfam and the Department of International Development.

Davidson, A. 2012: Vanessa Redgrave. *The Devils: DVD Booklet*. London: British Film Institute.

Davenport, L. 2009: *Jazz Diplomacy Promoting America in the Cold War Era*. Jackson Mississippi: University Press of Mississippi.

Davis, A. 2010a: *Political Communication and Social Theory*. London and New York: Routledge Taylor & Francis.

Davis, A. 2010b: Media and politics. In J. Curran (ed.), *Media and Society*. London and New York: Bloomsbury Academic.

de Tocqueville, A. 1830: *Democracy in America*. Cambridge: Sever and Francis, trans. Henry Reeve. http://ebooks.adelaide.edu.au/t/tocqueville/alexis/democracy/ (accessed 7.3.2013).

Devereaux, R. 2012: George Clooney arrested in planned protest at Sudanese embassy. Actor intended to be arrested in Washington, DC demonstration to plea for action against human rights abuses in Sudan. The *Guardian*, 16 March. www.guardian.co.uk/world/2012/mar/16/george-clooney-arrested-sudanese-embassy (accessed 17.3.12).

Dickenson, B. 2003: Tongues untied: art, politics and business collide. *Bright Lights Film Journal* 40. www.brightlightsfilm.com/40/oscars.htm (accessed 12.9.10).

Dickenson, B. 2006: *Hollywood's New Radicalism: War, Globalisation and the Movies from Reagan to George W. Bush*. London: I.B. Tauris.

Dideon, J. 1998: Vacant fervor. In C. Sylvester (ed.), *The Grove Book of Hollywood*. New York: Grove Press.

Dieter, H. and Kumar, R. 2008: The downside of celebrity diplomacy: the neglected complexity of development. *Global Governance* 14(3): 259–64.

Doggett, P. 2007: *There's a Riot Going On: Revolutionaries, Rock Stars and the Rise and Fall of the '60s*. Edinburgh, New York, Melbourne: Canongate.

Dowd, M. 1999: Liberties: Will you, Warren? *New York Times*, 15 August: 15.

Drake, P. and Higgins, M. 2006: I'm a celebrity, get me into politics: The political celebrity and the celebrity politician. In S. Holmes and S. Redmond (eds), *Framing Celebrity: New Directions in Celebrity Culture*. London and New York: Routledge.

Drake, P. and Higgins, M. 2012: Lights, camera, election: celebrity performance and the 2010 UK General Election leadership debates, *British Journal of Politics and International Relations* 14(3): 375–91.

Drake, P. and Miah, A. 2010: The cultural politics of celebrity. *Cultural Politics: An International Journal* 6(1): 49–64.

Draper, R. 2008: The making (and remaking) of the candidate: when a campaign can't settle on a central narrative, does it imperil its protagonist. *New York Times Magazine*, 26 October: 52.

Dreyfuss, R. 2000: Interview. In K. Bowser, *Hollywood DC: A Tale of Two Cities*. Freemantle Corporation.

Drezner, D. W. 2007: Foreign policy goes glam. *National Interest online* 11 January. www.nationalinterest.org/Article.aspx?id=16012 (accessed 17.4.10).

Dunne, P. 1980: *Take Two: A Life on Movies and Politics*. New York, St Louis, San Francisco, Mexico, Toronto, Dusseldorf: McGraw-Hill.

Edwards, B. 2008: Green Party: Celebrity politics. *Liberation*. http://liberation.typepad.com/liberation/2008/10/green-party-cel.html (accessed 12.9.10).

Elmhirst, S. 2012: Matt Damon: actor and teachers' campaigner. *New Statesman*, 9 January: 27.

Evans, J. 2005: Celebrity, media and history. In J. Evans and D. Hesmondhalgh (eds), *Understanding Media Celebrity*. Maidenhead: Open University Press/McGraw Hill Education.

Evans, J. and Hesmondhalgh, D. (eds) 2005: *Understanding Media Celebrity*. Maidenhead: Open University Press/McGraw Hill Education.

Evans, T. W. 2008: *The Education of Ronald Reagan: The General Electric Years and the Untold Story of His Conversion to Conservatism*. Columbia Studies in Contemporary American History. New York: Columbia University Press.

Fall, P. L. and Tang, G. 2006: *Goodwill Ambassadors in the United Nations System*. UN Joint Inspection Unit, Geneva.

Fletcher, M. 2010: Barack Obama: Wire fan. In R. Alvarez, *The Wire: Truth be Told*. Edinburgh, London, New York, Melbourne: Canongate, pp. 37–41.

Franklin, B. 2004: *Packaging Politics: Political Communication in Britain's Media Democracy*, 2nd edn. London: Arnold.

Freedland, J. 2008: From *West Wing* to the real thing. The *Guardian*, 21 February 2008. www.guardian.co.uk/world/feb/21/barackobama.uselections2008/ (accessed 26.2.11).

Gaber, I. 2011: The transformation of political campaign reporting: the 2010 UK election, revolution or evolution. In D. Wring, R. Mortimore and S. Atkinson (eds), *Political Communication in Britain: The Leaders' Debates, the Campaign and the Media in the 2010 General Election*. Basingstoke: Palgrave Macmillan.

Gabler, N. 1998: *Life: The Movie: How Entertainment Conquered Reality*. New York: Alfred A. Knopf.

Gallagher, N. 1996: '1996 Brit Awards'. Quoted in Holz, K. (2007), *Power to the People*. Munich: GRIN Verlag, p. 8.

Garthwaite, C. and Moore, T. 2008: The role of celebrity endorsements in politics: Oprah, Obama, and the 2008 Democratic Primary. http://econserver.umd.edu/~garthwaite/celebrityendorsements_garthwaitemoore.pdf (accessed 12.9.10).

Geldof, B. 2005: Interview. In *Live Aid Rockin' all over the World*. BBC Television.

Gibson, R. K. 2010: Parties, social media and the rise of 'citizen-initiated' campaigning. Paper presented at the American Political Studies Association, 1 September.

Gibson, R. K., Williamson, A. and Ward, S. (ed.) 2010: *The Internet and the 2010 Election: Putting the Small p Back into Politics*. London: Hansard Society.

Giddens, A. 1991: *The Consequence of Modernity*. Stanford, CA: Stanford University Press.

Gimson, A. 2010: Leaders' TV debate: punches flew as the job interview turned nasty. The *Daily Telegraph*, 22 April.

Gottfried, M. 1994: *Nobody's Fool: The Lives of Danny Kaye*. New York, London, Toronto, Sydney, Tokyo, Singapore: Simon and Schuster.

Gray, M. 2005: Interview. In *Live Aid Rockin' all over the World*. BBC Television.

Green, P. M. 2011: Interview with the author. Roosevelt University, Chicago, 1 August.

Green, P. M. and Holli, M. G. 1991: *Restoration 1989: Chicago Elects a New Daley*. Chicago: Lyceum Books.

Greenberg, D. 2011: Beyond the bully pulpit: Theodore Roosevelt and the origins of presidential spin. Paper presented at the Institute for the Study of Americas History seminar, University of London, 5 December.

Habermas, J. 1992: *The Structural Transformation of the Public Sphere*. New York: Polity.

Harris, J. 2003: *The Last Party: Britpop, Blair and the Demise of English Rock*. London: Harper Perennial.

Harris, M. 2011: How to train your celebrity. *Fast Company*. July/August: 82–5.

Harrison, M. 2010. The X-Factor election: on the air. In D. Kavanagh and P. Cowley (eds), *The British General Election of 2010*. Basingstoke: Palgrave Macmillan.

Hatch, S. 1960: Religion of Celebrity. *New Left Review* 1(3): 64–5.

Hay, C. 2007: *Why We Hate Politics*. Cambridge: Polity.

Heilemann, J. and Halperin, M. 2010. *Race of a Lifetime: How Obama Won the White House*. New York: Viking Penguin.

Herman, L. 2003: Bestowing knighthood: the visual aspects of Bill Clinton's Camelot legacy. In P. C. Rollins and J. E. O'Connor (eds), *Hollywood's White House: The American Presidency in Film and History*. Kentucky: The University of Kentucky Press.

Hess, S. 2000: Political dynasties: an American tradition. www.tompaine.com (accessed 26.2.10).

Higgins, M. 2008: *Media and Their Publics*. Maidenhead and New York: McGraw-Hill/Open University Press.

HISC (Congress of the United States, House of Representatives Committee on Internal Security) 1972: Letter to Hon. Richard G. Kleindeinst, Attorney General of the United States, Department of Justice, Washington, DC, August 10. In D. Critchlow and E. Raymond (eds), *Hollywood and Politics: A Sourcebook*. New York and London: Routledge, pp. 173–4.

Hollingshead, I. 2011: The Gurkhas in Aldershot: Little Nepal. The *Daily Telegraph*, 21 February. www.telegraph.co.uk/news/uknews/defence/8339467/The-Gurkhas-in-Aldershot-Little-Nepal.html (accessed 9.2.12).

Holmes, S. 2005: 'Starring . . . Dyer?': Re-visiting star studies and contemporary celebrity culture. *Westminster Papers in Communication and Culture* 2(2): 2–61.

Holmes, S. and Redmond, S. (eds) 2006: *Framing Celebrity: New Directions in Celebrity Culture*. London and New York: Routledge.

Holtz-Bacha, C. 2003: The private life of politicians: new image-making strategies and how they have changed relations between politicians and the press in Germany. *Political Communications Report: International Communication Association & American Political Science Association* 13(2). www.ou.edu/policom/1302_2003_spring/commentary.htm (accessed 26.2.11).

Hopper, H. 1965: Interview with Ronald Reagan. Hedda Hopper Special Collection, Academy of Motion Picture Library, Beverly Hills, CA, 6 May.

Howe, G. 1990: House of Commons resignation speech. London: Hansard. 13 November.

Huddart, S. 2005 (2002): *Do We Need Another Hero? Understanding Celebrities' Roles in Advancing Social Causes*. Montreal, Canada: McGill University.

Huliaris, A. and Tzifakis, N. 2011: Bringing the individuals back in? Celebrities as transnational activists. In L. Tsaliki, A. Huliaras and C. A. Frangonikolopoulos (eds), *Transnational Celebrity Activism in Global Politics: Changing the World?* Bristol: Intellect.

Hyde, M. 2009: *Celebrity: How Entertainers Took Over the World and Why We Need an Exit Strategy*. London: Harvill Secker.

Inglis, F. 2010: *A Short History of Celebrity*. Princeton and Oxford: Princeton University Press.

Inthorn, S. and Street, J. 2011: Simon Cowell for Prime Minister. *Media, Culture and Society* 33(3): 1–11.

IPOS MORI Social Research 2010: General election 2010: the leaders' debates: the worm's final verdict – lessons to be learned. www.ipos-mori.com/Assets/Docs/News/ipos-mori-public-reaction-to-leaders-debate.pdf. (accessed 4.8.10).

Izzard, E. 2011: I will run for mayor, MP and MEP. *BBC News*, 28 September. www.bbc.co.uk/news/entertainment-arts-15088430 (accessed 30.3.12).

Jackson, N. 2008: *Bono's Politics: The Future of Celebrity Political Activism*. Saarbrucken: VDM Verlag.

Johnson, T. 2012: Mitt's trial by fire: celebrity associations haven't helped Romney. *Variety*, 2 June. www.variety.com/article/VR1118054910 (accessed 12.6.12).

Jones, S. 2008: Clegg tots up sex encounters in *GQ* interview. The *Guardian*, 1 April: 5.

Junod, T. 2007: Angelina Jolie dies for our sins. *Esquire*, 24 July. www.esquire.com/women/women-we-love/Jolie0707 (accessed 17.4.10).

Kapoor, I. 2011: Humanitarian heroes? Paper presented at the annual meeting of the International Studies Association Annual Conference 'Global Governance: Political Authority in Transition', Le Centre

Sheraton Montreal Hotel. Montreal, Quebec, Canada, 16 March. www.allacademic.com/meta/p501500_index.html (accessed 2.3.12).

Kapoor, I. 2012: *Celebrity Humanitarianism: The Ideology of Global Charity*. London and New York: Routledge.

Kavanagh, D. and Cowley, P. 2010: *The British General Election of 2010*. Basingstoke: Palgrave Macmillan.

Keane, J. 2002: *Whatever Happened to Democracy?* London: IPPR.

Keane, J. 2003: *Global Civil Society?* Cambridge: Cambridge University Press.

Keane, J. 2009a: *The Life and Death of Democracy*. New York: Simon and Schuster.

Keane, J. 2009b: Monitory democracy and media-saturated societies. *Griffith Review, Edition 24: Participation Society*. www.griffithreview.com/edition-24-participation-society/222-essay/657.html (accessed 20.11.10).

Kellner, D. 2005: *Media Spectacle and the Crisis of Democracy*. Boulder, CO: Paradigm Press.

Kellner, D. 2009: Barack Obama and celebrity spectacle. *International Journal of Communication* 3(1): 715–41.

Kellner, D. 2010a: Celebrity diplomacy, spectacle and Barack Obama. *Celebrity Studies* 1(1): 121–3.

Kellner, D. 2010b: *The Cinema Wars: Hollywood Film and Politics in the Bush–Cheney Era*. Malden, Oxford, Chichester: Wiley-Blackwell.

Kellner, D. 2010c: Michael Moore and the aesthetics and politics of contemporary documentary film. In M. H. Bernstein (ed.), *Michael Moore: Filmmaker, Newsmaker, Cultural Icon*. Ann Arbor: University of Michigan Press, pp. 79–104.

Kenski, K., Hardy, B. W. and Jamieson, K. H. 2010: *The Obama Victory: How Media, Money and Message Shaped The 2008 Election*. Oxford, New York: Oxford University Press.

Keyishian, H. 2011: The 'confidence' president: Franklin D. Roosevelt in film. In I. W. Morgan (ed.), *Presidents in the Movies: American History and Politics on Screen*. New York: Palgrave Macmillan.

Kuhn, R. 2007: *Politics and the Media in Britain*. Basingstoke: Palgrave Macmillan.

Kuhn, R. 2010: Les médias, c'est moi: Presidential media management in Sarkozy's France. *French Politics* 8: 355–76.

Lai Stirland, S. 2008: Obama's secret weapons: internet, databases and psychology. *Wired Magazine*, 29 October. www.wired.com/threatlevel/2008/10/obamas-secret-w/ (accessed 20.11.10).

Lash, S. 1990: *The Sociology of Postmodernism*. London: Routledge.

Lees-Marshment, J. 2008: *Political Marketing and British Political Parties: The Party's Just Begun*, 2nd edn. Manchester: Manchester University Press.

Levinson, B. 2009a: *Poliwood: The Collision and Collusion between Politics, Hollywood and Media*. Screen Media Films.

Levinson, B. 2009b: Participant. *Poliwood: When Politics Meets Culture.* Moderator: Robin Bronk, 29 October. National Museum of Television and Radio, New York, NY.

Life Magazine 1944: Political potpourri: Broadway and Hollywood contribute skits and slapstick to enliven Democratic campaign, 23 October: 32–3. http://books.google.co.uk/books?id=BkIEAAAAMBAJ&printsec=frontcover&source=gbs_ge_summary_r&cad=O#v=onepage&q&f=false (accessed 7.3.2013).

Life Magazine 1968: The stars leap into politics: actor Paul Newman showing support for presidential candidate Eugene McCarthy, 10 May: 52.

Ling, J. 1984: Interview with Mr Jack Ling conducted by Judith Spiegelman at UNICEF HQ, 5 June. www.unicef.org/thailand/UNICEF_in_Thailand_Fifty_Years.pdf (accessed 17.4.10).

Long, R. E. (ed.) 2006: *Liv Ullman: Interviews.* Jackson: University of Mississippi Press.

Louw, P. E. 2005: *The Media and Political Process.* London, Thousand Oaks, New Delhi: Sage Publications.

Lowenthal, L. 1944: The triumph of mass idols. In *Literature, Popular Culture and Society.* Palo Alto, CA: Pacific Books.

Lynskey, D. 2010: *33 Revolutions per Minute: A History of Protest Songs.* London: Faber and Faber.

Lyons, J. 2012: Livid Mick Jagger snubs David Cameron after Tory 'stitch up'. The *Daily Mirror,* 25 January. www.mirror.co.uk/news/politics/2012/01/25/livid-mick-jagger-snubs-david-cameron-after-tory-stitch-up-115875-23718836/#ixzz1kbhysmuY (accessed 25.1.12).

Macintyre, B. 2000: Clinton: doing it his way to the last note. *The Times,* 12 August: 18.

Major, J. 2011: What took so long? The late arrival of TV debates in the UK General Election of 2010. Quoted by R. Bailey in D. Wring, R. Mortimore and S. Atkinson (eds), *Political Communication in Britain: The Leaders' Debates, the Campaign and the Media in the 2010 General Election.* Basingstoke: Palgrave Macmillan.

Marsh, D., 't Hart, P. and Tindall, K. 2010: Celebrity politics: the politics of the late modernity? *Political Studies Review* 8(3): 322–40.

Marshall, P. D. 1997. *Celebrity and Power: Fame in Contemporary Culture.* Minneapolis: University of Minnesota.

Martins, H. 1964: The celebrity syndrome. *New Left Review* I(26): 74–7.

May, L. 2002 (2000): *The Big Tomorrow: Hollywood and the Politics of the American Way.* Chicago and London: University of Chicago Press.

McDonald, P. 2008: The star system: production of Hollywood stardom in the post-studio era. In P. McDonald and J. Wasko (eds), *The Contemporary Hollywood Film Industry.* Malden, MA, Oxford, Carlton Victoria: Blackwell Publishing.

McDougal, D. 1998: *The Last Mogul: Lew Wasserman, MCA, and the Hidden History of Hollywood.* New York: Crown Publishers.

McDougall, D. 2006: Do celebrities help NGOs? The *Guardian*, 8 December. www.guardian.co.uk/world/2006/dec/08/outlook.development (accessed 2.3.11).

McKernan, B. 2011: Politics and celebrity: a sociological understanding. *Sociology Compass* 5(3): 190–202.

Medavoy, M. with Young, J. 2002: *You're Only as Good as Your Next One.* New York, London, Toronto, Sydney, Singapore: Atria Books.

Meyer, D. and Gamson, J. 1995: The challenge of cultural elites: celebrities and social movements. *Sociological Inquiry* 65(2): 181–206.

Meyer, T. with Hinchman, L. 2002: *Media Democracy: How the Media Colonize Politics.* Cambridge, UK: Polity.

Mills, C. W. 1956: *The Power Elite.* New York: Oxford University Press.

Mitchell, G. 1998: *Tricky Dick and the Pink Lady: Richard Nixon vs. Helen Gahagan Douglas – Sexual Politics and the Red Scare, 1950.* New York: Random House.

Monbiot, G. 2005: Bards of the powerful: Far from challenging G8's role in African poverty, Geldof and Bono are giving legitimacy to those responsible. The *Guardian*, 21 June. www.guardian.co.uk/politics/2005/jun/21/development.g8 (accessed 17.4.11).

Morgan, S. 2010: Historicising celebrity. *Celebrity Studies* 1(3): 366–8.

Morini, M. 2011: The 'Celebrity Obama' strategy: the 2008 presidential campaign's attack ads. *International Journal of Humanities and Social Science* 1(12): 33–42.

Mullin, C. 2010: *Decline and Fall: Diaries 2005–2010.* London: Profile Books.

Naughton, P. 1992: Sophie Loren becomes goodwill ambassador for refugees. *Reuters*, 18 November.

Neve, B. 2011: 'The 'Picture Man': cinematic strife of Theodore Roosevelt. In I.W. Morgan (ed.), *Presidents in the Movies: American History and Politics on Screen.* New York: Palgrave Macmillan.

Neveu, E. 2005: Politicians without politics, a polity without citizens: the politics of the chat show in contemporary France. *Modern and Contemporary France* 13: 323–35.

Newman, B. (ed.) 1999: *The Handbook of Political Marketing.* London, Thousand Oaks, New Delhi: Sage Publications.

Newman, B. 2011: Interview with the author. De Paul University, Chicago. 2 August.

Newman. N. 2010: *#UKelection2010, mainstream media and the role of the internet: how social and digital media affected the business of politics and journalism.* Oxford: Reuters Institute for the Study of Journalism.

Nye, J. 2004: *Soft Power: The Means to Success in World Politics.* New York: Public Affairs.

Orth, M. 1972: Will they snort coke in the White House? *The Village Voice.*

XVII(17), April 27. http://blogs.villagevoice.com/runninscared/2011/02/warren_beatty_s.php (accessed on 18.3.11).

Palin, S. 2008: Palin's speech at the Republican National Convention: The following is a transcript of Gov. Sarah Palin's speech at the Republican National Convention in St Paul, as provided by CQ Transcriptions. *New York Times*, 3 September 2008. http://elections.nytimes.com/2008/president/conventions/videos/transcripts/20080903_PALIN_SPEECH.html (accessed 12.9.11).

Parker, F. 1972: *FTA: The Show the Pentagon Couldn't Stop*. Stoney Road Films.

Parry, K. and Richardson, K. 2011: Political imagery in the British general election of 2010: The curious case of 'Nick Clegg'. *British Journal of Politics and International Relations* 13(4): 474–89.

Parsons, T. 2008: Toff Cam's just a flash in the pan. The *Daily Mirror*, 7 January. www.mirror.co.uk/news/top-stories/2008/01/07/toff-cam-s-just-a-flash-in-the-pan-115875-20277256/ (accessed 22.10.11).

Paterson, T. 2010: The iron frau: Angela Merkel. The *Independent*, 12 April. www.independent.co.uk/news/world/europe/the-iron-frau-angela-merkel-1941814.html (accessed 12.9.11).

Perkins, A. 2010: The celebrity debasement of politics. The *Guardian*, 15 February. www.guardian.co.uk/commentisfree/2010/feb/15/gordon-brown-piers-morgan (accessed 1.10.11).

Philips, F. 2010: Prime Minister Gordon Brown opens his heart to Fiona Phillips on the woman he says was the biggest influence in his life – his mother Bunty. The *Daily Mirror*, 19 February. www.mirror.co.uk/news/top-stories/2010/02/19/pm-gordon-brown-opens-his-heart-to-fiona-phillips-on-the-woman-he-says-was-the-biggest-influence-in-his-life-my-mother-115875-22053833/ (accessed 1.11.11).

Pidd, H. 2012: George Galloway shows his star power in Bradford West: Not many middle-aged politicians can draw dozens of fans to a late night election count, but Galloway is far from normal. The *Guardian*, 30 March. www.guardian.co.uk/politics/2012/mar/30/george-galloway-star-power-bradford?newsfeed=true (accessed 30.3.12).

Pleios, G. 2011: Fame and symbolic value in celebrity activism and diplomacy. In L. Tsaliki, A. Huliaras and C. A. Frangonikolopoulos (eds), *Transnational Celebrity Activism in Global Politics: Changing the World?* Bristol: Intellect.

Plouffe, D. 2009: *The Audacity to Win: How Obama Won and How We Can Beat the Party of Limbaugh, Beck and Palin*. London: Penguin.

Postman, N. 1987: *Amusing Ourselves to Death: Public Discourse in the Age of Show Business*. London: Methuen.

Purdum, T. S. 2011: From that day forth. *Vanity Fair*, February. www.vanityfair.com/society/features/2011/02/kennedy-201102 (accessed 25.6.11).

Purnell, S. 2011: *Just Boris: The Irresistible Rise of a Political Celebrity*. London: Aurum Press.

Putnam, R. D. 1995: Bowling alone: America's declining social capital. *Journal of Democracy* 6(1): 65–78.

Putnam, R. D. 2000: *Bowling Alone*. New York: Simon and Schuster.

Rabidoux, G. R. 2009: *Hollywood Politicos, Then and Now: Who They Are, What They Want, Why It Matters*. Lanham, Boulder, New York, Toronto, Plymouth, UK: University Press of America.

Rajan, A. 2011: True colours? Is Blue Labour the way forward for the Left? The *Independent*, 6 June. www.independent.co.uk/news/uk/politics/true-colours-is-blue-labour-the-way-forward-for-the-left-2293425.html (accessed 10.6.11).

Redmond, S. 2010: Avatar Obama in the age of liquid celebrity. *Celebrity Studies* 1(1): 81–95.

Redmond, S. and Holmes, S. 2008: *Stardom and Celebrity: A Reader*. London, Thousand Oaks, New Delhi: Sage Publications.

Renshon, S. A. 2008: Psychological reflections on Barack Obama and John McCain: assessing the contours of a new presidential administration. *Political Science Quarterly* 123(3): 391–432.

Repo, J. and Yrjölä, R. 2011: The gender politics of celebrity humanitarianism in Africa. *International Feminist Journal of Politics* 13(1): 44–62.

Richardson, K., Parry, K. and Corner, J. 2011: Genre and the mediation of election politics. In D. Wring, R. Mortimore and S. Atkinson (eds), *Political Communication in Britain: The Leaders' Debates, the Campaign and the Media in the 2010 General Election*. Basingstoke: Palgrave Macmillan.

Richey, L. A. and Ponte, S. 2011: *Brand Aid: Shopping Well to Save the World*. Minneapolis, London: University of Minnesota Press.

Robinson, N. 2012: Bradford – An extraordinary one-off. *BBC News*, 30 March www.bbc.co.uk/news/uk-politics-17559759 (accessed 30.3.12).

Robinson, J. and Teather, D. 2010: Cameron – the PR years. The *Guardian*, 20 February. www.guardian.co.uk/politics/2010/feb/20/david-cameron-the-pr-years (accessed 7.10.11).

Rojek, C. 2001: *Celebrity*. London: Reaktion Books.

Ross, S. J. (ed.) 2002: *Movies and American Society: Blackwell Readers in American Social and Cultural History*. Oxford, Malden: Blackwell Publishers.

Ross, S. J. 2011: *Hollywood Left and Right: How Movie Stars Shaped American Politics*. Oxford, New York: Oxford University Press.

Roth, P. 2005: *The Plot Against America*. London: Vintage Books.

Sanders, K. 2009: *Communicating Politics in the Twenty-First Century*: Basingstoke: Palgrave Macmillan.

Scammell, M. 1995: *Designer Politics: How Elections are Won*. London: Macmillan.

Schama, S. 2008: *The American Future: A History*. British Broadcasting Corporation (BBC).

Schroeder, A. 2004: *Celebrity in Chief: How Show Business Took Over the White House*. Boulder, CO and Oxford: Westview Press.

Scott, I. 2000: *American Politics in Hollywood Film*. Edinburgh: Edinburgh University Press.

Scott, I. 2011a: *American Politics in Hollywood Film*, 2nd edn. Edinburgh: Edinburgh University Press.

Scott, I. 2011b: Transition: the making of screen presidents. In I. W. Morgan (ed.), *Presidents in the Movies: American History and Politics on Screen*. New York: Palgrave Macmillan.

Scott, J. 2007: The long run: in 2000, a streetwise veteran schooled a bold young Obama. *New York Times*, 9 September. www.nytimes.com/2007/09/09/us/politics/09obama.html?pagewanted=all (accessed 19.1.13).

Selter, B. 2008: Following the script: Obama, McCain and the 'West Wing'. *New York Times*, 30 October. www.nytimes.com/2008/10/30/arts/television/30wing.html? (accessed 26.2.11).

Seymour-Ure, C. 2003: *Prime Ministers and the Media*. Oxford: Blackwell Publishers.

Sherrill, M. 1998: The hardest working man in show business: the president as celebrity. *Esquire*, April: 74.

Shiel, M. 2007: Hollywood, the New Left and *FTA*. In F. Krutnik et al. (eds), *'UnAmerican' Hollywood: Politics and Film in the Blacklist Era*. New Brunswick, NJ and London: Rutgers University Press.

Sinatra, F. 1944: Quoted in 'Sinatra's Politics.' *The Pop History Dig: Exploring the History and Power of Popular Culture*. www.pophistorydig.com/?p=9361 (accessed 31.7.12).

Smith, S. 2007: Angelina Jolie wants to save the world. 'A Mighty Heart' is the story of Mariane Pearl's unquenchable spirit. It's not a bad description of the actress who plays her, either. *Newsweek*, 25 June. www.highbeam.com/doc/1G1-165293677.html (accessed 19.1.13).

Snow, J. 2010: The internet election that never happened. The *Sunday Times*, 1 May. www.timesonline.co.uk/tol/comment/columnists/guest_contributors/article7113351.ece (accessed 1.10.11).

Stanyer, J. 2007: *Modern Political Communication*. Cambridge: Polity Press.

Stanyer, J. and Wring, D. 2004: Public images, private lives: an introduction. *Parliamentary Affairs* 57(1): 1–8.

Stokes, W. 2011: Democratization and gender. In J. Haynes (ed.), *Routledge Handbook of Democratization*. Oxford: Routledge.

Straw, W. 2010: Yes we did? What Labour learned from Obama. In R. K. Gibson, A. Williamson and S. Ward (eds), *The Internet and the 2010 Election: Putting the Small p Back in Politics*. London: Hansard Society.

Street, J. 2002: Bob, Bono and Tony B: the popular artist as politician. *Media, Culture and Society* 24(3): 433–41.

Street, J. 2003: The celebrity politician: political style and popular culture.

In J. Corner and J. Pels (eds), *The Media and the Restyling of Politics*. London, Thousand Oaks, New Delhi: Sage Publications.

Street, J. 2004: Celebrity politicians: popular culture and political representation. *The British Journal of Politics and International Relations* 6(4): 435–52.

Street, J. 2010: *Mass Media, Politics and Democracy*, 2nd edn. Basingstoke: Palgrave Macmillan.

Street, J. 2011: *Music and Politics*. Cambridge: Polity Press.

Street, J. 2012: Do celebrity politics and celebrity politicians matter? *British Journal of Politics and International Relations: Celebrity Politics* 14(2) (special edn). http://onlinelibrary.wiley.com/doi/10.1111/j.1467-856X.2011.00476.x/abstract (accessed 12.3.12).

Street, J., Hague, S. and Savigny, H. 2008: Playing to the crowd: the role of music and musicians in political participation. *British Journal of Politics and International Relations* 10(2): 269–85.

Summers, D. 2009: Politics blog: Gordon Brown has the worst smile in the world. The *Guardian*, 5 May. www.guardian.co.uk/politics/blog/2009/may/05/brown-smile-prescott (accessed 22.10.11).

't Hart, P. and Tindall, K. 2009: Leadership by the famous: celebrity politics in democracy (with K. Tindall). In J. Kane, H. Patapan, P. 't Hart (eds), *Dispersed Democratic Leadership*. Oxford: Oxford University Press.

Thompson, J. 1995: *The Media and Modernity: A Social Theory of the Media*. Cambridge: Polity.

Thorpe, V. 2011: Hugh Grant and Steve Coogan join war on red tops. The *Guardian*, 9 July. www.guardian.co.uk/media/2011/jul/09/hugh-grant-steve-coogan-news (accessed 9.2.11).

Thrall, A. T., Lollio-Fakhreddine, J., Berent, J., Donnelly, L., Herrin, M., Paquette, Z., Wenglinski, R. and Wyatt, A. 2008: Star power: celebrity advocacy and the evolution of the public sphere. *The Harvard International Journal of Press/Politics* 13: 362.

Traub, J. 2008: The celebrity solution. *New York Times*, 9 March: 38.

Tsaliki L., Frangonikolopoulos, C. A. and Huliaras, A. (eds) 2011: *Transnational Celebrity Activism in Global Politics: Changing the World?* Bristol: Intellect.

Turner, G. 2004: *Understanding Celebrity*. London, Thousand Oaks, New Delhi: Sage Publications.

Turner, G., Bonner, F. and Marshall, P. D. 2000: *Fame Games: The Production of Celebrity in Australia*. Cambridge: Cambridge University Press.

Twain, M. 1901: To the Person sitting in Darkness. *North American Review*, February: 161–76.

Ullman, L. 1993: Women and children make up 80 per cent of the world's refugees. CNN. 8 February.

UNICEF 2006: *A Guide to Working with Goodwill Ambassadors*. New York: UNICEF.

United Nations 1958: The Report of the Expert Committee on United

Nations Public Information. 28 August, United Nations Archive, New York. S-0540-DAG-12/1.0 Box 13.

United Nations 2007: *United Nations Messengers of Peace*. UN Web Services, Department of Public Information, New York. www.un.org/sg/mop/ (accessed 12.9.08).

Usborne, D. 2012: Obama steers clear of Hollywood as he set off fundraising. *The Independent on Sunday*, 1 January: 30.

Ustinov, P. 1977: *Dear Me*. New York: Penguin Books.

Valenti, J. 2007. *This Time, This Place: My Life in War, White House and Hollywood*. New York: Three Rivers Press.

Vallely, P. 2009: From A-lister to aid worker: does celebrity diplomacy really work? The *Independent*, 17 January. www.independent.co.uk/news/people/profile/from-alister-to-aid-worker-does-celebrity-diplomacy-really-work-1365946.html (accessed 26.2.10).

van Zoonen, L. 2005: *Entertaining the Citizen: When Politics and Popular Culture Converge*. Lanham, Boulder, New York, Toronto, Oxford: Rowman & Littlefield Publishers.

van Zoonen, L. 2006: The personal, the political and the popular: a woman's guide to celebrity politics. *European Journal of Cultural Studies* 9(3): 287–301.

Vaughn, R. 2008: *A Fortunate Life*. New York: Thomas Dunne/St Martin's Press.

Vaughn, S. 1994: *Ronald Reagan in Hollywood: Movies and Politics*. Cambridge: Cambridge University Press.

Vendel, C. 2005: Spitting by Vietnam vet dismissed. *Kansas City Star*, 26 August. www.kansascity.com/mld/kansascity/news/local/12479774.htm%22 (accessed 12.9.10).

Vogler, C. 2009: Quoted in Svetkey, B., Labreque J. and Pastorek, W. President Rock Star. *Entertainment Weekly*, 30 September: 22–6.

Watson, T. and Hickman M. 2012: *Dial M for Murdoch: News Corporation and the Corruption of Britain*. London: Allen Lane Penguin Books.

Weintraub, J. with Cohen R. 2010: *When I Stop Talking, You'll Know I'm Dead: Useful Stories From A Persuasive Man*. New York, Boston: Twelve Hachette Group.

West, D. M. 2003: *Arnold Schwarzenegger and Celebrity Politics*. www.insidepolitics.org/heard/westreport903.html (accessed 12.9.10).

West, D. M. and Orman, J. 2003: *Celebrity Politics*. Upper Saddle River, NJ: Prentice Hall.

Wheeler, M. 2006: *Hollywood: Politics and Society*. London: British Film Institute.

Wheeler, M. 2011: Celebrity diplomacy: United Nations' Goodwill Ambassadors and Messengers of Peace. *Celebrity Studies: Special Edition on Celebrity and the Transnational* 2(1): 6–18.

Wheeler, M. 2012: Bill Clinton: courting the Hollywood film industry.

In M. White (ed.), *Bill Clinton: Dominating the Nineties*. London: I.B. Tauris.

White, M. 2011: The cinematic Kennedy: Franklin D. Roosevelt in film. In I. W. Morgan (ed.), *Presidents in the Movies: American History and Politics on Screen*. New York: Palgrave Macmillan.

Wilbekin, E. 2008: Leader of the new school: a look at the impact of the celebrity, style and culture of Barack Obama. *Giant*, October–November: 86.

Wills, G. 1997: *John Wayne: The Politics of Celebrity*. London: Faber and Faber.

Wilson, J. 2011: A new kind of star is born: Audrey Hepburn and the global governmentalisation of female stardom. *Celebrity Studies: Special Edition on Celebrity and the Global* 2(1): 56–68.

Wiseman, G. 2009: Celebrity diplomacy: the effectiveness and value of celebrity diplomacy. An edited transcript of a Panel Discussion at the USC Center on Public Diplomacy at the Annenberg School, Norman Lear Center, 21 April.

Wolfsfeld, G. 2011. *Making Sense of Media and Politics: Five Principles in Political Communication*: New York, London: Routledge.

Woods, J. 2010: Election 2010: The big fight for the support of celebrities. The *Daily Telegraph*, 16 February. www.telegraph.co.uk/news/election-2010/7248132/Election-2010-The-big-fight-for-the-support-of-celebrities.html (accessed 16.1.12).

Wring, D. 2005: *The Politics of Marketing the Labour Party*. Basingstoke: Palgrave Macmillan.

Wring, D. 2011: Introduction. In D. Wring, R. Mortimore and S. Atkinson (eds), *Political Communication in Britain: The Leaders' Debates, the Campaign and the Media in the 2010 General Election*. Basingstoke: Palgrave Macmillan.

Yrjölä, R. 2011: The global politics of celebrity humanitarianism. In L. Tsaliki, C. A Frangonikolopoulos and A. Huliaras (eds), *Transnational Celebrity Activism in Global Politics: Changing the World?* Bristol: Intellect.

Yrjölä, R. 2012: From street into the world: towards a politicised reading of celebrity humanitarianism. *British Journal of Politics and International Relations: Celebrity Politics* 14(2) (special edn): http://onlinelibrary.wiley.com/doi/10.1111/j.1467-856X.2011.00476.x/abstract (accessed 12.3.12).

Zaleski, K. 2008: Participant. *Youthquake: Elections, Media and Voters*, 12 November. New York: Paley Center.

Index